The Behavior Management Handbook

Setting Up Effective Behavior Management Systems

The Behavior Management Handbook

Setting Up Effective Behavior Management Systems

Thomas McIntyre

Allyn and Bacon
Boston   London   Sydney   Toronto

Copyright © 1989 by Allyn and Bacon
A Division of Simon & Schuster
160 Gould Street
Needham Heights, Massachusetts 02194

Library of Congress Cataloging-in-Publication Data

McIntyre, Thomas, 1952–
    The behavior management handbook : setting up effective behavior management systems / Thomas McIntyre.
        p.   cm.
    Bibliography: p.
    ISBN 0-205-11709-0
    1. Problem children—Education—United States—Handbooks, manuals, etc. 2. Learning disabled children—Education—United States—Handbooks, manuals, etc. 3. Behavior modification—United States—Handbooks, manuals, etc. 4. Classroom management—United States—Handbooks, manuals, etc. I. Title.
    LC4802.M35 1989
    371.93—dc19   88-15526
                                                                    CIP

Printed in the United States of America
10 9 8 7 6 5 4 3 2 1   92 91 90 89 88

To America's teachers,
who, under great constraints,
continue to educate and enlighten our youth.

Contents

3   Symptom Checklists   37

Preface

Some teachers make behavior management look so easy, and perhaps, for some, it develops naturally. Certain educators have a headstart on others—a greater confidence, more charisma, a quick wit, or a subject of interest to students that involves various hands-on activities. All of these make the control of undesirable behavior a bit easier. However, *everyone* can become an effective behavior manager. If your skills in this area are not yet honed to a fine edge, do not despair. Often, the most difficult task is to decide to implement a new technique, or change a personal style that is presently timid or abrasive. You have probably become accustomed to a certain routine, as have your students, and it is difficult to walk in the classroom one day and make changes. However, for the benefit of our students (and our own sanity) it is important that we discontinue ineffective techniques and implement ideas that work.

Over the years, nationwide polls of teachers and the general public arrive at the same consensus: Discipline is the major issue facing education. Increasingly, we teachers are confronted by students who have not learned proper respectful behavior or who lack the motivation to give education its proper place in their lives. Whether this is due to upbringing, the neighborhood environment, societal pressures, emotional turmoil, or peer influences, there appears to be more of these students in the schools now than ever before. Many of these students will display behavior that is so severe that they will be labeled *handicapped*. Due to legal decisions and recent legislation, schools can no longer expel or refuse to serve this population. Because their behavior is a handicapping condition, they must be served. But whether the behavior of our students is mild or severe in nature, we need to be familiar with numerous behavior management techniques in order to deal with their varied personalities and behaviors.

The *Behavior Management Handbook* will address that need. Section One provides an overview regarding students who misbehave or experience emotional difficulties. Section Two reviews the various ways in which students are identified as having behaviors that are inappropriate. Activities are presented at the end of each chapter to familiarize the teacher or future teacher with the numerous concepts and the use of identification procedures. References are provided if more information on these topics is desired.

Sections Three, Four, and Five contain chapters that provide an overview of various behavior management approaches and a checklist of steps to assist you in implementing and using each one. Every chapter in these sections contains activities that allow you to practice each intervention technique before actually implementing it in the classroom. As in the previous sections, references are listed at the end of each chapter if more information is desired.

Section Six provides chapters on issues related to the education of students who are experiencing emotional/behavioral difficulties. These include information on legal implications of behavior management, mainstreaming, the management of stress, and assisting parents in their efforts at home. Again, activities are given at the end of each chapter to assist you in applying this information, and references are listed if more information is desired.

This book can help make teachers and future teachers better behavior managers. It is directed primarily toward those who teach students with intellectual levels ranging from mildly retarded to gifted, be it in the regular classroom or a special education setting. Those who teach students of lower intellectual abilities will also find this text to be helpful. All that is required to make this book useful to all is to modify the activities and suggestions to apply to one's specific situation. For certain behaviors that prove resistant to your comprehensive behavior management system, refer to my companion edition to this book, *A Resource Book for Remediating Common Behavior and Learning Problems* (Allyn and Bacon, 1989). It provides numerous strategies for remediating some 350 different behaviors or academic difficulties.

Many other educational professionals can benefit from the information presented in this book. For university faculty, we offer practical information and activities for training teachers in behavior management and issues regarding the education of students who misbehave. The step-by-step approach for using each method would fit nicely with a theoretical overview by the faculty member. The suggested activities and discussion questions assist in making the learning of this material more interesting. Inservice coordinators will find the implementation steps and activities invaluable in teaching new approaches to their colleagues. Schools might house a copy of this book in their library for use by teachers.

In summary, you can learn how to reach your students and assist them in becoming better adjusted, more productive members of society. It is only a matter of finding the optimal intervention for each of them.

For ease in reading, and due to the overwhelming prevalence of males exhibiting emotional/behavioral difficulties, we have chosen to refer to the student as being male. Sometimes, however, we refer to a female student when conditions that pertain predominantly to females are discussed.

Acknowledgments

I am indebted to Dr. Larry Janes for sharing his vast knowledge of education law and to Dr. Herbert Foster for sharing his expertise in the education of street-corner youths in their respective chapters. I am also greatly indebted to Karol Cowell, who coauthored Chapter 26, The IRS Plan for Parents, a program that she developed. Additionally, my thanks extend to Valerie Croll, Kathleen Kramer, and Debra Wolfson for writing the hypothetical case studies included in Chapter 1. Thank you to Karol Cowell and Dr. Richard Schwab for their support and critique of this book. Last, many thanks to Dr. A. J. Pappanikou, Dr. Melvin Reich, and Dr. Spencer Gibbons for the knowledge they imparted to me.

SECTION ONE

An Overview

1

Emotional/Behavioral Problems

We tend to glorify and rejoice in defiance and inappropriate behavior when it is removed from our personal lives. Consider the many books, movies, and television shows that frighten us, make us laugh, or otherwise keep our interest due in large part to the inappropriate behavior that is shown or described. However, when this same behavior occurs in our classrooms, it loses its humorous or appealing nature. Surveys conducted in the last fifteen years indicate that parents and teachers agree: Discipline is the biggest problem faced by our schools.

For you as a teacher, students with emotional/behavioral problems occupy much of your time and thought. They may learn less efficiently because of the time they spend off task. Other students may also learn less efficiently because of classroom disturbances and the distraction of the teacher from his or her duties. Additionally, the perceptions of your peers regarding your ability as a teacher will be influenced by how well you manage your students' behavior. School principals report that they fire more first-year teachers for lack of behavior management skills than for any other reason. Thus, as you might suspect, surveys of teachers consistently report discipline problems in the classroom as being one of the major causes of stress and burnout among educators.

Prevalence

Although most of your students will display some degree of undesirable behavior during the school year, it is estimated that 6 to 15 percent of school-age students are in need of special services due to their misbehavior. However, nationwide, only 2 to 3 percent of pupils are identified as needing these services. Those identified are usually the students with the most severe problems. The others are oftentimes not served due to financial concerns and lack of available services. It is estimated that the cost of educating students with a behavioral/emotional disability in a special program is two to three times what it costs to educate less disruptive students. Most schools are reluctant to implement a special program complete with teacher, aide, classroom materials, and supportive help for only a few students. Therefore, most students with behavior problems are educated in the regular classroom, where it is estimated that teachers will have 60 to 90 percent more interaction with these pupils than with others in the room. In fact, it was reported that teachers in urban areas may spend up to 80 percent of instructional time attempting to manage misbehavior.

Other factors impinge upon the prevalence figures. Five times as many boys than girls are identified as having emotional/behavioral problems. Additionally, blacks are twice as likely as whites, proportionately, to be identified as being in need of specialized services. This is especially true of blacks from urban areas who are bused to suburban schools where their value system and behavior may be at odds with middle-class expectations. They are often placed in special education classes because of this. This phenomenon has come to be known as *re-segregation*.

One thing is certain. You, as a teacher, will be dealing with inappropriate behavior, and skill in the area of behavior management is an important part of effective teaching.

Terminology

Although the federal government refers to emotionally/behaviorally handicapped students as "severely emotionally disturbed," the terminology used by the various states differs. Some states feel that the word *disturbed* has a negative connotation. Other states believe that *emotions* cannot be observed and measured, thus we can label someone only by their behavior. Other states feel that students who have mild and moderate problems are also in need of services. Therefore, depending on the state in which you teach or the literature that you read, you may see these or other terms used to describe similar students:

Severely emotionally disturbed

Emotionally disturbed

Emotionally disordered

Emotionally impaired

Emotionally handicapped

Behaviorally disordered

Behaviorally handicapped

Socially-emotionally maladjusted

Socially-emotionally disordered

Causation

Many factors have been proposed as possible causes of undesirable behavior. Depending on the type and severity of the emotional/behavioral abnormality, the following possible causes have been suggested:

Family interaction

Nutrition

Abuse or neglect at home

Chemical imbalances

Brain damage

Reaction to medication

Genetics

Peer pressure or modeling

Frustration in learning

Radiation from neon lights

Daily pressures of life

Need for attention or love

In most cases, however, it is difficult, if not impossible, to identify a specific cause for aberrant behavior in children, youths, and adults.

Treatment

Depending on one's training and personal philosophy, any number of remedial efforts might be recommended. Those who subscribe to the psychodynamic school of thought believe that misbehavior is due to emotional difficulties resulting from unresolved stages and/or crises. Counseling and various types of therapies (e.g., art therapy, play therapy, dance therapy) might be recommended to assist the person in resolving this inner turmoil.

Behaviorists have proven that behavior can be controlled or changed by the use of punishment, rewards, or ignoring. Whereas psychodynamic people insist that this does not resolve the precipitating inner emotional turmoil, behaviorists respond that improved behavior improves self-concept as the person functions better in society. They also counter that psychodynamic practitioners cannot prove the effectiveness of their approaches and that the results take too long.

Those with a medical orientation might recommend the use of medication, surgery, or modification in diet to obtain desired behavioral changes, whereas those of other orientations, depending on their beliefs, would implement other intervention procedures.

Although most teachers develop an eclectic approach that promotes "using whatever works," we are oftentimes confronted by choices offered by different viewpoints and must make our decisions based on our personal views of causation, the perceived needs of the student and the class, and the constrictions of our classroom environment.

Categorizing Behavior

Depending on a specialist's viewpoint, you may see behavior classified in a number of ways. Some view behavior as being either functional or organic in origin. Behavior is organically based if a physical cause can be found for the behavior. All nonorganically based behavior is labeled as being functional. Other authors would label behavior as being either overcontrolled or undercontrolled. Overcontrolled behavior is withdrawn or overly quiet and noninteractive in nature, and undercontrolled behavior is more active, aggressive, or acting-out in form. Certain other theorists would describe behavior as being either disturbed or disturbing. Disturbed behavior insinuates emotional imbalance or turmoil as the cause of behavior, whereas disturbing behavior is that which is upsetting to others in the environment, yet is not due to psychological imbalance. Other systems, categories, and terms exist. You may hear of conditions such as autism and schizophrenia, which often fall into the category of psychotic behavior, meaning that the student is out of touch with or misrepresenting reality. (For federal funding purposes, autism is considered to be a health impairment.) You might read of the less severe category of neurosis, which includes phobias (fears) and manias (compulsive behaviors). Many other descriptors, too numerous to mention, are used to identify various types of behavior.

Definitions

In order to receive federal funding (40 percent of the *excess* costs for educating a student), schools must indicate on special forms that a certain student is in need of services due to his or her behavior. The federal definition states that in order to be identified as severely emotionally disturbed, a student must possess:

An unexplained inability to achieve

An inability to establish and maintain relationships

Inappropriate affect or feelings

Unhappiness or depression

Physical symptoms due to emotional upset

This definition is vague and certainly not comprehensive. Most school systems probably do not use the above definition in identifying emotionally/behaviorally disordered pupils. A more common basis for identification criteria would probably include the degree to which the student disrupts the classroom environment, prevents others from learning, interferes with the teachers' ability to teach, is a danger to self or others, or displays any behavior that is inappropriate in a given situation.

As you can see, much subjectivity is involved in the identification of pupils with emotional/behavioral disorders. Tolerance on the part of the teacher is certainly a factor. Two teachers might disagree as to whether a certain student is in need of special services such as counseling or special classes. Availability of funding and services also affect the number of students served. Therefore, behavior that results in special services in one school district may not result in these same services in another. Whatever services are provided, most students who are labeled as being *behavior disordered* spend at least part of the day in the regular classroom. Various other students do not display behavior serious enough to receive a label, but do show a level or type of behavior that concerns us.

This means that all teachers must possess strong skills in behavior management if they are to be effective in educating our young people.

Activities and Discussion Questions

1. When deciding if a student's behavior is in need of remediation, a number of factors must be considered: the frequency and duration of the behavior, how chronic the behavior has been, the context (e.g., who, what, when, where, why, and how), and the teacher's tolerance. Decide under which circumstances the behaviors below would be considered to be normal, and when they would be considered to be abnormal.

   Screaming

   Scratching

   Interrupting conversations

   Biting one's self

   Making animal noises

   Refusing to follow the directions of someone in charge of a situation

2. Below are excerpts from case histories of hypothetical students. Decide whether the student's behavior in the following situations is: (a) disturbed or disturbing, (b) functional or organic, and (c) overcontrolled or undercontrolled. Decide, in your own mind, whether the students described below are in need of special services and, if so, which ones? Should these students be placed in a regular education or special education classroom? Would you label each student's problems as being of no concern, mild, moderate, or severe in nature? Is the federal definition of *severe*

emotional disturbance helpful in these cases? What should the school program include? How can you involve the parents in the program?

Case History: Bruce Baker

Reason for Referral

Bruce regularly exhibits aggressive and defensive behavior, and his reading achievement gain scores are progressively decreasing.

Health and Developmental History

Bruce Baker is now nine years and five months old and in the third grade. He was the last of five children born to his mother, who experienced great difficulty during pregnancy, partly due to the fact that she was forty-two years old. Bruce's birth weight was six pounds. He was hospitalized for pneumonia and had frequent ear infections thereafter. He walked at age nineteen months and spoke intelligibly at age thirty-two months. When he was three years old, tubes were inserted in both ears, and at age seven they were removed.

He is allergic to dairy products, dust, and pollen, and frequently complains of headaches. His speech patterns are immature, and his few playmates are six to seven years old. He is a handsome boy of average intelligence though small for his age.

Family History

Bruce's fifty-two-year-old father is a factory worker for a farm implement company, and his mother works part time as a cashier at a discount department store. All grandparents except his maternal grandfather are alive and live within thirty miles of Bruce's home in a small city. He has three brothers, aged twelve, fifteen, and sixteen, and one sister, aged thirteen, who have little to do with him and regard him as a nuisance. The main family pastime is watching television with a beer-drinking father and a mother who is preoccupied with housework. Family recreation consists of church attendance and activities, and visits to the grandparents' farm.

Bruce's leisure activities consist of watching television, particularly violent comedies; drawing (often on walls) with felt pens; and building structures with Lego parts, which he destroys immediately after completion. His favorite toys are cars and trucks. He eats an inordinate amount of candy and chewing gum. He is easily frustrated and cries often. He shows aggressive behavior with his playmates, who are usually two or three years younger than he, and he frequently abuses the family dog. He seems unaware of the feelings of others, and his parents have little control over his behavior.

Since both parents' working hours end at 5:00 P.M., they are rarely home before evening mealtime. Thus, Bruce is often home alone for three hours each afternoon and receives little or no help with his homework assignments. No regular chores are assigned to Bruce. His mother cleans his room, makes his bed, and puts away his belongings.

School History

Bruce entered kindergarten at age five, and was described by his teacher as being immature, aggressive, and demanding of individual attention. These traits have persisted throughout his school career. After spending two years in second grade, he is now half way through third grade and is described as having a short attention span, high distractability, and a continuing need for the teacher's attention. His mathematics achievement scores are in the average range, but he has problems in reading and has been placed in the lowest reading group. Specifically, his word attack and identification skills are on grade level, but comprehension of passages is on second-grade level. His handwriting is poor and he does not know all the cursive letters. Spelling is on second-grade level. In art class, the predominant color used for his artwork is black.

Bruce frequently daydreams, and his conversation typically resolves around television characters whom he speaks of as his friends. He often hides in the classroom, under desks, tables, or in the closet. His favorite period is the story-telling session at the end of the day.

Over the past three years, there have been a number of negative classroom incidents that have caused concern: scribbling in other students' workbooks, scribbling on desks and refusing to wash them, writing foul language on the chalkboard, placing thumbtacks on chairs of students and teachers, and stealing classmates' crayons and lunchboxes. In addition, he once kicked the vice-principal when he was sent to the office for inappropriate behavior during a physical education class.

Playground incidents include regularly using foul language toward the playground attendant, taking away equipment from younger children during recess games, fighting for possession of the ball while playing games, and pushing a boy off the jungle gym, causing the child to need ten stitches in his chin.

Case History: Lynn Schefer

Reason for Referral

Lynn has a low self-concept, has exhibited tendencies of self-destructive behavior, and is considered to be a high risk for delinquency.

Health and Developmental History

Lynn is now fourteen years and ten months of age and in the ninth grade. Her mother's pregnancy was normal, but Lynn was born with her left foot curved inward (clubfoot), a condition that required a leg brace for eighteen months. She had the usual childhood diseases—chicken pox, mumps, and German measles—with normal recovery. Her parents have had her immunized regularly for diphtheria, whooping cough, tetanus, polio, and red measles.

Her birth weight was eight pounds, three ounces, and her physical development was normal. She walked at age thirteen months and talked intelligibly at age twenty-eight months. She has required correctional lenses since age six and is now able to wear soft contact lenses. For the past year, she has complained of chronic pain in the left knee, but no organic causes have been determined.

Family History

Lynn is the second of four children. She has one eighteen-year-old brother and two sisters aged thirteen and eight. Both parents have university degrees in education, and her father teaches at a nearby university. Her maternal grandparents are deceased. Her paternal grandparents are retired and live in a large city 100 miles away, as do her father's siblings, with whom there are strong family ties.

Lynn's parents were divorced when she was eight years old and she lived with her mother in a town of 1,000 residents until she was thirteen. Her mother then sold the house to her father and moved with the children to a large city 150 miles away. Six months later, her mother, who was living on social assistance, asked her father to take all four children to live with him temporarily. Lynn's reaction was to attempt suicide by swallowing an assortment of pills, mostly aspirin. No professional help was solicited by either parent.

During the first six months of living with her father, there were few restrictions on Lynn's activities. She was dating nineteen- and twenty-year-old boys who rarely called for her at home. At the end of the summer, her father imposed limits on social activities and issued a number of rules regarding household chores and family responsibilities. This action resulted in Lynn's brother moving away from home, and rebellion from Lynn. She was spanked with a belt for going out while "grounded," and a total lack of communication developed between her and her father. A month later, she used foul language to her father, who then, according to Lynn, chased her, shook her, and choked her. The incident was reported to the child abuse hot line, subsequently investigated, and recorded. No other action was implemented.

Lynn is tall, very attractive, of normal intelligence, and considers herself knowledgeable about sex. She has one close girlfriend and dates different boys each week. She judges her personal popularity by how many boys like her. Her thirteen-year-old sister includes her in activities with her friends and protects Lynn in confrontations with others, particularly her father. Lynn appears to have little concept of empathy for others. Her common verbal expressions are abusive and include "hate" and "kill" in reference to family and peers. When asked to explain her actions, her usual response is, "I don't know."

In the past two months, Lynn has had a serious physical fight with another girl, has come home drunk twice, has "made out" with strange boys, has sneaked out of the house late at night to be with them, and lies about her whereabouts and activities. These actions have resulted in her being slapped and grounded by her father.

School History

Lynn has always been a low-average student in comparison to her siblings, who maintain straight As. She had reading resource help in fifth and sixth grades, but made little effort on her own. Her reading is presently on the fifth-grade level. In ninth grade, she is getting extra help in mathematics (her skills are on the fourth-grade level) upon the insistence of her father. She is described by her teachers as uncommunicative, lazy, and uncooperative. Their judgment is that she would achieve better if she tried. Lynn considers herself dumb, and is satisfied with C and D grades because they require little effort.

She has no real friends at school and has been involved in several incidents of physical and verbal abuse of other girls. Her peers call her Ozone Girl and Space Cadet, referring to her tendency to talk irrelevantly. Although her school counselor has advised referral to the school social worker, her father has not felt such action necessary.

3. The following is a page from a pamphlet that was given to teachers in an urban school system. Discuss with others the accuracy of this information and its implications. This information is said to be of use in curriculum planning. Is this indeed useful? Should this be included in literature given to teachers?

Profile of the Typical Disruptive Student

Purpose: To provide information on the attitudes, performance, and home environment common to disruptive students, this can be of use in curriculum planning and specialized intervention.

Personal	Age range of thirteen to seventeen years; male; minority group member; athletic
Home Situation	From a single-parent home, foster home, and/or low-income family
Interaction Patterns	Repeated conflicts with teachers, authority figures, and peers; socially immature and incompetent
School Performance	Low academic achievement; enrolled in basic-level classes; frequent disciplinary referrals to school administration; frequently absent from school and tardy to class; cuts one or more classes during the day; prone to drop out of school; on free or reduced lunch program

Attitudes   Views school in a "hostile" environment;
                             fluctuates between periods of being with-
                             drawn and outspoken; lacks a feeling of
                             identity with the school; fails to accept re-
                             sponsibility for own behavior; always
                             reacts in same way when faced with var-
                             ious types of frustration

4. Have any of the students with whom you have worked
   been identified as being emotionally/behaviorally disordered? Should some of your past students have been identified as possessing a behavior problem? Which points, if
   any, of the federal definition would apply to these
   students?

5. What reasons might explain why males and minorities are
   overrepresented in the incidence figures?

For More Information

Newcomer, P. L. (1980). *Understanding and teaching emotionally disturbed children.* Boston: Allyn and Bacon.

Reinhart, H. R. (1980). *Children in conflict.* St. Louis: Mosby Company.

Swanson, H. L., and Reinhart, H. R. (1984). *Teaching strategies for children in conflict: Curriculum methods and materials.* St. Louis: Times Mirror/ Mosby.

SECTION TWO

Identifying Problem
Behaviors

There may come a time when a student's behavior becomes so severe in nature that you must ask that the student be evaluated for special services (e.g., special education placement, counseling, a systematic discipline approach). Deciding when to start the referral process is not an easy decision. However, the following behaviors are often cited as reasons for referral:

1. The student's behavior is demanding an inordinate amount of your time and attention.

2. The student's behavior is disrupting the class and preventing others from learning.

3. The student's behavior is resistant to your attempts to control it or the behavior is becoming more severe in nature.

4. The student's behavior is more like that of a younger child than someone of his age.

5. The student perceives himself negatively.

6. The student is perceived negatively by the majority of his classmates.

7. The student is a danger to himself or others.

In addition to the above guidelines, numerous instruments and techniques have been devised to assist you in your decision to enter the referral process.

2

Behavior Checklists

Many quick and easy-to-complete checklists have been developed to assist you in identifying whether a student has a behavioral problem. The various scales typically include many items or questions which, when rated and categorized, will indicate whether a student has a behavioral or emotional problem of a certain type. Even if the student in question does not display a pattern of behavior that is, according to the instruments, severe enough to bring a referral and possible services, these instruments can identify which specific behaviors are in need of remediation. They are also useful in providing supportive evidence for your viewpoint regarding the severity of a student's condition. These instruments allow comparisons between past and present behavior and comparisons among students, which may assist in placement decisions. They will also be useful in devising Individualized Education Plan (IEP) goals in that you know which behaviors need remediation.

However, the educational significance of the information gained from the scales is limited. None of the instruments make any remedial suggestions for the identified behaviors. The validity (the degree to which the instrument really measures what it claims to measure) and reliability (the degree to which the same results are attained in repeated use) of these instruments has also been questioned. Therefore, the results obtained from the behavior checklists may not always be accurate. These instruments merely provide you with additional information on the student in question. They should never be used as the sole criterion for labeling a student as having a behavior problem.

Thirteen of the major behavior rating scales are presented and reviewed.

AAMD Adaptive Behavior Scales

The public school version of the AAMD scale (AAMD, 1981) contains 110 questions and has norms for persons three to eighteen years of age. Several weighted choices (assigned point values) are provided for each question, which are later summed to obtain scores for the various subtests. These subtest scores are then converted into percentile ranks for comparison with other students of the same age and grade. This scale is designed for use with students who are labeled as Educable or Trainable Mentally Retarded. The AAMD scale is divided into two parts and corresponding subtests as follows:

Adaptive Behavior	**Maladaptive Behavior**
Independent Functioning (21 items)	Violent and Destructive Behavior (5 items)
a. Eating	Antisocial Behavior (6 items)
b. Toilet use	Rebellious Behavior (6 items)
c. Not applicable to schools	Untrustworthy Behavior (2 items)
d. Appearance	
e. Care of clothing	
f. Dressing and undressing	Withdrawal (3 items)
g. Travel	Stereotyped Behavior and
h. Other independent functioning	Odd Mannerisms (2 items)

Adaptive Behavior

Physical Development
(6 items)

   a. Sensory development
   b. Motor development

Economic Activity (4 items)

   a. Money handling
   b. Shopping skills

Language Development
(9 items)

   a. Expression
   b. Comprehension
   c. Social language
     development

Numbers and Time (3 items)

Not Applicable to Schools

Vocational Activity (3 items)

Self Direction (5 items)

   a. Initiative
   b. Perseverance
   c. Leisure time

Responsibility (2 items)

Socialization (7 items)

Maladaptive Behavior

Inappropriate Interpersonal
Manners (1 item)

Unacceptable Vocal Habits
(1 item)

Unacceptable or Eccentric
Habits (4 items)

Not Applicable to Schools

Hyperactive Tendencies
(1 item)

Not Applicable to Schools

Psychological Disturbances
(7 items)

Use of Medications (1 item)

Behavior Problem Checklist

The Behavior Problem Checklist (BPC) (Peterson and Quay, 1979) contains 55 items divided into five areas:

   Conduct Problems

   Personality Problems

   Inadequate-Immature Behavior

Socialized Delinquent Behavior

Psychotic Behavior

Raw scores are translated into grade equivalents so that the student can be compared with others of his age. This checklist is intended for use with students in the elementary grades although norms are given for a few other populations. A good amount of research has been conducted on the BPC. Generally, the research is favorable and supports the use of this instrument as a screening device.

Behavior Rating Profile

The Behavior Rating Profile (BRP) (Brown and Hammill, 1978) has four major sections:

Teacher Rating Scale—The teacher rates the student in question according to how similar he is to each of thirty descriptions of negative behavior.

Student Rating Scales—The student rates himself as to how similar he is to each of sixty negative statements. There are twenty items each in the areas of peer relations, home problems, and school behavior.

Parent Rating Scales—The parent rates the student regarding his home behavior.

Sociogram—Classmates are asked which three students they would most like, and least like, to have as friends. Students are rank-ordered according to the responses of others.

The BRP is designed for use with students aged six to thirteen years. It is more comprehensive than most checklist instruments in that it assesses the student's behavior in a number of settings from various viewpoints.

Bower-Lambert Scales

The Bower-Lambert Scales (Bower and Lambert, 1982) are a comprehensive set of instruments designed to assess the behavior of students from kindergarten through high school. The scales assess the students from three perspectives:

Teacher Rating

> *Teacher Rating* (all grades)—Upon reading each of eight descriptions of behavior, the teacher rank orders students as being most like the description.

Peer Rating

> *Class Pictures* (grades K–3)—Students view pictures of pupils engaging in negative, neutral, or positive behavior and identify classmates who are similar to the children in the pictures.

> *Class Play* (grades 3–7)—Students identify classmates as being appropriate for casting in negative and positive dramatic roles.

> *Student Survey* (grades 7–12)—Students identify classmates who are most like the descriptions of negative, neutral, or positive behavior.

Self-Rating

> *A Picture Game* (grades K–3)—The student places pictures of home and school situations into piles by whether they are "happy" or "sad" pictures.

> *Thinking About Yourself* (grades 3–7)—Given descriptions of hypothetical students, the student tells whether he is like that student and whether he wishes to be like that student.

> *A Self Test* (grades 7–12)—Same as *Thinking About Yourself* except that the descriptions are oriented more to students in high school.

Answers are weighted and a certain number of students with the highest scores on each of the ratings are identified. If the student is identified in two of the three ratings, he is considered to have an emotional/behavioral problem.

The Bower Lambert Scales provide a comprehensive picture of students, yet tend to be more combersome and time consuming than other checklists.

Burks Behavior Rating Scales

The Burks Behavior Rating Scales (BBRS) (Burks, 1977) contains 110 items that are divided into nineteen categories:

Excessive Self Blame (5 items)

Excessive Anxiety (5 items)

Excessive Withdrawal (6 items)

Excessive Dependency (6 items)

Poor Ego Strength (7 items)

Poor Physical Strength (5 items)

Poor Coordination (5 items)

Poor Intellectuality (7 items)

Poor Academics (5 items)

Poor Attention (5 items)

Poor Impulse Control (5 items)

Poor Reality Contact (8 items)

Poor Sense of Identity (6 items)

Excessive Suffering (7 items)

Poor Anger Control (5 items)

Excessive Sense of Persecution (5 items)

Excessive Aggressiveness (6 items)

Excessive Resistance (4 items)

Poor Social Conformity (8 items)

The BBRS is designed for use with students in grades 1 through 8. Each item is scored on a one to five scale with a score of five indicating a more severe behavior. To score the BBRS, the scores of the items for each category are summed and plotted on a profile graph. The profile identifies the score for each behavior category as being "not significant," "significant," or "very significant." The student's profile is then compared with other typical profile patterns presented in the manual. Additionally, the manual presents remedial activities for students who score high in various categories.

Due to a lack of standardization and research information, this instrument's usefulness to teachers is somewhat limited, except in identifying behaviors in need of change.

Devereux Adolescent Behavior Rating Scale

The Devereux Adolescent Behavior Rating Scale (DAB) (Spivak, Spotts, and Haimes, 1967) is designed for use with students who are thirteen to eighteen years of age. It focuses on nonacademic aspects of emotional/behavioral development. The DAB consists of eighty-four items divided into fifteen categories:

Unethical (4 items)

Defiant-Resistive (4 items)

Domineering-Sadistic (4 items)

Heterosexual Interest (6 items)

Hyperactivity-Expansive (6 items)

Poor Emotional Control (5 items)

Needs Approval Dependency (4 items)

Emotional Distance (4 items)

Physical Inferiority-Timidity (5 items)

Schizoid Withdrawal (4 items)

Bizarre Speech and Cognition (7 items)

Bizarre Action (5 items)

Inability to Delay (6 items)

Paranoid Thinking (4 items)

Anxious Self Blame (5 items)

Devereux Child Behavior Rating Scale

The Devereux Child Behavior Rating Scale (DCBR) (Spivak and Spotts, 1966) is designed for use with students who are eight to twelve years of age. It focuses on nonacademic aspects of emotional/behavioral development, which makes it useful for rating the behavior of children who are mentally retarded. It can be completed by persons who have had close contact with the youth over a period of time. The DCBR consists of ninety-seven items divided into seventeen categories:

Distractibility (4 items)

Poor Self Care (2 items)

Pathological Use of Senses (3 items)

Emotional Detachment (6 items)

Social Isolation (3 items)

Poor Coordination and Body Tonus (4 items)

Incontinence (3 items)

Messiness, Sloppiness (3 items)

Inadequate Need for Independence (4 items)

Unresponsiveness to Stimulation (4 items)

Proneness to Emotional Upset (8 items)

Need for Adult Contact (5 items)

Anxious-fearful Ideation (7 items)

"Impulse" Ideation (5 items)

Inability to Delay (6 items)

Social Aggression (4 items)

Unethical Behavior (4 items)

The scores for each category are plotted on a profile sheet. If the score is plotted beyond a certain cutoff line (one standard deviation from the mean), the student is considered to have a problem in that area.

Devereux Elementary School
Behavior Rating Scale

The Devereux Elementary School Behavior Rating Scale (DESB) (Spivak and Swift, 1967) is designed for use with students in kindergarten through sixth grade. The DESB has eleven major sections:

Classroom Disturbance (4 items)

Impatience (4 items)

Disrespect-Defiance (4 items)

External Blame (4 items)

Achievement Anxiety (4 items)

External Reliance (5 items)

Comprehension (3 items)

Inattentive-Withdrawn (4 items)

Irrelevant-Responsiveness (4 items)

Creative Initiative (4 items)

Needs Closeness to Teacher (4 items)

Scores for the various categories are plotted on a profile sheet. If the student's score in a category is plotted beyond a cutoff line provided (one standard deviation), he is considered to have a problem in that area.

Hahnemann Elementary School
Behavior Rating Scale

The Hahnemann Elementary School Behavior Rating Scale (HESB) (Spivak and Swift, 1975) contains sixty items describing desirable and undesirable behavior. The items are separated into fourteen major categories:

Originality (4 items)

Independent Learning (5 items)

Involvement (5 items)

Productive with Peers (3 items)

Intellectual Dependency (4 items)

Failure Anxiety (5 items)

Unreflectiveness (3 items)

Irrelevant Talk (4 items)

Social (Over) Involvement (4 items)

Negative Feelings (5 items)

Holding Back-Withdrawn (5 items)

Critical-Competitive (4 items)

Blaming (4 items)

Approach to Teacher (4 items)

Category scores are plotted on a profile sheet. A score that exceeds a provided cutoff line (one standard deviation from the mean) identifies the student as having a problem in that area.

Hahnemann High School
Behavior Rating Scale

The Hahnemann High School Behavior Rating Scale (HHSB) (Spivak and Swift, 1971) is designed for use with adolescents. It contains forty-five items describing negative and positive behavior. The questions are divided into thirteen categories:

Reasoning Ability (4 items)

Originality (4 items)

Verbal Interaction (3 items)

Rapport with Teacher (3 items)

Anxious Producer (3 items)

General Anxiety (3 items)

Quiet-Withdrawn (4 items)

Poor Work Habits (4 items)

Lacks Intellectual Independence (4 items)

Dogmatic-Inflexible (3 items)

Verbal Negativism (3 items)

Disturbance-Restlessness (4 items)

Expressed Inability (3 items)

Scores for each category are plotted on a profile sheet. Scores that exceed a provided cutoff line (one standard deviation from the mean) indicate a problem for the student in that area.

Louisville Behavior Checklist

The Louisville Behavior Checklist (Miller, 1981) is designed for use with students four to seventeen years of age. This instrument is completed by parents and returned to an outside agency for analysis. The checklist contains 123 to 164 items separated into twenty categories for ages four to six, nineteen categories for ages seven to twelve, and thirteen categories for ages thirteen to seventeen. The categories are:

Ages Four to Six

Infantile Aggression (24 items)

Hyperactivity (17 items)

Antisocial Behavior (13 items)

Aggression (47 items)

Social Withdrawal (18 items)

Sensitivity (15–16 items depending on sex)

Fear (18 items)

Inhibition (43–47 items depending on sex)

Intellectual Deficit (16 items)

Immaturity (10 items)

Cognitive Disability (26 items)

Normal Irritability (24 items)

Prosocial Deficit (13 items)

Rare Deviance (21 items)

Neurotic Behavior (26 items)

Psychotic Behavior (21 items)

Somatic Behavior (12 items)

Sexual Behavior (9 items)

School Disturbance Predictor (16 items)

Severity Level (123 items)

Ages Seven to Twelve

Infantile Aggression (24 items)

Hyperactivity (17 items)

Antisocial Behavior (13 items)

Aggression (47 items)

Social Withdrawal (18 items)

Sensitivity (15–17 items depending on sex)

Fear (18 items)

Inhibition (44–47 items depending on sex)

Academic Disability (14 items)

Immaturity (10 items)

Learning Disability (23 items)

Normal Irritability (14–16 items depending on sex)

Prosocial Deficit (13 items)

Rare Deviance (22–32 items depending on sex)

Neurotic Behavior (23 items)

Psychotic Behavior (14 items)

Somatic Behavior (19 items)

Sexual Behavior (11 items)

Severity Level (143 items)

Ages Thirteen to Seventeen

Egocentric-Exploitive (21 items)

Destructive-Assaultive (16 items)

Social Delinquency (24 items)

Adolescent Turmoil (13 items)

Apathetic Isolation (13 items)

Neuroticism (24 items)

Dependent Inhibited (12 items)

Academic Disability (9 items)

Neurological or Psychotic Abnormality (17 items)

General Pathology (18 items)

Longitudinal (97 items)

Severity (80 items)

Total Pathology (164 items)

Ottawa School Behavior Checklist

The Ottawa School Behavior Checklist (OSBCL) (Pimm and McClure, 1978) contains 100 items that assess academic performance, physical problems, self-care difficulties, aggression and withdrawn behavior, and other traits. Although it is completed by the teacher, it must be sent to an outside agency for scoring.

Walker Problem Behavior
Identification Checklist

The Walker Problem Behavior Identification Checklist (Walker, 1983) is designed for use with students in preschool through grade 6. It consists of fifty items divided into five categories of behavior:

Acting Out (14 items)

Withdrawal (5 items)

Distractibility (11 items)

Disturbed Peer Relations (10 items)

Immaturity (10 items)

The scores for each category are plotted on a profile sheet. A score that exceeds a provided cutoff line indicates that the student has a problem in that area. Different profile scales are provided for males and females.

How to Use Behavior Checklists

1. Decide which checklist(s) is most appropriate for use with your students. Consider the age, mental abilities, and sex of the pupils. Scrutinize the format of the instrument. Decide whether you wish also to use self and peer ratings.

2. Purchase or obtain the desired instrument, administration manuals, and scoring sheets. (Sources for purchasing these materials are listed in the References at the end of this book.)

3. Complete the scales according to directions.

4. Use the information as supporting evidence for decisions

regarding this student or to identify specific behaviors in need of remediation.

Activities and Discussion Questions

1. Obtain different behavior checklists. Compare them, focusing on a certain student with whom you are familiar. Would this student be labeled as *behavior disordered* in a certain area if the checklists were the only criteria for labeling? Do you agree with the ratings given by each instrument?

2. Think of three behaviors displayed by a former student that are not listed on the instruments. Write items or questions for these behaviors. Within which subscale on each behavior checklist would they be included?

3. Obtain different behavior checklists. Compare them for ease of administration, scoring, and wording of items or questions. What are the positive points and drawbacks to each instrument?

4. Complete different behavior checklists. Find the student's behaviors that are most bothersome to you. Go to the strategy sheet section of this book's companion text, entitled *A Resource Book for Remediating Common Behavior and Learning Problems* (Allyn and Bacon, 1989), which contains remedial ideas for various behaviors. Find the proposed solutions for each behavior. Decide which techniques might work with this student.

5. The Walker Problem Behavior Identification Checklist has different scores for identifying males and females as having emotional/behavioral problems. It is possible that even though both obtain the same score on a subtest, the female may be identified as having a problem in need of reme-

diation whereas the male is not identified as such. Is this sexist or is it merely a reflection of our society which gives more behavioral leeway to boys?

6. What are the benefits and drawbacks of using instruments that include the observations of the parent, child, and other professionals?

For More Information

Taylor, R. L. (1980). *Assessment of exceptional students.* Englewood Cliffs, N.J.: Prentice-Hall.

3

Symptom Checklists

The following checklists were developed to *assist* you in determining if a student has a condition that *may* be in need of specialized intervention. Although the proper identification of these conditions may require medical or psychological evaluation, these checklists can assist you in determining whether to refer a student for further evaluation.

The checklists contain items that are indicators of certain behavioral or learning patterns along with characteristics that often accompany that state. They are *not* listed in any hierarchical order; rather, they are listed in random order.

There is no score or scoring pattern that will indicate that the student has a condition in need of remediation, instruction, or assistance. You must make the referral decision based on your perception of the severity of the condition. Be aware that some symptoms can be indicative of numerous conditions or can exist in isolation with no connection to any condition listed. The following conditions are addressed:

Achievement Anxiety

Alcoholism

Anorexia Nervosa

Asthenic Personality

Autism

Bulimia

Child Abuse and Neglect Victimization

Delinquency

Depression

Dropout Proneness

Giftedness

Hyperactivity

Hyperactivity Medication Side Effects

Kleptomania

Learning Disabilities

Manic-Depressive Personality

Marijuana Abuse

Passive-Aggressive Personality

Pinball or Video Game Addiction

Poor Self-Concept

Pregnancy

Premenstrual Syndrome (PMS)

Pyromania

Schizophrenia

School Phobia

Shoplifting

Social Overinvolvement

Social Withdrawal

Suicide Proneness

Test Anxiety

Achievement Anxiety

_____ Says and does things that display a low self-esteem (Gaudry and Spielberger, 1971; Niles and Mustachio, 1978).

_____ Has a tendency to choose easy tasks because success is more certain (Gaudry and Spielberger, 1971; Hill and Wigfield, 1984).

_____ Has difficulty communicating with others (Gaudry and Spielberger, 1971).

_____ Parents indicate their child had difficulty learning to read (Gaudry and Spielberger, 1971).

_____ Discrepancies exist between the student's potential and actual performance (Dowdall and Colangelo, 1982).

_____ Low standardized test scores coupled with high performance (Hegeman, 1981).

_____ Will not give obvious answers to easy questions, fearing the tester might be playing a trick on him. The student subscribes to the theory, "It can't be this easy or they wouldn't have asked it." This applies to achievement and IQ tests (Holt, 1969).

_____ Parents push the child mercilessly to achieve.

_____ Falling grades from early kindergarten or first grade through the intermediate grades. This may or may not occur gradually (Rimm, 1984).

_____ Inconsistent work (Rimm, 1984).

_____ Poor study habits (Rimm, 1984).

———— Lack of concentration (Rimm, 1984).

———— Hyperactivity (Rimm, 1984).

———— Perfectionism (Rimm, 1984).

———— Pokiness (Rimm, 1984).

———— Noncompletion of assignments (Rimm, 1984).

———— Disorganization (Deffenbacher and Kemper, 1974; Rimm, 1984).

———— Inability to think clearly when confronted with test materials (Rogers, 1977).

———— Total blocking of thoughts in testing situations (Rogers, 1977).

———— Extreme nervousness during testing situations (Rogers, 1977).

———— Short attention span during testing situations (Deffenbacher and Kemper, 1974).

———— Easily distracted while taking a test (Deffenbacher and Kemper, 1974).

———— Experiences difficulty reading and comprehending simple sentences on a test (Deffenbacher and Kemper, 1974).

———— Unable to recall and organize materials in an orderly fashion during testing (Deffenbacher and Kemper, 1974).

———— May "draw a blank" in testing situations (Deffenbacher and Kemper, 1974).

———— May display disruptive attention-getting behavior (Nicholls, 1976).

———— Tends to depend on teachers for guidance (Nicholls, 1976).

———— Exhibits an extreme reluctance to go to school (Kelly, 1973).

———— Attempts to avoid highly evaluative situations (Hill and Wigfield, 1984).

_____ Displays more persistence on easy tasks in which success is more certain (Hill and Wigfield, 1984).

_____ Asks many questions concerning homework assignments (Doll and Fleming, 1966).

_____ Is very concerned about completing assignments correctly (Doll and Fleming, 1966).

_____ Indulges in daydreaming (Gaudry and Spielberger, 1971; Rimm, 1984).

_____ Describes himself negatively (Deffenbacher and Kemper, 1974).

_____ Has a tense posture during testing situations (Gaudry and Spielberger, 1971).

_____ Heart beats rapidly during testing situations (Rogers, 1977).

_____ Faints when given tests (Rogers, 1977).

_____ Becomes nauseous and lightheaded when given a test (Deffenbacher and Kemper, 1974).

_____ Becomes shaky when given a test (Deffenbacher and Kemper, 1974).

_____ Complains of aches or pains in the stomach in the morning before school (Lall and Lall, 1979).

_____ Becomes pale (Lall and Lall, 1979).

_____ Has problems with diarrhea (Lall and Lall, 1979).

_____ Has trouble sleeping at night (Lall and Lall, 1979).

_____ Wets the bed at home (Lall and Lall, 1979).

_____ Refuses to eat breakfast on the days he goes to school (Lall and Lall, 1979).

_____ Reports to the nurse's office for some accident or physical complaint (Gaudry and Spielberger, 1971).

_____ Less secure than other students (Faudry and Spielberger, 1971).

———   Receives less favorable sociometric rankings from peers (Nicholls, 1976).

———   Is seen in a negative way by peers (Gaudry and Spielberger, 1971).

———   Parents report that their child worries about missing school if ill (Gaudry and Spielberger, 1971).

———   Parents report that their child has many negative feelings about starting school at the beginning of the year (Gaudry and Spielberger, 1971).

———   Feels he must be perfect on work or achieve perfect scores on tests (Rogers, 1977).

———   Expects to fail tests (Sepie and Keeling, 1978).

———   On the way to school, he worries that the teacher might give the class a test (Sepie and Keeling, 1978).

———   Is so preoccupied with thoughts of approaching tests, he excludes other thoughts (Rogers, 1977).

———   Feels that failing a test is the worst experience one can have (Rogers, 1977).

———   Even after a good test performance, the student feels he must do better (Rogers, 1977).

———   Feels that he has never done well on tests, therefore he will not do well on upcoming tests (Rogers, 1977).

———   Feels it is awful or terrible to take tests (Rogers, 1977).

———   Correlates his test score with feelings of being a success or failure. Low scores reveal failure and high scores reveal success (Rogers, 1977).

———   Fear of failing, or uncertainty about the unfamiliar, making him uncomfortable and tense (Chen, 1982).

———   Instead of facing challenges, he builds a shelter to protect himself with a false sense of security (Chen, 1982).

———   Parents have overexpectations or underexpectations for their child.

———— Feels that the classroom is "closing in" on him (Rogers, 1977).

———— Feels inadequate compared to other students (Rogers, 1977).

———— Feels unable to compete with other students (Rogers, 1977).

———— Has a fear of separation from his mother or either of the parents (Kelly, 1973).

———— Overly concerned with parents' and teachers' evaluations of his performance (Hill and Wigfield, 1984).

Alcoholism

———— Severe headaches (Ingalls, 1983; Royce, 1981).

———— Nausea (Ingalls, 1983; Lake, 1983; Baron, 1983).

———— Vomiting (Ingalls, 1983; Lake, 1983; Baron, 1983).

———— Diarrhea (Baron, 1983).

———— Passing out (Marks, 1983).

———— Blackouts. Episodes of amnesia (Marks, 1983).

———— Unsteady gait or wobbly walk (Coffey, 1971).

———— Nail biting (Tahka, 1966).

———— Slurred speech.

———— Stammering (Tahka, 1966).

———— Bed wetting (Tahka, 1966).

———— Insomnia (Tahka, 1966).

———— Unclear eyes (Coffey, 1971).

———— Shaky hands (Coffey, 1971).

———— Slight increase of puffiness about the face (Coffey, 1971).

———— Tiny beads of sweat clustered under the eyes (Coffey, 1971).

_____ Neglect of physical cleanliness (Royce, 1981).

_____ Weight gain in a puffy fashion (Royce, 1981).

_____ Severe acne (Bucky, 1978).

_____ Flushed skintone (Bucky, 1978).

_____ Shortness of breath (Bucky, 1978).

_____ Severe stomach cramps (Bucky, 1978; NEFA, 1983).

_____ Morning cough, raspy voice, huskiness in throat (Bucky, 1978).

_____ Lowered tolerance to physical pain (Coffey, 1971).

_____ Smell of liquor on breath (Coffey, 1971).

_____ Malnutrition.

_____ Difficulty in swallowing.

_____ Dry heaves (Bucky, 1978).

_____ Erratic eating patterns (Coffey, 1971).

_____ Dehydration.

_____ Increase in blood pressure.

_____ DTs (Delirum Tremens) (Baron, 1983).

_____ Misses classes (Ingalls, 1983).

_____ Fighting (Ingalls, 1983).

_____ Loss of job (Ingalls, 1983).

_____ Damages property (Ingalls, 1983).

_____ Erratic behavior (Kiechel, 1982).

_____ Capacity for drinking declines (Kiechel, 1982).

_____ Cannot predict his actions when drinking (Kiechel, 1982).

_____ Consistently finishes a drink ahead of others. Draws ahead of others in consumption (Mann, 1950).

_____ Under stress, drink is used as a medicine (Kessel and Walton, 1967; Alcoholics Anonymous, 1983).

_____ Constant gum or mint chewing (Coffey, 1971).

_____ Becomes loud, argumentative, belligerent, or violent (Mann, 1950).

_____ Irritability (Clinebell, 1968).

_____ Compulsive lying/covering up (Marks, 1983).

_____ Preoccupation with alcohol (Lake, 1983).

_____ Deterioration of social relationships (Carroll, 1970).

_____ Recurrent periods of irritability, flashes of temper, unreasonable ideas (Mann, 1950).

_____ Problems with spouse or boyfriend/girlfriend (Cahalcon, 1970).

_____ Problems with work/boss (Cahalcon, 1970).

_____ Hides bottles.

_____ Drop in grades.

_____ Change in friendships.

_____ Work begins to slide.

_____ Drinks on weekdays.

_____ Makes excuses to drink.

_____ Thought, judgment, and restraint impaired.

_____ Immature behavior (Kessel and Walton, 1967).

_____ Drinks before facing certain situations (NIMH, 1969).

_____ Frequent drinking sprees (NIMH, 1969).

_____ Steady increase in intake (NIMH, 1969).

_____ Solitary drinking (NIMH, 1969).

_____ Early morning drinking (NIMH, 1969).

_____ Monday morning absenteeism (NIMH, 1969).

_____ Frequent outbursts of temper (Mittenthal, 1983).

_____ A generally resentful attitude (Mittenthal, 1983).

_____ Overreaction to minor mishaps (Mittenthal, 1983).

_____ Drop in performance levels at school (Mittenthal, 1983).

_____ Lack of interest in formerly favored hobbies, sports, or activities (Mittenthal, 1983).

_____ Lack of energy (Carroll, 1970).

_____ Sudden interest in a new group of friends and new hangouts (Mittenthal, 1983).

_____ Loss of short-term memory (Mittenthal, 1981).

_____ Mental fatigue.

_____ Noticeable drop in attention span; lack of concentration (Mittenthal, 1983).

_____ Distorted sense of time (Mittenthal, 1983).

_____ Vague or secretive attitudes about friends and activities (Mittenthal, 1983).

_____ Stealing money or salable items from home (Mittenthal, 1983).

_____ Recognizes there is a problem but cannot stop drinking (Kessel and Walton, 1967; AA, 1983).

_____ Lack of motivation (Mittenthal, 1983).

_____ "Couldn't care less" attitude about everything (Coffey, 1971).

_____ Mind seems fogged, confused at times (Royce, 1981).

_____ Psychological dependence on alcohol (Cahalcon, 1970).

_____ Resentment toward the world (Mann, 1950).

_____ Erratic emotions (Coffey, 1971).

_____ Extended periods of moddiness (Mittenthal, 1983).

_____ Low self-esteem (Kiechel, 1982).

Anorexia Nervosa

_____ A drop in body weight of at least 25 percent (MacLeod, 1981).

_____ Lack of menstral periods (Knickerbocker, 1983).

_____ Constipation (Baker and Bayner, 1984).

_____ Loss of hair and lowered nail quality (Baker and Bayner, 1984).

_____ Dental cavities and peridontal disease from vomiting (Bruch, 1973).

_____ Slow pulse and respiration (Bruch, 1973).

_____ Failure of sexual functioning (Bruch, 1973).

_____ Easily bruised with cuts and sores taking months to heal (Liu, 1979).

_____ Use of large, loose-fitting clothes to hide thinness (Shainess, 1984).

_____ Often cold (Shainess, 1984).

_____ Insomnia (MacLeod, 1981).

_____ Anenorrhea.

_____ Hypothermia (Bruch, 1973).

_____ Appearance of being "deathly" skinny (Shainess, 1984).

_____ Skin rash and dry skin (Liu, 1979).

_____ Persistent denial of the problem (MacLeod, 1981).

_____ Excessive use of laxatives, diuretics, emetics, and diet pills (MacLeod, 1981).

_____ Unusual eating habits or refusal to eat (Bruch, 1973).

_____ Secretive about how much has been eaten (Liu, 1979).

_____ Increased isolation (Liu, 1979; Bruch, 1978).

_____ Pronounced hyperactivity (Bruch, 1973).

_____ Self-induced vomiting after eating.

_____ Compulsive perfectionism (Shainess, 1984).

_____ Denial of fatigue (Bruch, 1973).

_____ Close analyzation of food intake.

_____ Overestimation of weight (Bruch, 1973).

———— Obsession with weighing oneself on scales (Shainess, 1984).

———— Increased interest in cooking or meal preparation (Mallick, 1984).

———— Distorted body image; insists she cannot "see" the extent of the thinness (Bruch, 1978).

———— Disturbed sense of time (Bruch, 1978).

———— Becomes completely self-absorbed, ruminating only about weight and food (Bruch, 1978).

———— Thinking and goals become bizarre. May construct unusual ideas about what happens to food (Bruch, 1978).

———— Hyperacuity of senses (Bruch, 1978).

———— Enormous display of self-discipline (Shainess, 1984).

———— Distorted sense of body functions (Shainess, 1984).

———— Avoidance of all food and food-related activities (Shainess, 1984).

———— Change in eating habits (Liu, 1979).

———— Believes that thinness is its own reward (Shainess, 1984).

———— Unconscious fantasies that all food is poison (Shainess, 1984).

———— Chemical imbalances may distort thinking to a degree that the individual can no longer rationally evaluate the dangers of the behavior (Mallick, 1984).

———— Inability to deal with stress (Mallick, 1984).

———— Inability to separate from parents (Mallick, 1984).

———— Recently rejected by peers (Mallick, 1984).

———— Sudden interest in diet books (Mallick, 1984).

———— Withdrawal from peer relationships (Mallick, 1984).

———— Experiences highly obsessive or ritualistic behaviors in relationship to activities other than those that are related to food (Mallick, 1984).

_____ Increased participation in school activities, decreasing the time available to eat (Mallick, 1984).

_____ Recognizes the dangers of the behavior, but denies the possibility that she will be the one to experience the fatal consequences (Mallick, 1984).

_____ Believes she will be able to recognize the danger signs in time to control the behavior (Mallick, 1984).

_____ Has a love/hate relationship with food.

_____ Has a need to be "perfect" in the eyes of others.

_____ Feels lonely or excluded and not truly valued (Bruch, 1978).

_____ Extraordinary pride and pleasure taken in being able to do something so difficult as losing weight (Bruch, 1978).

_____ Low sense of self-worth (Liu, 1979).

_____ Fear of puberty (Mallick, 1984).

_____ Need for a sense of identity (Bruch, 1973).

Asthenic Personality

"A personality disorder, characterized by low energy level, easy fatigability, incapacity for enjoyment and lack of enthusiasms, and oversensitivity to physical and emotional stress" (Hinsie and Campbell, 1970).

_____ Temper displays (Millon, 1969).

_____ Shows malice toward others (Wolman, 1965).

_____ Slow speech and movement (Millon, 1969).

_____ Finds it hard to complete tasks (Goldenson, 1970).

_____ Tries to escape responsibility (Goldenson, 1970).

_____ Lack social interaction (Millon, 1969).

_____ Lack of spontaneity (Millon, 1969).

———— Appears to be involved in own preoccupations (Millon, 1969).

———— Hypochondriac (Eidelberg, 1968).

———— Chroncially tired (Kretschmer, 1970).

———— Frail (Kretschmer, 1970).

———— Clumsy (Millon, 1969).

———— Low energy level (Hinsie and Campbell, 1970).

———— Quick mental fatigue (Slater and Roth, 1969).

———— Easy physical fatigue (Hinsie and Campbell, 1970).

———— Poor memory (Hinsie and Campbell, 1970).

———— Easily distracted (Coleman, 1964).

———— Irritable (Coleman, 1964).

———— Insensitive (Millon, 1969).

———— Depressed (Kisker, 1972).

———— Immature (Goldenson, 1970).

———— Frustrated (Goldenson, 1970).

———— Feels rejected (Goldenson, 1970).

———— Lack of initiative (Slater and Roth, 1969).

———— Fears exercise and injury (Goldenson, 1970).

———— Inability to concentrate (Goldenson, 1970).

———— Lacks enthusiasm and motivation (Hinsie and Campbell, 1970).

———— Overly dependent (Goldenson, 1970).

———— Weak willed (Millon, 1969).

———— Excessive concern with health (Wolman, 1965).

———— Lacks self-confidence (Millon, 1969).

———— Feels inadequate (Millon, 1969).

———— Easily discouraged (Goldenson, 1970).

———— Takes criticism poorly (Goldenson, 1970).

_____ Finds it difficult to make decisions (Goldenson, 1970).

Autism

_____ Intelligence is potentially normal (Koegel, Lovaas, and Schreibman, 1977).

_____ Symptoms present from beginning of life (Rimland, 1974).

_____ High levels of intellectual ability and achievement among parents (Rimland, 1974).

_____ Personality of parents is cold, bookish, formal, introverted, and rather humorless and detached (Rimland, 1974).

_____ Parents display rationality and objectivity, politeness, dignity, and seriousness (Rimland, 1974).

_____ Smiled, cut teeth, sat up, crawled, and walked at usual ages.

_____ Weight gain normal once early feeding problems have passed.

_____ Delay in fine motor development.

_____ Values sameness (Aptic and Conoley, 1973).

_____ Unstable and indefinite self-concept (Berry, 1969; Mussen, 1973).

_____ Forms no relationships with others (Mussen, 1973; Newcomer, 1980; Riess, 1968; Koegel, Lovaas, and Schreibman, 1977).

_____ Lonely, isolated, and withdrawn (Mussen, 1973; Berry, 1969; Koegel, Lovaas, and Schreibman, 1977).

_____ Appears aloof and disinterested in people (Aptic and Conoley, 1973; Newcomer, 1980; Riess, 1968; Berry, 1969).

_____ Irritable when confronted with stress (Riess, 1968; Newcomer, 1980).

_____ Deliberately does not follow orders.

_____ Shows no interest or sympathy for others (Riess, 1968).

_____ Absorption into fantasy as an escape from reality (Newcomer, 1980).

_____ Lack of creativity (Rutter, 1978).

_____ Placid and undemanding (Rutter, 1978).

_____ Cannot be comforted or soothed when crying.

_____ Does not cry when hungry.

_____ Needs a routine (Berry, 1969; Rutter, 1968).

_____ Resistent to change in menu.

_____ Loves music (Berry, 1969; Newcomer, 1980).

_____ Has a "distant" gaze (Koegel, Lovaas, and Schreibman, 1977).

_____ Does not gaze at people or objects for any length of time (Rutter, 1978).

_____ Likes mechanical toys (Newcomer, 1980; Riess, 1968).

_____ Interested in a special object.

_____ Bizarre and compulsive behavior (Berry, 1969; Aptic and Conoley, 1973; Rimland, 1974; Koegel, Lovaas, and Schreibman, 1977).

_____ Little variation of facial expression; no social smiles (Mussen, 1973).

_____ Quiet, passive, and inattentive (Rimland, 1974; Kogel, Lovaas, and Schreibman, 1977).

_____ Self-stimulation (Koegel, Lovaas, and Schreibman, 1977).

_____ Self-abusive (Gillman, 1981; Riess, 1968).

_____ Repeated arm and hand movements (Gillman, 1981; Berry, 1969).

_____ Rocking.

_____ Banging of head (Rimland, 1974).

_____ Repeated outbursts of laughter.

_____ Fluttering of eyelids (Berry, 1968).

_____ Hyperactivity (Riess, 1968).

_____ Fidgetiness (Riess, 1968).

_____ Ritualistic and compulsive behavior (Rimland, 1974).

_____ Nonresponsive or overresponsive to varying levels of sound (Gillman, 1981; Newcomer, 1980; Berry, 1969).

_____ Repetitive or stereotyped movements (Newcomer, 1980).

_____ Screams a great deal during both day and night.

_____ Screams especially upon awakening.

_____ Perseveration.

_____ Perseverates with a special object (Aptic and Conoley, 1973; Newcomer, 1980).

_____ Looks around the room.

_____ Avoidance of eye contact (Campbell, Scaturro, and Lickson, 1983).

_____ Collects items.

_____ Enjoys playing with water, sand, or mud.

_____ Enjoys watching patterns of movements.

_____ Odd posture when standing (Berry, 1969).

_____ Difficulty stopping movement.

_____ Absence or delay in movement.

_____ Motor and manual ability is excellent (Rimland, 1974).

_____ Resists being held (Rimland, 1974).

_____ Short attention span.

_____ Nonresponsive or overresponsive to touch and pain (Gillman, 1981; Riess, 1968).

_____ Pays close attention to visual details (Gillman, 1981).

———— Displays aggressive behaviors.

———— Twirls self.

———— Walks on tip toes.

———— Dry-eyed crying (Riess, 1968).

———— Sniffling and drooling (Riess, 1968).

———— Lack of initiative to communicate (Rimland, 1974).

———— Mutism (Kiernan, 1983).

———— Seems unaware that speech has a meaning.

———— Limited comprehension of oral language.

———— Echolalia (Rimland, 1974; Koegel, Lovaas, and Schreibman, 1977; Aptic and Conoley, 1973; Berry, 1969; Riess, 1968; Kiernan, 1983).

———— Learns only one name for items.

———— Difficulty controlling volume of his voice.

———— Lacking language and imagination (Newcomer, 1980; Kiernan, 1983).

———— Failure to develop the use of abstract terms, concepts, and reasoning (Gillman, 1981).

———— Failure to assign symbolic meanings to gestures (Gillman, 1981; Kiernan, 1983).

———— Hums or sings at perfect pitch (Rimland, 1974).

———— Early use of words before speech is usually discontinued (Rimland, 1974).

———— Uncommunicative speech (Rimland, 1974; Mussen, 1973; Rutter, 1978; Kiernan, 1983).

———— Pronominal reversal (Rimland, 1974; Aptic and Conoley, 1973).

———— Affirmation by repetition (Rimland, 1974).

———— Extreme literalness (Rimland, 1974).

———— Metaphorical use of language (Rimland, 1974; Aptic and Conoley, 1973).

_____ Disordered speech, omitting words, inverted word order (Aptic and Conoley, 1973).

_____ Inability to make meaningful identifications (Berry, 1969; Newcomer, 1980).

_____ Dull, meaningless intonation pattern and cluttered rhythm (Berry, 1969; Kiernan, 1983).

_____ Communicates through body gestures (Berry, 1969; Kiernan, 1983).

Bulimia

Binge-eating followed by self-initiated vomiting.

_____ Ulcers (Doane, 1983).

_____ Hernias (Seligman and Zabarsky, 1983).

_____ Hypothermia (Doane, 1983; Yudkovitz, 1983).

_____ Disturbance of the blood's chemical balance (Doane, 1983).

_____ Bloodshot eyes (Fischer, 1982; Yudkovitz, 1983).

_____ Dental problems due to acidity in vomitus (Doane, 1983; O'Neill, 1982; Seligmann and Zabarsky, 1983; Yudkovitz, 1983).

_____ Enamel coming off the teeth (Doane, 1983; O'Neill, 1982; Seligman and Zabarsky, 1983; Yudkovitz, 1983).

_____ Teeth feel loose (Fischer, 1982; Yudkovitz, 1983).

_____ Swollen parotid glands; cheeks swell (Doane, 1983; Landau, 1983; Yudkovitz, 1983).

_____ Numbness in feet and hands (Fischer, 1982).

_____ Has the chills (Padus, 1981; O'Neill, 1982).

_____ Irregular menstrual cycle (O'Neill, 1982; Yudkovitz, 1983).

_____ No menstrual cycle (Landau, 1983).

_____ Complains of dizziness (O'Neill, 1982; Yudkovitz, 1983).

_____ Stomach pains (Chernin, 1981; Doane, 1983; O'Neill, 1982).

_____ Weak (Doane, 1983; O'Neill, 1982; Yudkovitz, 1983).

_____ Constipation (O'Neill, 1982).

_____ Insomnia.

_____ Skin rash and dry skin.

_____ Loss of hair and nail quality.

_____ Heartbeat drops to 50 to 55 per minute (72 beats per minute is average for normal women) (Padus, 1981).

_____ Blood pressure drops to 80/50 (120/70 is normal for young women) (Padus, 1981).

_____ Eats compulsively (Lukeman and Sorensen, 1974).

_____ Binges on favorite foods (Landau, 1983; Garfinkel and Moldofsky, 1980).

_____ Binges on high-calorie foods (Landau, 1983; Yudkovitz, 1983).

_____ Eats one meal on top of the other (Landau, 1983; Yudkovitz, 1983).

_____ Binging on food is a ritual (Garfinkel and Moldofsky, 1980; Landau, 1983).

_____ Vomits in private several times a day (Garginkel and Moldofsky, 1980; Landau, 1983).

_____ Goes to the restroom each time after eating (Mayer, 1982).

_____ Has been on a stringent diet (Frumkes, 1982).

_____ Has a chronic sore throat (Landau, 1983; Yudkovitz, 1983).

_____ Excess use of laxatives, diuretics, emetics, and diet pills.

_____ Changes in personality or behavior (Garfinkel and Moldofsky, 1980).

_____ Use of street drugs (Garfinkel and Moldofsky, 1980).

_____ Suicide attempts (Garfinkel and Moldofsky, 1980).

_____ Stealing (Garfinkel and Moldofsky, 1980).

_____ Low self-esteem (Bauer, 1983; Katzman and Wolchik, 1983; Todt, 1983).

_____ Feels depressed (Fischer, 1982; Garfinkel and Moldofsky, 1980; Yudkovitz, 1983).

_____ Feelings of loneliness (Garfinkel and Moldofsky, 1980; Mayer, 1982; Yudkovitz, 1983).

_____ Fear (Garfinkel and Moldofsky, 1980; Mayer, 1982; Yudkovitz, 1983).

_____ Insecurity (Chernin, 1981; Garfinkel and Moldofsky, 1980; _Good Housekeeping_, 1982; Yudkovitz, 1983).

_____ Seeks attention from parents (Chernin, 1981; Katzman and Wolchik, 1983; Orbach, 1982).

_____ Dependent on others (Orbach, 1982).

_____ Perfectionist (Frumkes, 1982; Katzman and Wolchik, 1983; M.L.S., 1982; Yudkovitz, 1983).

_____ Feels "out of control" (Orbach, 1982).

Child Abuse and Neglect Victimization

Physical Abuse: Includes any nonaccidental, physical injury caused by the child's caretaker (Broadhurst, Edmunds, and MacDicken, 1979).

_____ Unexplained bruises or welts (Broadhurst, Edmunds, and MacDicken, 1979).

_____ Unexplained burns suggestive of smoking materials, iron or stove burns, or hot liquids (Broadhurst, Edmunds, and MacDicken, 1979).

_____ Swollen or tender spots on limbs (McIntyre, 1982).

_____ Fear of adults (McIntyre, 1982).

_____ Injuries appearing to be inflicted by an instrument (e.g., belt buckle, rope, or cord) (McIntyre, 1982).

_____ Human bites appearing as crescent or oval shaped bruises (Faller, 1981).

_____ Pain, swelling, and discoloration over a bone or joint (Faller, 1981).

_____ Internal injuries appearing as pain, fever, vomiting, respiratory distress, drowsiness, and nonresponsiveness (Faller, 1981).

_____ Scars in unusual areas or of unique shapes (Faller, 1981).

_____ Unusually docile behavior (Faller, 1981).

Emotional Abuse: Parental behavior that leads to psychological as opposed to physical harm to the child (Faller, 1981).

_____ Ticks (Faller, 1981).

_____ Low self-esteem (Faller, 1981).

_____ School failure (Faller, 1981).

_____ Hyperactivity (Faller, 1981).

_____ Aggressive behavior (Faller, 1981).

_____ Bizarre behavior (Faller, 1981).

Neglect: Inattention to the basic needs of the child, such as food, clothing, shelter, medical care, and supervision.

_____ Extremely unkept appearance, poor hygiene (McIntyre, 1982).

_____ Constant hunger (Broadhurst, Edmunds, and MacDicken, 1979).

_____ Untreated scrapes or cuts (Broadhurst, Edmunds, and MacDicken, 1979).

_____ Repeated truancy (McIntyre, 1982).

_____ Odor of alcohol on student's breath (McIntyre, 1982).

_____ Inappropriate clothing for the season.

Sexual Abuse: Any contacts or interactions between a child and an adult in which the child is being used for the sexual stimulation of the adult.

_____ Difficulty in walking or sitting (Broadhurst, Edmunds, and MacDicken, 1979).

_____ Stained, bloody, or torn underwear (Broadhurst, Edmunds, and MacDicken, 1979).

_____ Venereal disease (McIntyre, 1982).

_____ Pregnancy in early adolescence (McIntyre, 1982).

_____ Unwillingness to disrobe for gym, showers, or physical examinations (McIntyre, 1982).

_____ Intimate knowledge about sexual matters beyond his or her developmental level (Faller, 1981).

Delinquency

_____ Restless and energetic (Gavain, 1954).

_____ Adventurous and inclined toward activities that offer risk and excitement (Gavain, 1954).

_____ Doesn't get along with other students of the same age (Gavain, 1954).

_____ Associates mainly with other students who are delinquent (Gavain, 1954).

_____ Unsuccessful in school (Gavain, 1954; Polk and Schaefer,

1972; Empey and Hubeck, 1971; Frease, 1973; Jensen, 1976).

_____ Has repeated several grades (Gavain, 1954).

_____ Chronically truant (Gavain, 1954).

_____ Rejects school authority figures (Hindeland, 1973; Jensen, Erickson, and Gibbs, 1978).

_____ Gives in easily to peer pressure (Jensen and Rojek, 1980).

_____ Impulsive (Gavain, 1954).

_____ Brags about his criminal or immoral behavior.

_____ Has been apprehended by the police for misbehavior.

_____ Belongs to a "gang."

_____ Stays out late.

_____ Is internally disturbed by unhappy family relationships (Gavain, 1954).

_____ Feels rejected in home, school, and community (Gavain, 1954).

_____ Dislikes school intensely and intends to drop out as soon as the law allows (Gavain, 1954; Hindeland, 1973; Jensen, Erickson, and Gibbs, 1978).

_____ Has low aspirations for himself (Hirschi, 1969).

_____ In suspicious and distrustful of others (Jesness, 1963).

Depression

_____ Withdrawn (Morse, 1975).

_____ Cries often (Stumphauzer, 1977).

_____ Talks about suicide (Stumphauzer, 1977).

_____ Frequent temper tantrums (Gordon, 1981).

_____ Disobedient (Gordon, 1981).

_____ Truant (Gordon, 1981).

_____ Runs away from home (Gordon, 1981).

_____ Fails to achieve in school (Gordon, 1981).

_____ Inhibited (Gordon, 1981).

_____ Lacks interest in activities (Gordon, 1981).

_____ Listless or bored (Gordon, 1981).

_____ Aggressive behavior (Gordon, 1981).

_____ Change in school performance (Gordon, 1981).

_____ Diminished socialization (Gordon, 1981).

_____ Regression from social contact (Gordon, 1981).

_____ Participates in excessive activity to mask depression (Derdeyn, 1983).

_____ Hypoactive (Kashani and Ray, 1983).

_____ Hyperactive (Kahani and Ray, 1983).

_____ Socially isolated (Berndt and Kaiser, 1983).

_____ Frequent physical complaints (Gordon, 1981).

_____ Sleep disturbances (Gordon, 1981).

_____ Loss of usual energy (Gordon, 1981).

_____ Unusual changes in appetite or weight (Gordon, 1981).

_____ Fatigue (Kashani and Ray, 1983).

_____ Low self-esteem (Morse, 1975; Ornstein, 1975).

_____ Drifts into a world of fantasy (Morse, 1975).

_____ Feels demoralized (Ornstein, 1975).

_____ Low and unrealistic aspiration levels (Ornstein, 1975).

_____ Generally sad, depressed, and unhappy (Gordon, 1981).

_____ Angry (Derdeyn, 1983; Berndt and Kaiser, 1983).

_____ Irritable (Kashani and Ray, 1983).

_____ Apathetic (Kashani and Ray, 1983).

_____ Feelings of hopelessness (Butler and Whipple, 1983).

_____ Negative attitudes (Butler and Whipple, 1983).

——— Extremely shy (Callahan, 1979).

——— Psychoneurotic (Callahan, 1979).

——— Extremely fearful (Callahan, 1979).

——— Irrational beliefs (Kelly and Lahey, 1983).

——— Lonely (Berndt and Kaiser, 1983).

——— Feeling very stressed (Berndt and Kaiser, 1983).

——— External as opposed to internal locus of control. Believes he has little control over what happens to him (Banks and Goggin, 1983).

Dropout Proneness

——— Lack of proper parental direction, concerns, and motivation (Drummie, 1970).

——— Complains about home, community, parents, and peers (Lindsay, 1977).

——— Has older siblings who have dropped out (Martin, 1981).

——— Incompatibility with siblings (Drummie, 1970).

——— Unclean, disorderly home with lack of cultural refinement (Glueck and Gluech, 1970).

——— Father has poor work habits and lack of ambition (Glueck and Glueck, 1970).

——— Family is in the low socioeconomic status (Drummie, 1970; Jablonsky, 1970; Martin, 1981).

——— Parent achieved a low-grade level education (Jablonsky, 1970).

——— Lack of parental/community direction, concern, or motivation toward higher education (Drummie, 1970).

——— Family has lack of group recreation (Glueck and Glueck, 1970).

_____ Parents are not involved in school activities (Martin, 1981).

_____ Student has excessive street life (Hardy and Cull, 1974).

_____ Lack of friends (Young and Reich, 1974).

_____ Discourages easily (Merrill, 1947).

_____ Poor recreation habits and delinquent companions (Hardy and Cull, 1974).

_____ Frequently absent (Carroll, 1981).

_____ Unexcused absences (Carroll, 1981).

_____ Does not bring necessary materials to class (Beck, 1981).

_____ Does less than half of his homework (Wrieley, 1982).

_____ Experiences difficulty in many academic subjects (Simon, 1980).

_____ Often off-task (Carroll, 1981).

_____ Usually the last student to return to the classroom after recess (Giffin, 1980).

_____ Needs much more time to complete an assignment when compared to the rest of the class (C. Calvano, personal communication, 1983).

_____ Often in trouble and spends a large percentage of time in the principal's office (C. Calvano, personal communication, 1983; Martin, 1981).

_____ Not interested in class projects in which he must create his own work (Simon, 1980).

_____ Retained in lower grades (Martin, 1981).

_____ Poor work and study habits (Young and Reich, 1974).

_____ Is not involved in school activities (Young and Reich, 1974).

_____ Frequently moves from school to school (Glueck and Glueck, 1970).

_____ Tends to isolate himself in class (Wirtanen, 1969; Beck, 1981; Lindsay, 1977; Sewell, 1981).

_____ Not liked by other classmates (Wirtanen, 1969; Giffin, 1980).

_____ Older than his classmates (C. Calvano, personal communication, 1983).

_____ Failure in school (Wirtanen, 1969).

_____ Rejected by school (Jablonsky, 1970).

_____ Rejected by peers and teachers (Young and Reich, 1974).

_____ Low vocational maturity (Sewell, 1981).

_____ Seldom volunteers to answer questions or display work (Wrieley, 1982).

_____ Indifferent towards the activities occurring in the classroom (C. Calvano, personal communication, 1983).

_____ Resents authority. Must repeatedly be told to do a particular task (Carroll, 1981).

_____ Sees little importance in education. Feels he can survive without it (Young and Reich, 1974; Giffin, 1980).

_____ Fabricates stories about health problems so that he is frequently excused from class and sent to the nurse (Carroll, 1981).

_____ Feelings of being a competent adult. Thinks "Who needs school?" (Wirtanen, 1969).

Giftedness

_____ Large vocabulary. Knows and uses advanced terminology (Ehrlich, 1982).

_____ Expresses self well; both orally and written. Uses longer sentences than peers (Ehrlich, 1982).

_____ Good memory for details (Ehrlich, 1982).

_____ More socially mature than nongifted peers (Terman and Oden, 1976).

_____ Advanced skills in music, writing, poetry, and/or art at an early age (Cox, 1976).

_____ Variety of interests (Terman and Oden, 1976).

_____ Displays leadership capabilities (Hewett and Forness, 1977).

_____ Sensitive and alert to the environment (Hewett and Forness, 1977).

_____ Persistent. Intense application of energies (Hewett and Forness, 1977).

_____ Displays originality (Hewett and Forness, 1977).

_____ Creative (Ehrlich, 1982).

_____ Interested in unusual, esoteric subjects (Hewett and Forness, 1977).

_____ Is an avid reader; reads a broad variety of materials (Ehrlich, 1982).

_____ Long attention span (Ehrlich, 1982).

_____ High academic grades.

_____ Usually high ability in one or more areas.

_____ Parents report quick understanding, insatiable curiosity, extensive information, retentive memory, large vocabulary, and unusual interest in number relations, atlases, and encyclopedias (Terman and Oden, 1976).

_____ Has intelligent parents (Cox, 1976).

Hyperactivity

_____ Physically aggressive (Conrad, 1976).

_____ Poor focusing on concentration (Taylor, 1980).

_____ Won't take "No" for an answer (Sugarman and Stone, 1974).

———— Makes disruptive noises (Barkley, 1982).

———— Extremely curious (Taylor, 1980).

———— Cries easily or often (Barkley, 1982).

———— Extremely talkative (Wender, 1973).

———— Easily distracted (Wender, 1973).

———— Very short attention span (Sugarman and Stone, 1974).

———— Problems with making and keeping friends (Barkley, 1982).

———— Gets into fights (Safer and Allen, 1976).

———— Teeth grinding (Taylor, 1980).

———— Frequently scratches himself (Sugarman and Stone, 1974).

———— Rocking or wiggling motions (Taylor, 1980).

———— Temper outbursts (Safer and Allen, 1976).

———— Influences others to misbehave (Barkley, 1982).

———— Demands teacher's attention (Barkley, 1982).

———— Openly defiant (Barkley, 1982).

———— Seems to be driven (Sugarman and Stone, 1974).

———— Quick mood changes (Safer and Allen, 1976).

———— Compulsiveness (Sugarman and Stone, 1974).

———— Lacks flexibility; rigid in approach to others (Taylor, 1980).

———— Poor self-image (Alabiso, 1977; Hansen, 1976).

———— Poor memory (Sugarman and Stone, 1974).

———— Impulsive (Wender, 1973).

———— Nervous and tense (Safer and Allen, 1976).

———— Restless and overactive (Safer and Allen, 1976; Conrad, 1976).

———— Immature (Wender, 1973).

Hyperactivity Medication
Side Effects

Ritalin

_____ Insomnia (Gadow, 1979).

_____ Anorexia; loss of appetite (Gadow, 1979).

_____ Headache (Gadow, 1979).

_____ Stomachache (Gadow, 1979).

_____ Nausea (Gadow, 1979).

_____ Moodiness (Gadow, 1979).

_____ Irritability (Gadow, 1979).

_____ Increased talkativeness (Gadow, 1979).

_____ Dyskinesia; impaired or abnormal motion of voluntary or involuntary muscles (Gadow, 1979).

_____ Hallucinations (Gadow, 1979).

_____ Marked decrease in activity (Gadow, 1979).

_____ Suppression of growth (Gadow, 1979).

_____ Difficulty with visual accommodation; blurring of vision (Gadow, 1979).

_____ Nervousness (Gadow, 1979).

_____ Dizziness (Gadow, 1979).

_____ Palpitations (Gadow, 1979).

_____ Drowsiness (Gadow, 1979).

_____ Blood pressure and pulse changes (Gadow, 1979).

_____ Tachycardia; abnormally fast heartbeat (Gadow, 1979).

_____ Angina; heart pain (Gadow, 1979).

_____ Cardiac arythmia (Gadow, 1979).

_____ Weight loss (Gadow, 1979).

_____ Scalp hair loss (Gadow, 1979).

_____ Leukopenia (Gadow, 1979).

_____ Anemia (Gadow, 1979).

_____ Abdominal pain (Gadow, 1979).

_____ Skin rash (Gadow, 1979).

_____ Fever (Gadow, 1979).

Dexedrine

_____ Insomnia (Gadow, 1979).

_____ Anorexia; loss of appetite (Gadow, 1979).

_____ Headache (Gadow, 1979).

_____ Dyskinesia; impaired or abnormal motion of voluntary of involuntary muscles (Gadow, 1979).

_____ Dizziness (Gadow, 1979).

_____ Palpitations (Gadow, 1979).

_____ Blood pressure and pulse changes (Gadow, 1979).

_____ Tachycardia; abnormally fast heartbeat (Gadow, 1979).

_____ Overstimulation (Gadow, 1979).

_____ Restlessness (Gadow, 1979).

_____ Euphoria (Gadow, 1979).

_____ Dysphoria (Gadow, 1979).

_____ Tremors (Gadow, 1979).

_____ Dryness of mouth (Gadow, 1979).

_____ Unpleasant taste in mouth (Gadow, 1979).

_____ Diarrhea (Gadow, 1979).

_____ Constipation (Gadow, 1979).

_____ Gastrointestinal disturbances (Gadow, 1979).

Cylert

_____ Insomnia (Gadow, 1979).

_____ Anorexia; loss of appetite (Gadow, 1979).

_____ Headache (Gadow, 1979).

_____ Stomachache (Gadow, 1979).

_____ Nausea (Gadow, 1979).

_____ Irritibility (Gadow, 1979).

_____ Hallucinations (Gadow, 1979).

_____ Dizziness (Gadow, 1979).

_____ Drowsiness (Gadow, 1979).

_____ Skin rashes (Gadow, 1979).

_____ Mild depression (Gadow, 1979).

Kleptomania

_____ Steals compulsively (Ramelli and Mapelli, 1979).

_____ Missing items are found on him or in his possession (C. Gingerich, personal communication, 1984).

_____ Steals from other individuals, even the most insignificant items (C. Gingerich, personal communication, 1984).

_____ History of stealing (C. Gingerich, personal communication, 1984).

_____ Has cash on his person, yet steals the items rather than purchasing them (C. Gingerich, personal communication, 1984).

_____ Apprehended often for shoplifting (C. Gingerich, personal communication, 1984).

_____ Steals the same type of article repeatedly (Goldenson, 1970).

_____ Does not sell or use the stolen articles (Goldenson, 1970; World Book, 1983).

_____ Accumulates, discards, or anonymously returns the stolen items (Goldenson, 1970).

_____ Does not plan the stealing episodes (Goldenson, 1970).

_____ Steals items he does not need (World Book, 1983).

_____ Makes resolutions to stop stealing, but continues to do so (Nicholi, 1978).

_____ Steals precious objects of sentimental value to others (Podolsky, 1953).

_____ Steals worthless articles that have only an emotional value (Podolsky, 1953).

_____ Steals many different times in one day (Taylor, 1979).

_____ Unconcerned about security measures (Taylor, 1979).

_____ Has been asked not to enter certain stores due to suspicion of theft (J. Steele, personal communication, 1985).

_____ Is of average to above average intelligence, yet steals clumsily (*Time*, 1980).

_____ Steals items for no obvious reasons (C. Gingerich, personal communication, 1984).

_____ Cannot explain why he steals items (C. Gingerich, personal communication, 1984; Goldenson, 1970).

_____ Realizes that the stealing endangers his social life (Nicholi, 1978).

_____ May not be consciously aware that he or she is stealing, and if apprehended, expresses shock or amazement at what has been stolen (Taylor, 1979).

_____ Steals more when depressed (Ramelli and Mapelli, 1979).

_____ Is obsessively preoccupied with articles that have direct or indirect erotic significance (e.g., compacts, brassieres, handbags) (Goldenson, 1970).

_____ Feels an overwhelming impulse to steal, which he usually tries in vain to resist (Podolsky, 1953; Goldenson, 1970; Keutzer, 1972; Taylor, 1979; Rosenblatt, 1981).

_____ Has feelings of humiliation, guilt, and remorse after the stealing episode (Goldenson, 1970; *Time*, 1980).

_____ The act of stealing itself arouses sexual fantasies or leads to sexual gratification (Goldenson, 1970).

_____ The danger and excitement associated with the stealing contribute to sexual stimulation (Podolsky, 1953; Goldenson, 1970; Nicholi, 1978).

_____ Steals for rebellion against parental figures (Goldenson, 1970).

_____ Feels a need to be punished (Podolsky, 1953; Goldenson, 1970; World Book, 1983).

_____ Has poor impulse control (Goldenson, 1970).

_____ Is envious of others and their possessions (World Book, 1983).

_____ Is greedy (World Book, 1983).

_____ The impulse to steal is rooted in childhood sexuality (i.e., is a mode of reclaiming affection that has been withheld or is symbolic of a definite repressed wish often associated with penis envy) (Keutzer, 1972).

_____ Experiences an irresistible, repetitious impulse to steal (Keutzer, 1972).

_____ Stolen objects possess a libidinal value (Hinsie and Campbell, 1970).

_____ Is secretively defensive of his actions (Nicholi, 1978).

_____ Relief or sense of fulfillment follows the act (Nicholi, 1978).

_____ Is relieved after arrest (Nicholi, 1978).

_____ Punishment that follows stealing is a source of pleasure (Podolsky, 1953).

_____ Is fully aware that punishment follows detection of the act of stealing (Podolsky, 1953).

_____ Is pleased that thefts cause pain and distress to others (Podolsky, 1953).

_____ Feels a need to compensate for the affection and sense of self-worth he never had (Kopecky, 1980).

_____ Has an unconscious drive to steal (Kopecky, 1980).

_____ Steals for neurotic rather than economic motives (_Time_, 1980).

_____ Is under emotional stress (_Time_, 1980).

_____ Is suffering from depression and a sense of entitlement (i.e., he may feel that he has been treated harshly and therefore deserves the items stolen) (_Time_, 1980).

_____ Believes himself to have been the victim of theft in the past, and is simply evening the score (_Time_, 1980).

_____ Impulse to steal is strongest during the menstrual period (Goldenson, 1970; Podolsky, 1953).

Learning Disabilities

_____ Low academic performance (Bryan and Bryan, 1975; Duhl, 1983).

_____ Short memory (Duhl, 1983).

_____ Excellent memory in one modality, but not in the other modalities (Myers and Hammill, 1976; Bush and Waugh, 1976).

_____ Language impairments including difficulties in: inner language, auditory receptive language, reversals of letters or words, inversion of letters, poor or slow word recognition, immature expressive language, or difficulty in comprehending or the memory of spoken language (Miller, 1973; Bryan and Bryan, 1975; Myers and Hammill, 1976; Wallace and McLoughlin, 1975; Bush and Waugh, 1976; Gearheart, 1976).

_____ Reading impairments including difficulties in: sound blending, poor sequential memory skills, word analysis skills, sight words, literal comprehension skills, or interpretive comprehension skills (Meyers and Hammill, 1976; Miller, 1973; Bryan and Bryan, 1975; Wallace and McLoughlin, 1975).

_____ Student will give correct answer, but will not be able to tell how he arrived at that conclusion (Duhl, 1983).

_____ Will given responses that are unrelated to what is being discussed (Duhl, 1983).

_____ Absent-minded; forgets important details (Wallace and Kauffman, 1973; Bush and Waugh, 1976).

_____ Uses fingers to count (Miller, 1973).

_____ Inability to follow directions.

_____ Disorders of symbolization (Hammill and Myers, 1976).

_____ Special learning difficulties in performing certain learned tasks involving reading, speaking, listening, writing, and calculating (Wallace and McLoughlin, 1975; Hewett and Forness, 1977; Sampson and Velten, 1978; Duhl, 1983).

_____ Auditory perception impairments including auditory memory and auditory blending of sounds (Wallace and McLoughlin, 1975; Bush and Waugh, 1976; Gearheart, 1977).

Characteristics That Commonly Accompany Learning Disabilities

_____ Hyperactivity (Gearheart, 1977; Hewett and Forness, 1977; Myers and Hammill, 1969; Sampson and Velten, 1978).

_____ Hypoactivity (Myers and Hammill, 1976; Sampson and Velten, 1978).

_____ Impulsivity (Hewett and Forness, 1977).

_____ General clumsiness or awkwardness (Myers and Hammill, 1976).

_____ Equivocal neurological signs; neurological signs not clearly associated with a particular neurological problem, but not within the normal range of functioning (Byran and Byran, 1975; Hewett and Forness, 1977).

_____ Poor eye-hand coordination (Miller, 1973; Hewett and Forness, 1977).

_____ Emotional liability (Bryan and Bryan, 1975; Hewett and Forness, 1977).

_____ Low self esteem (Duhl, 1983).

_____ Lack of motivation (Gearheart, 1976).

_____ Aggression (Miller, 1973; Gearheart, 1976).

_____ Social immaturity (Miller, 1973; Bryan and Bryan, 1975).

_____ Disorganization (Wallace and McLoughlin, 1975; Duhl, 1983).

_____ Appears to daydream often (Duhl, 1983).

_____ Perseveration (Myers and Hammill, 1976; Hewett and Forness, 1977; Gearheart, 1976; Sampson and Velten, 1978).

_____ Inability to match different sizes (Bush and Waugh, 1976).

_____ Inattentive (Gearheart, 1976).

_____ Overattentive and unable to break focus on one particular object (Gearheart, 1976).

_____ Problems in left to right progression (Bush and Waugh, 1976).

_____ Irregular eye movements (Duhl, 1983).

_____ Difficulty in completing work on time (Gearheart, 1976).

_____ Inability to match colors (Bush and Waugh, 1976).

_____ Inability to match shapes (Bush and Waugh, 1976).

_____ Confusion in handedness (Duhl, 1983).

_____   Difficulty with space and time perception; estimating time (Wallace and McLoughlin, 1975; Hewett and Forness, 1977).

_____   Poor figure-ground discrimination (Wallace and McLoughlin, 1973).

_____   Motor impairments including difficulties in: fine motor, gross motor, blance, rhythm, laterality, directionality, body image awareness, or perceptual motor (Myers and Hammill, 1976; Miller, 1973; Bush and Waugh, 1976; Hewett and Forness, 1977; Gearheart, 1976).

_____   Short attention span (Sampson and Velten, 1978; Duhl, 1983).

_____   Distractability (Wallace and Kauffman, 1973; Hewett and Forness, 1977; Gearheart, 1976).

Manic-Depressive Personality

A group of affective psychotic reactions characterized by a predominant mood of elation or depression, accompanied by related disturbances of thought and activity (Goldenson, 1970).

_____   Sudden oscillation of emotion or mood. Alternates between cheerful and outgoing to withdrawn and suspicious (Eidelberg, 1968; Beck, 1967; Wiley, 1974).

_____   Preaches a sermon one moment and tells a vulgar joke the next (Eidelberg, 1968).

Manic Stage

_____   Vulgar tirades and tells crude jokes (Goldenson, 1970).

_____   Witty (Goldenson, 1970).

_____   Resorts to joking and making puns when cornered (Beck, 1967).

——— Sings, laughs, rhymes, and hums in excess (Goldenson, 1970).

——— Talks in theatrical tones (Goldenson, 1970).

——— Dominates the conversation and talks incessantly (Goldenson, 1970).

——— Denies all problems and blames others (Beck, 1967).

——— Overdresses and is overly decorative.

——— Spends money recklessly (Goldenson, 1970).

——— Increased narcissism (Goldenson, 1970).

——— Aggressiveness (Gallant and Simpson, 1976).

——— Temper tantrums (Gallant and Simpson, 1976).

——— Increased sexuality (Gaylin, 1968).

——— Destructiveness (Gallant and Simpson, 1976).

——— Tears clothes to pieces (Goldenson, 1970).

——— Energetic and hyperactive (Beck, 1967; Gallant and Sampson, 1976).

——— Flight of ideas, and increased errors because of distractibility (Beck, 1967).

——— Delusions of grandeur; unrealistic ambitions (Aaron and Beck, 1967; Goldenson, 1970).

——— Positive self-image and feels good about himself (Beck, 1967).

——— Intolerant to criticism (Goldenson, 1970).

——— Impatient (Goldenson, 1970).

——— Shows arbitrary decision making (Beck, 1967).

——— Unrealistic feelings of strength (Messinger, 1973).

——— Decreased sleep; insomnia.

——— High tolerance for fatigue (Aaron and Beck, 1967).

——— Has large expansive handwriting (Messinger, 1977).

Depressive Stage

_____   Avoids social contact (Messinger, 1973; Derdeyn, 1983).

_____   Appears sad (Kashani and Ray, 1983).

_____   Feelings of hopelessness (Derdyn, 1983).

_____   Fear of competition (Wiley, 1974).

_____   Withdrawal (Kashani and Ray, 1983).

_____   Indifference to immediate surroundings (Kashani and Ray, 1983).

_____   Underselling of the self (Wiley, 1974).

_____   Wishing to be dead (Kashani and Ray, 1983).

_____   Hypoactivity (Kashani and Ray, 1983).

_____   Decreased energy level (Derdyn, 1983).

_____   Somatic complaints (Derdyn, 1983).

Other

_____   Decrease in school performance (Derdeyn, 1983).

_____   Confused about time and people (Goldenson, 1970).

_____   Drinks to excess (Goldenson, 1970).

_____   Tendencies toward envy of others (Wiley, 1974).

_____   Appetite disturbance (Kashani and Ray, 1983).

_____   Abnormal weight gain or loss (Brunch, 1978).

Marijuana Abuse

_____   Lowered physical activity (Lamanna, 1981).

_____   Numbed senses (Lamanna, 1981).

_____   Numbness of body parts (Halikas, Goodwin, and Guze, 1973).

——— Reaction-response patterns impaired (Lamanna, 1981).

——— Accelerated heart beat (Dornbush, Fink, and Freedman, 1973; Halikas, Goodwin, and Guze, 1973; Margolis and Popkin, 1980; Oursler, 1968; Robbins, 1976).

——— Sluggish in physical responses (Kolansky and Moore, 1978; Margolis and Popkin, 1980).

——— Lethargic (Goode, 1970; Halikas, Goodwin, and Guze, 1973).

——— Doesn't realize that coordination is altered (Halikas, Goodwin, and Guze, 1973; Margolis and Popkin, 1980; Miller, 1974).

——— Feels drowsy (Goode, 1970; Halikas, Goodwin, and Guze, 1973; Lamanna, 1981; Rublowsky, 1983).

——— Feels hungry (Dorbush, Fink, and Freedman, 1973; Fidel, 1981; Goode, 1970; Halikas, Goodwin, and Guze, 1973; Hollister, 1973; Oursler, 1968; Robbins, 1976; Rublowsky, 1983).

——— Muscular twitching (Rublowsky, 1983).

——— Pupils dialate (Goode, 1970; Halikas, Goodwin, and Guze, 1973).

——— Perceived heaviness of extremities (Halikas, Goodwin, and Guze, 1973).

——— Loss of pain sensation (Halikas, Goodwin, and Guze, 1973).

——— Sudden cravings for sweets (Goode, 1970; Halikas, Goodwin, and Guze, 1973; Oursler, 1968).

——— Sudden cravings for liquids (Lamanna, 1981; Goode, 1970; Halikas, Goodwin, and Guze, 1973; Robbins, 1976).

——— Dry mouth and throat (Halikas, Goodwin, and Guze, 1973).

——— Red or bloodshot eyes (Fidel, 1981; Goode, 1970; Halikas, Goodwin, and Guze, 1973; Robbins, 1976).

_____ Sense of touch is more exacting or sensual (Fidel, 1981; Goode, 1970).

_____ Odor of marijuana is noticeable as it clings to clothing or body (Gordon, 1979).

_____ Impaired reaction time (Margolis and Popkin, 1980).

_____ Inconsistencies in auditory-signal detection (Lamanna, 1981).

_____ Visual perception impaired (Margolis and Popkin, 1980).

_____ Decreased hand and body steadiness (Halikas, Goodwin, and Guze, 1973; Hanteen et al., 1976).

_____ Sense of taste intensified (Robbins, 1976).

_____ Sense of sounds intensified (Goode, 1970, Halikas, Goodwin, and Guze, 1973; Robbins, 1976).

_____ Increased sex drive (Halikas, Goodwin, and Guze, 1973; Oursler, 1968; Robbins, 1976).

_____ Increased blood pressure (Ousler, 1968).

_____ Frequent urination (Halikas, Goodwin, and Guze, 1973; Oursler, 1968).

_____ Cough (Halikas, Goodwin, and Guze, 1973).

_____ Flushing (Halikas, Goodwin, and Guze, 1973).

_____ Shortness of breath (Halikas, Goodwin, and Guze, 1973).

_____ Headaches (Halikas, Goodwin, and Guze, 1973).

_____ Swollen eyelids (Goode, 1970; Halikas, Goodwin, and Guze, 1973).

_____ Chills (Halikas, Goodwin, and Guze, 1973).

_____ Nausea (Halikas, Goodwin, and Guze, 1973).

_____ Vomiting (Halikas, Goodwin, and Guze, 1973).

_____ Diarrhea (Halikas, Goodwin, and Guze, 1973).

_____ Constipation (Halikas, Goodwin, and Guze, 1973).

_____ Impaired ability to concentrate (Gordon, 1979; Halikas, Goodwin, and Guze, 1973; Lamanna, 1981).

_____ Loss of self-control (Halikas, Goodwin, and Guze, 1973; Lamanna, 1981; Robbins, 1976).

_____ Overly silly (Goode, 1970; Halikas, Goodwin, and Guze, 1973; Lamanna, 1981).

_____ Loss of judgment (Brooks, Lukoff, and Whiteman, 1980; Lamanna, 1981).

_____ Releases inhibitions (Lamanna, 1981).

_____ Damages school property (Lamanna, 1981).

_____ Performance of previously learned functions show some impairment (Lamanna, 1981).

_____ Disoriented (Lamanna, 1981; Rosenthal, 1972).

_____ Shortened attention span (Brooks, Lukoff, and Whiteman, 1980; Margolis, 1980; Robbins, 1976).

_____ Distractibility (Brooks, Lukoff, and Whiteman, 1980; Margolis and Popkin, 1980).

_____ Imparied communication skills (Margolis and Popkin, 1980).

_____ Lack of goals (Margolis and Popkin, 1980).

_____ Lack of concern for physical appearance (Margolis and Popkin, 1980).

_____ Difficulty with recent memory (Abel, 1983; Clark, Hughes, and Nakashima, 1973; Dornbush, Fink, and Freedman, 1973; Goode, 1980; Halikas, Goodwin, and Guze, 1973; Margolis and Popkin, 1980; Robbins, 1976).

_____ Incapability of completing thoughts during verbal communications (Kolansky and Moore, 1978; Margolis and Popkin, 1980).

_____ Quiet and dreamy (Jones, Shainber, and Byer, 1969).

_____ Overly aggressive (Lamanna, 1981; Oursler, 1968; Halikas, Goodwin, and Guze, 1973).

_____ Problems operating equipment and vehicles (Goode, 1970; Lamanna, 1981; Oursler, 1968; Robbins, 1976).

_____ Talkative (Goode, 1970; Halikas, Goodwin, and Guze, 1973; Jones, Shainber, and Byer, 1969).

_____ Says time passes very slowly (Fidel, 1981; Kolansky and Moore, 1978).

_____ Forgets; absent minded (Darley and Tinklenberg, 1974; Kaplan, 1970).

_____ Inability to organize work (Gordon, 1979).

_____ Impaired search and recognition skills (Lamanna, 1981).

_____ Sluggish in mental response (Kolansky and Moore, 1978).

_____ Recall impairment (Darley and Tinklenberg, 1974).

_____ Inability to carry out mental tasks.

_____ Increased creativity (Robbins, 1976).

_____ Decision making decreased (Clark, Hughes, and Nakashima, 1973).

_____ Heightened mental powers (Halikas, Goodwin, and Guze, 1973).

_____ Best friend known to use marijuana (Ramsey, 1974).

_____ Tendency to be influenced more by friends than parents (Lamanna, 1981).

_____ Impaired depth perception (Oursler, 1968).

_____ More intense color perception (Keller, Ewing, and Rouse, 1973).

_____ Objects seem clearer or sharper (Keeler, Ewing, and Rouse, 1973).

_____ Senses in general are more sensitive, perceptive (Goode, 1970).

_____ Stimulation of senses more enjoyable (Goode, 1970).

_____ Sense of touch more acute (Goode, 1970).

_____ Floating sensation (Halikas, Goodwin, and Guze, 1973).

_____ Loss of or low self-esteen (Lamanna, 1981).

_____ Unpleasant feelings (Lamanna, 1981).

_____ Depressed (Goode, 1980; Lamanna, 1981).

_____ Confused (Goode, 1980; Halikas, Goodwin, and Guze, 1973; Kolansky, 1978; Lamanna, 1981; Rosenthal, 1972).

_____ Afraid (Kolansky and Moore, 1978; Lamanna, 1981).

_____ Easily irritable (Lamanna, 1981; Miller, 1974; Halikas, Goodwin, and Guze, 1973).

_____ Impulsive (Lamann, 1981; Rosenthal, 1972).

_____ Decreased motivation (Brook, Lukoff, and Whiteman, 1980; Margolis and Popkin, 1980).

_____ Magical thinking (Margolis and Popkin, 1980).

_____ Flattening of emotional expressions (Margolis and Popkin, 1980).

_____ Progressive loss of insight (Margolis and Popkin, 1980).

_____ Feeling on inner joy (Jones, Shainber, and Byer, 1969).

_____ Mood reactions highly variable and unpredictable (Rosenthal and Mothner, 1972).

_____ Shy (Kellam, 1982).

_____ Paranoid (Goode, 1970; Lamanna, 1981).

_____ Apathy (Brooks, Lukoff, and Whiteman, 1980).

_____ Experiences a "high" feeling (Fidel, 1981).

_____ Nervous feeling (Goode, 1970).

_____ Decreased tension (Robbins, 1976).

_____ More understanding and compassionate with others (Oursler, 1968).

_____ Feeling of fearlessness (Oursler, 1968).

_____ Sad or despondent (Halikas, Goodwin, and Guze, 1973).

_____ Crys (Halikas, Goodwin, and Guze, 1973).

Passive-Aggressive Personality

_____ Takes a long time to do what is asked.

_____ Argues a point for the sake of arguing.

_____ When asked to do something, he does the opposite.

_____ Follows directions so precisely that the final product is not what was desired by the instructor.

_____ When directions are followed so closely that the product is undesirable, he blames the work product on the instructor.

_____ Rather than trying, the student says, "I can't."

_____ Often complains about rules.

_____ Requests often have to be repeated by the instructor.

_____ Appears lazy and physically lethargic.

_____ Remains silent when asked for an explanation of some misbehavior.

_____ Has many excuses for why he cannot do what was requested.

_____ Complains about punishment given to classmates.

_____ Student offers unacceptable excuses for not doing homework.

_____ Uses school failure as a way of passively expressing aggression against parents and other authority figures (Davids, 1974).

_____ Impulsive; has hostile-aggressive drives (Davids, 1974).

_____ Plays the part of class clown (N. Hammerschmidt, personal communication, 1984).

_____ Knowingly gives inappropriate responses (N. Hammerschmidt, personal communication, 1984).

_____ Does not ask questions (N. Hammerschmidt, personal communication, 1984).

_____ Acts as a nonconformist (N. Hammerschmidt, personal communication, 1984).

_____ Does not take responsibility for own actions (N. Hammerschmidt, personal communication, 1984).

Pinball or Video Game Addiction

_____ Calluses on his hand(s) (K. Sepich, personal communication, 1985).

_____ Tension, sleeplessness, and dreams that have to do with the games played that day (*Awake*, 1983).

_____ Maintains a unique stance while playing the video game (D. Maloney, personal communication, 1985).

_____ When walking past a video game, stops to play at least one game (C. Simmons, personal communication, 1985).

_____ States that he will play only one game, but plays two or more times (C. Simmons, personal communication, 1985).

_____ Regularly averages two or more hours a day playing video games (Blotnick, 1984).

_____ Looks to see if a personal score is still recorded on the board when walking by the machine that he plays (P. Traywick, personal communication, 1985).

_____ Repeatedly plays the same video game (E. Connelly, personal communication, 1985).

_____ Regularly plays video games at the same time daily (J. Koehler, personal communication, 1985).

_____ Will promote a contest to determine the best player of his favorite video game (J. Koehler, personal communication, 1985).

_____ Regularly talks about video games (E. Connelly, personal communication, 1985).

_____ Tells anyone and everyone his highest score (E. Connelly, personal communication, 1985).

_____ Claims that video games improve eye-hand coordination, and therefore, because of this, he is not wasting time or money by playing video games (J. Koehler, personal communication, 1985).

_____ Surrounded by several other people when playing a video game (J. Koehler, personal communication, 1985).

_____ Watches other people playing video games (J. Koehler, personal communication, 1985).

_____ Uses lunch money to play video games.

_____ Sells possessions to obtain money for video games.

_____ Uses a string tied to a quarter in order to drop the quarter into the machine and pull it out again (J. Koehler, personal communication, 1985).

_____ Carries quarters (C. Simmons, personal communication, 1985).

_____ Frequently borrows quarters (K. Woolridge, personal communication, 1985).

_____ Uses his last twenty-five cents on a video game (P. Traywick, personal communication, 1985).

_____ Cashes in pennies, nickels, and dimes for quarters (J. Koehler, personal communication, 1985).

_____ Generally obtains change in quarters for two dollars or more at one time (C. Simmons, personal communication, 1985).

_____ Requests rolls of quarters at the bank to play video games (J. Koehler, personal communication, 1985).

_____ Instead of using exact change when purchasing an item, he will break another dollar to obtain more quarters (J. Koehler, personal communication, 1985).

_____ Able to detect any small problem with the machine, such as a burnt out light, and makes a point to tell someone about it (C. Simmons, personal communication, 1985).

_____ Able to tell that the flippers have been tightened, and will relay this information to someone else (C. Simmons, personal communication, 1985).

Poor Self-Concept

———— Communicates the messages "I can't do it" and "He's better than me" (Shea, 1978).

———— Expresses feelings of inferiority (Shea, 1978).

———— Resists independent functioning (Shea, 1978).

———— Frequently immobilized when confronted with new or different problems and situations (Shea, 1978).

———— Lacks self-confidence (Biehler, 1974; Shea, 1978).

———— Fears the unfamiliar (Shea, 1978).

———— Poor estimate of self (Biehler, 1974).

———— Fear of failure (Biehler, 1974).

———— Mumbles, grunts, or talks into his sleeves (Swift and Spivak, 1970).

———— Acts out to receive attention from the teacher (Wolfgang, 1980).

———— Complains that others are laughing and making fun of him (Sprick, 1981).

———— Blames self for anything that goes wrong (Sprick, 1981).

———— Becomes embarrassed and flustered unnecessarily (Sprick, 1981).

———— Sits by himself (Collins, 1981).

———— Lack of responsibility (Reinhart, 1980).

———— Compulsive eating (Reinhart, 1980).

———— Says "I'm too tired" or "I can't remember" (Reinhart, 1980).

———— Depreciates and distrusts own abilities (M. Burns, personal communication, 1983).

———— Needs to be approved by others (Burton and Daily, 1983).

_____ Obsessive anxiety about possible calamities in the future (Burton and Daily, 1983).

_____ Often afraid others are talking about him. Claims others don't like him (M. Burns, personal communication, 1983).

_____ Needs to excel in all endeavors in order to feel worthwhile as a person (Burton and Daily, 1983).

_____ Daydreaming or apathetic inattention.

_____ Believes it's better to avoid problems than face them (Burton and Daily, 1983).

_____ Projects negative feelings about self in an aggressive manner. Believes it is best to "get them before they get me" (Burton and Daily, 1983).

_____ Claims to be sick when unpleasant experiences occur in school (M. Burns, personal communication, 1983).

_____ Tries "too hard" to make friends to the point where he becomes a nuisance to peers (M. Burns, personal communication, 1983).

_____ Selectively mute at school while able and willing to converse at home (Reinhart, 1980).

_____ Takes a long time to recover following disappointment (Epstein, 1982).

_____ Pessimistic view of life (Epstein, 1982).

_____ Intolerant of own and others mistakes (Epstein, 1982).

_____ Brags and makes extravagant claims about self (Epstein, 1982).

_____ Dogmatic in his views and opinions (Epstein, 1982).

_____ Desire for power and leadership in the classroom (Epstein, 1982).

_____ Inordinate desire for prestige which may result in tales of fantasy (Epstein, 1982).

_____ Dwells on problems and weaknesses, and feels that he has no strengths or resources (Canfield and Wells, 1976).

_____ Feelings of jealousy about other family members and/or other classmates (Canfield and Wells, 1976).

_____ Verbally abuses others (*Today's Education*, 1982–83).

_____ Passive, shy, compliant, lacks a conspicuous presence in the classroom. Is ignored by classmates on the playground (Byrnes, 1984).

_____ Must be reassured constantly about his work and the daily routine (K. Fisher, personal communication, 1984).

Pregnancy

_____ Missed menstrual period (Tippelt, 1983; Brinkley, Goldberg, and Kukar, 1982).

_____ Tests positive on a home pregnancy test.

_____ Implantation bleeding. Spots slightly on the day the ovum attaches to uterine wall (Brinkley, Goldberg, and Kukar, 1982).

_____ Vagina thickens and softens (Brinkley, Goldberg, and Kukar, 1982).

_____ Vagina becomes blue to violet in color as the result of increased supply of blood to the area (Brinkley, Goldberg, and Kukar, 1982).

_____ Vaginal secretions become more noticeable (Brinkley, Goldberg, and Kukar, 1982).

_____ Tingling or prickling sensation in breasts during early weeks of pregnancy (Russell, 1977; Brinkley, Goldberg, and Kukar, 1982).

_____ Breasts enlarge (Brinkley, Goldberg, and Kukar, 1982).

_____ Veins may become visible under the skin of breasts (Brinkley, Goldberg, and Kukar, 1982).

_____ Small round elevated areas appear on the dark part of

the nipple, the areola (Smith, 1979; Brinkley, Goldberg, and Kukar, 1982).

_____ Needs to urinate more frequently (Russell, 1977; Smith, 1979; Brinkley, Goldberg, and Kukar, 1982).

_____ Feels nauseous or vomits (Smith, 1979; Russell, 1977; Brinkley, Goldberg, and Kukar, 1982).

_____ Trouble with indigestion and heartburn (Russell, 1977; Brinkley, Goldberg, and Kukar, 1982).

_____ Constipation (Brinkley, Goldberg, and Kukar, 1982).

_____ Tires and becomes fatigued easily (Tipelt, 1983; Brinkley, Goldberg, and Kukar, 1982).

_____ Headaches may occur more frequently (Gillespie, 1977; Mitchell and Klein, 1969).

Premenstrual Syndrome (PMS)

_____ Engages in child abuse (Norris and Sullivan, 1983).

_____ Engages in alcohol abuse (Norris and Sullivan, 1983).

_____ Assaults others (Norris and Sullivan, 1983).

_____ Attempts suicide (Norris and Sullivan, 1983).

_____ Irritability (Norris and Sullivan, 1983).

_____ Tension (Norris and Sullivan, 1983).

_____ Depression (Norris and Sullivan, 1983).

_____ Panic attacks (Norris and Sullivan, 1983).

_____ Psychotic episodes (Norris and Sullivan, 1983).

_____ Increased sex drive (Norris and Sullivan, 1983).

Physical Symptoms That Often Accompany PMS

_____ Headache (Norris and Sullivan, 1983).

_____ Fatigue (Norris and Sullivan, 1983).

_____ Breast swelling and tenderness (Norris and Sullivan, 1983).

_____ Abdominal bloating (Norris and Sullivan, 1983).

_____ Weight gain of six or more pounds (Norris and Sullivan, 1983).

_____ Increased thirst (Norris and Sullivan, 1983).

_____ Increased appetite (Norris and Sullivan, 1983).

_____ Cravings for sweet or salty foods (Norris and Sullivan, 1983).

_____ Acne (Norris and Sullivan, 1983).

_____ Asthma (Norris and Sullivan, 1983).

_____ Constipation (Norris and Sullivan, 1983).

_____ Boils, herpes, hives (Norris and Sullivan, 1983).

_____ Epilepsy, migranes, dizziness (Norris and Sullivan, 1983).

_____ Conjunctivities, sties, uveitis (Norris and Sullivan, 1983).

_____ Hoarseness, sore throat, sinusitis, rhinitis (Norris and Sullivan, 1983).

_____ Cystitis or urethritis (Norris and Sullivan, 1983).

Pyromania

_____ History of fire setting (Wooden, 1985).

_____ Fascinated with matches and fires (Wooden, 1985).

_____ Compulsive urge to set fires (Wesley, 1972; Bakwin and Bakwin, 1972).

_____ Desire to be a hero (Bakwin and Bakwin, 1972).

_____ Sexual immaturity/sexual conflicts/fear of opposite sex (Vandersall and Wiener, 1970; Bakwin and Bakwin, 1972; Wesley, 1972).

_____ Sexual pleasure derived from setting fires (Wesley, 1972).

_____ Impulsive (Stein and Davis, 1982; Wooden, 1985).

_____ Guiltless (Verville, 1967).

_____ Has matches in possession (Wooden, 1985).

_____ Discovered near scene of fire (Wooden, 1985).

_____ Involved in other illegal activities (Abrahamsen, 1980; Kaufman, Heims, and Reiser, 1961; Bartol, 1980; Strachen, 1981; Gruber, Heck, and Mintzer, 1981; Bumpass, Fagelman, and Brix, 1983).

_____ Fantasizes about burning someone (MacDonald, 1920).

_____ Interest in becoming a firefighter (Wooden, 1985; Bakwin and Bakwin, 1972).

_____ Emotionally disturbed/socially maladjusted (MacDonald, 1920; Wooden, 1985).

_____ Can't express anger appropriately (MacDonald, 1920; Chess and Massibi, 1978; Stein and Davis, 1982).

_____ Seeks revenge (Bakwin and Bakwin, 1972; Chess and Massibi, 1978).

_____ Isolated or rejected by others (Vandersall and Wiener, 1970; Bromberg, 1972; Chess and Massibi, 1978).

_____ Unable to relate to others (Chess and Massibi, 1978; Vandersall and Wiener, 1970).

_____ Poor academic performance of achievement (Gruber, Heck, and Mintzer, 1981; Verville, 1967; Fine and Louie, 1979).

Schizophrenia

_____ Delusional beliefs (Macnab, 1968).

_____ Hallucinations (Redd, Porterfield, and Anderson, 1979).

_____ Attention or thought processes impaired (Rosenbaum, 1970).

_____ Preoccupation with the same topic (Rosenbaum, 1970).

_____ Indecisive (Rosenbaum, 1970).

_____ Focuses attention on internal feelings and blocks of attention to the external environment (Macnab, 1968).

_____ Disturbances of memory (Rosenbaum, 1970).

_____ Talks to self or unseen others (Redd, Potterfield, and Anderson, 1979).

_____ Muteness (Redd, Potterfield, and Anderson, 1979).

_____ Mumbles, swears, or screams (Macnab, 1968).

_____ Incoherent or bizarre speech (Macnab, 1968).

_____ Echolalic speech (Rosenbaum, 1970).

_____ Peculiar giggling, smiling, frowning, and grimacing that is inconsistent with present happenings (Rosenbaum, 1970).

_____ Excitable or euphoric (Wolf and Berle, 1976).

_____ Freezing in strange positions for hours or days (Redd, Potterfield, and Anderson, 1979).

_____ Incessant agitation (Redd, Potterfield, and Anderson, 1979).

_____ Bizarre, stereotyped movements (Wolf and Berle, 1976).

_____ Blank staring (Redd, Potterfield, and Anderson, 1979).

_____ Withdrawal of interest from interpersonal dealings (Rosenbaum, 1970; Wolf and Berle, 1978).

_____ Unwilling to initiate behavior (Rosenbaum, 1970).

_____ Unreliable (Wolf and Berle, 1976).

_____ Unable to work (Wolf and Berle, 1976).

_____ Makes heartless accusations (Wolf and Berle, 1976).

_____ Neglects family (Wolf and Berle, 1976).

_____ Misinterprets situations.

School Phobia

_____ Prolonged absence from school (Johnson, 1978).

_____ Severe emotional upset before school including excessive fearfulness and temper outbursts (Wheeler and Wheeler, 1974; Johnson, 1978; Lall and Lall, 1979).

_____ Stays at home with the knowledge of the parent (Johnson, 1978).

_____ Separation anxiety on part of mother (Boyd, 1980).

_____ Complaints of a physical nature including stomachaches, pains, nausea, vomiting, paleness, trembling, inability to move, dizziness, enuresis, and diarrhea (Johnson, 1978; Lall and Lall, 1979).

_____ Sleeping disturbances (Harris, 1980).

_____ Eating disturbances (Harris, 1980).

_____ Crying, screaming, or whining in the classroom (Gresham and Nagle, 1981).

_____ Frequent runs from the classroom (Gresham and Nagle, 1981).

_____ Breaks out in a cold sweat at the words _math_, _English_, _spelling_, and so on (Lall and Lall, 1979).

Shoplifting

_____ Has enough money to pay for items at the time of apprehension.

_____ Items are taken for personal use.

_____ Done to "prove" onseself to peers.

_____ Steals in order to gain membership to groups.

_____ Travels in a pair or groups in the store.

_____ Stealing done in a childish or silly manner.

_____ Carries a handbag or a paper bag.

_____ Carries a coat over arm.

_____ In department without a hat, purse, and so on, where such merchandise is sold.

_____ Shabbily or poorly dressed.

_____ Loose or unnaturally fitting garments.

_____ Wears unseasonable clothing.

_____ Carries many items into the dressing room.

_____ Takes a baby carriage to the store.

_____ Starts a commotion with the salesperson while a friend is at a distance in order to draw attention away from the friend.

_____ Handles a lot of merchandise at different counters.

_____ Holds merchandise below counter level.

_____ Places merchandise in pocket.

_____ Leaves the store but returns in a few minutes.

_____ Aimless walking up and down aisles.

_____ Unusual actions in store.

_____ Appears nervous.

_____ Always has something new in his or her possession (S. Winkler, personal communications, 1984).

_____ Collects things just for the sake of acquiring possessions (Mack, 1970).

_____ If people won't let him or her borrow an item, it is taken from a store (Mack, 1970).

_____ Previous problems with shoplifting (S. Winkler, personal communication, 1984).

_____ Tries to impress others with possessions (S. Winkler, personal communication, 1984).

_____ Does not respect other's property (Sprick, 1981).

_____ Has a poor self-image (Sprick, 1981).

_____ Feels insecure (Sprick, 1981).

_____ Does not know the difference between desires and needs (Sprick, 1981).

_____ Shoplifting is viewed as being fun (Mack, 1970).

_____ Jealous of other's belongings (S. Winkler, personal communication, 1984).

Social Overinvolvement

_____ Joins a majority of school clubs and organizations (T. Marlier, personal communication, 1984).

_____ Runs for office positions in school clubs and organizations (T. Marlier, personal communication, 1984).

_____ Participates in sports (T. Marlier, personal communication, 1984).

_____ Attends many sports events and other activities of which he or she is not a participant (T. Marlier, personal communication, 1984).

_____ Significant decrease in school achievement and grades (T. Marlier, personal communication, 1984).

_____ Inability to complete homework on time (T. Marlier, personal communication, 1984).

_____ Tends to be more aggressive in asking for help and more successful in obtaining it (Webb, 1982).

_____ Participates in active social involvement with others through body contact or talk (Swift and Spivack, 1975).

_____ Often misses regularly scheduled classes due to other commitments in extracurricular activities (Mendez, 1984).

_____   Is popular and well-known by other students and faculty (T. Marlier, personal communication, 1984).

_____   Drawn to activities around him or her during class (Swift and Spivack, 1975).

_____   Prone to dominate class discussions (T. Marlier, personal communication, 1984).

_____   Tends to be ignored less often than other students (Webb, 1982).

_____   Is unable to accept being ignored (Swift and Spivack, 1975).

_____   Parental pressure to be involved is evident (Buser, Long, and Tweedy, 1975).

_____   Overinvolved to gain social status and acceptance among peers (Gholson and Buser, 1981).

_____   Appears irritable and easily frustrated when things don't go as planned (K. Webster, personal communication, 1985).

_____   Appears tired in class from activities impinging on sleep (K. Webster, personal communication, 1985).

Social Withdrawal

_____   Shy and introverted (Noshpitz, 1971; Cohen, Millman, and Schaefer, 1981).

_____   Few friends (Cohen, Millman, and Schaefer, 1981).

_____   Self-conscious (Cohen, Millman, and Schaefer, 1981).

_____   Unassertive (Cohen, Millman, and Schaefer, 1981).

_____   Lonely (Cohen, Millman, and Schaefer, 1981).

_____   Depressed (Cohen, Millman, and Schaefer, 1981).

_____   Low self-concept (Cohen, Millman, and Schaefer, 1981).

_____ Excessively cooperative (Cohen, Millman, and Schaefer, 1981).

_____ Passive (Cohen, Millman, and Schaefer, 1981).

_____ Poor eye contact (Cohen, Millman, and Schaefer, 1981).

_____ Short speech duration (Cohen, Millman, and Schaefer, 1981).

_____ Inaudible responses (Cohen, Millman, and Schaefer, 1981).

_____ Inability to make requests (Cohen, Millman, and Schaefer, 1981).

_____ Overdependent upon adults (Cohen, Millman, and Schaefer, 1981).

_____ Frequently seeks teacher contact (Cohen, Millman, and Schaefer, 1981).

_____ Intimidated or frightened by peers (Cohen, Millman, and Schaefer, 1981).

_____ Rarely initiates conversation (Cohen, Millman, and Schaefer, 1981).

_____ Little or no interaction with peers (Callahan, 1979; Cohen, Millman, and Schaefer, 1981).

_____ Rarely volunteers for assignments or special activities (Cohen, Millman, and Schaefer, 1981).

_____ Tends to daydream (Cohen, Millman, and Schaefer, 1981).

_____ Tends to doodle (Cohen, Millman, and Schaefer, 1981).

_____ Lacking in social skills (Bornstein, 1977).

_____ Tries to avoid calling attention to self (Kerr and Nelson, 1983).

_____ Doesn't protest when hurt, teased, or criticized by others (Noshpitz, 1971; Callahan, 1979; Kerr and Nelson, 1983).

_____ Last to be chosen for team activities (Kerr and Nelson, 1983).

_____ Not liked by other children (Kerr and Nelson, 1983).

_____ Lacks energy (Kerr and Nelson, 1983).

_____ Does not ask for help when needed.

_____ Fearful of being hurt during play (Ross, Lacy, and Parlor, 1965).

_____ Trembles when called upon to recite (Ross, Lacy, and Parlor, 1965).

_____ Embarrasses easily (Ross, Lacey, and Parlor, 1965).

_____ Sits or stands by self on playground (C. Walters, personal communication, 1984).

Suicide Proneness

_____ Lack of satisfying relationships with adults (Orbach, Gross, and Glaubman, 1981).

_____ Poor self-image (Dugan, 1976).

_____ Death of a loved one (Bush, 1980; Miller, 1984).

_____ Breakup of a relationship; separation or divorce (Bush, 1980; Miller, 1984; Pfeffer, Conte, Plutchik, and Jerrett, 1979; Smith, 1981).

_____ Consistent failure in meeting present goals.

_____ Doing poorly in school (Smith, 1981).

_____ Marital discord (Pfeffer, Conte, Plutchik, and Jerrett, 1979).

_____ Recent move (Deykin, 1984).

_____ Previous suicide attempt (Miller, 1984; Resnik and Hawthorne, 1974; Deykin, 1984).

_____ Changes in sleeping habits/sleeping disturbances (e.g., insomnia, early waking, excessive sleeping) (Deykin, 1984; Miller, 1984; Pfeffer, Conte, Plutchik, and Jerrett, 1979; Pfeffer, 1981).

_____ Change in eating habits (e.g., loss of appetite, compulsive eating) (Miller, 1984; Pfeffer, Conte, Plutchik, and Jerrett, 1979; Pfeffer, 1981).

_____ General bodily complaints (Dugan, 1976).

_____ Crying for no apparent reason (Miller, 1984).

_____ Chronic fatigue and lack of energy (Deykin, 1984; Miller, 1984; Pfeffer, Conte, Plutchik, and Jerrett, 1979).

_____ Digestive problems (stomach pain, nausea, indigestion, and/or change in bowel habits).

_____ Weight loss (Miller, 1984; Pfeffer, Conte, Plutchik, and Jerrett, 1979).

_____ Feelings of loneliness.

_____ Feelings of worthlessness (Miller, 1984; Pfeffer, 1981).

_____ Feelings of hopelessness (Miller, 1984; Pfeffer, 1981).

_____ Exaggerated guilt or self-blame (Pfeffer, Conte, Plutchik, and Jerrett, 1979; Pfeffer, 1981).

_____ Sadness (Miller, 1984; Pfeffer, Conte, Plutchik, and Jerrett, 1979).

_____ Loss of interest in friends and activities (Deykin, 1984; Pfeffer, Conte, Plutchik, and Jerrett, 1979).

_____ Lack of emotional responsiveness (Miller, 1984).

_____ Inability to find pleasure in anything (Deykin, 1984; Miller, 1984; Pfeffer, Conte, Plutchik, and Jerrett, 1979).

_____ Loss of sexual desire (Miller, 1984).

_____ A sudden, unexplainable lift in spirits (Miller, 1984).

_____ Loss of warm feelings toward family or friends.

_____ Dissatisfaction of life in general.

_____ Reduced ability to cope on daily basis.

_____ Indecisive and confused.

_____ Impaired memory.

_____ Inability to concentrate (Miller, 1984; Pfeffer, Conte, Plutchik, and Jerrett, 1979; Pfeffer, 1981).

_____ Apathetic (Miller, 1984).

_____ Seems withdrawn (Miller, 1984).

_____ Dwells on problems (Miller, 1984).

_____ Preoccupied (Miller, 1984).

_____ Bored (Deykin, 1984; Dugan, 1976; Miller, 1984).

_____ Easily discouraged (Miller, 1984).

_____ Low frustration tolerance (Miller, 1984; Pfeffer, Conte, Plutchik, and Jerrett, 1979).

_____ Moody (Pfeffer, Conte, Plutchik, and Jerrett, 1979).

_____ Mistrust of the world (Pfeffer, Conte, Plutchik, and Jerrett, 1979).

_____ Morbid thoughts and views (Deykin, 1984; Miller, 1984; Pfeffer, Conte, Plutchik, and Jerret, 1979).

_____ Feels unloved (Pfeffer, Conte, Plutchik, and Jerret, 1979).

_____ Continuously depressed (Bush, 1980).

_____ General angry attitude (Dugan, 1976).

_____ Intensely ambivalent about parents (Pfeffer, Conte, Plutchik, and Jerrett, 1979).

_____ Worries about doing poorly in school (Pfeffer, Conte, Plutchik, and Jerrett, 1979).

_____ Diminished attention span (Deykin, 1984).

_____ Sudden resigning from clubs, church groups, fraternal orders (Miller, 1984).

_____ Withdrawal from activities.

_____ Neglect of responsibilities.

_____ Neglect of appearance (Miller, 1984).

_____ Irritability and complaints about matters previously taken in stride (Miller, 1984).

_____ Doesn't want to converse (Miller, 1984).

_____ Gives terse replies when asked questions (Miller, 1984).

_____ Avoids friends and insists on being alone.

_____ Spends most of time watching television (Smith, 1981).

_____ Marked decrease in academic performance (Deykin, 1984).

_____ Unexplained impulsive behavior resulting in physical injuries, frequent accidents (Deykin, 1984).

_____ Getting one's affairs in order (e.g., preparing will, reviewing insurance papers, patching up bad feelings with others, writing long overdue letters, giving away personal possessions with sentimental value) (Miller, 1984; Resnik and Hawthorne, 1974).

_____ Preparing for suicide (e.g., buying a gun, a cache of pills, rubber hose for car exhaust, etc.) (Deykin, 1984; Miller, 1984; Resnik and Hawthorne, 1974).

_____ Planning own funeral after the death of a loved one (Deykin, 1984; Miller, 1984).

_____ Makes a suicide threat or writes a note (Bush, 1980; Deykin, 1984; Miller, 1984).

_____ By direct or indirect statement, essays, or poems, indicates a desire or intention to die (Deykin, 1984; Miller, 1984; Pfeffer, Conte, Plutchik, and Jerrett, 1979; Resnik and Hawthorne, 1974).

_____ Is truant from school (Dugan, 1976).

_____ Runs away from home (Dugan, 1976).

Test Anxiety

_____ Attempts to avoid testing situations (Turner, 1982).

_____ Possesses test-taking skill deficits (Hill, 1982).

_____ Tense stomach or stomach churning before a test (Hayward, 1982; Petersen, 1982).

_____ Tingling sensations in the limbs before a test (Hayward, 1982).

_____ Muscular tension in the shoulder and neck area before and during tests (Hayward, 1982).

_____ Nervousness before and during tests (Rogers, 1977; Turner, 1982).

_____ Sweaty palms before and during tests (Petersen, 1982).

_____ Faster heartbeat as test approaches (Turner, 1982).

_____ Gets an uneasy feeling when tests are mentioned (Turner, 1982).

_____ Perspires before and during tests (Turner, 1982).

_____ Needs to urinate frequently before and during tests (Turner, 1982).

_____ Mouth gets dry before and during tests (Turner, 1982).

_____ Gets a full feeling in the stomach before and during tests (Turner, 1982).

_____ Has tense posture during testing situations (Gaudry and Speilberger, 1971).

_____ Increased mental confusion before and during tests (Rogers, 1977; Hayward, 1982).

_____ Expects to fail tests (Sepie and Keeling, 1978; Hayward, 1982; Hagtvet, 1982).

_____ Negative self-talk regarding test taking ability (Hayward, 1982).

_____ Engages in reality testing or quizzing of others (Mayward, 1982).

_____ Negatively affected by testing instructions (Buckley, and Ribordy, 1982).

_____ Correlates test scores with feelings of being a success or failure (Rogers, 1977).

_____ Easily distracted while taking a test (Deffenbacher and Kemper, 1974).

_____ Impaired recall during test taking (Deffenbacher and Kemper, 1974).

_____ Shows much concern for level of performance and has negative task expectations (Turner, 1982).

_____ Performance expectancy is set high (Hagtvet, 1982).

_____ Low motivation (Hill, 1983).

_____ Anxiety relates strongly to report card grades and academic progress (Hill, 1983).

_____ Teacher feels the repeated necessity of "refocusing" the student's attention on critical information (Turner, 1982).

4

Sociograms

A sociogram is a teacher-made device that is used to provide additional information regarding a student and how he interacts with peers. It is valuable in determining how a student is viewed by his classmates. Students respond to a teacher-provided direction such as, "List the two classmates with whom you would most like to sit" or "Write the name of the person with whom you would enjoy working on a project." You may also assess interaction and social perceptions by using negatively worded statements or questions such as, "Who would you not want to play with during recess?" The results are then tabulated to determine how many times each student was chosen and by whom. This is graphically plotted to identify social isolates, popular students, and interaction patterns. The sociogram can be useful in a number of ways:

1. Allowing a student to work with a chosen peer may be a motivational tool.

2. Social isolates (those not chosen by others) could be placed in interaction situations with accepting peers or could be made the center of attention in positions such as charades leader or team captain.

3. By developing good rapport with class leaders, you can be more influential in convincing them to comply with directions, and others will be more likely to follow.

4. Interaction and friendship changes can be monitored via frequent administration of the sociogram technique.

How to Use Sociograms

1. Devise a question. State it in simple, easy-to-understand language. Word your question to be consistent with the information you desire to obtain (e.g., who to assign as field trip partners; who is unpopular).

2. Have students write their answers to your question or statement. Allow and encourage your students to make their choices privately. Clearly explain any limitations on choices (e.g., number of choices, classmates only).

3. On a list of the names of your students, write the number of times each student was chosen next to his name.

4. Make a large diagram of concentric rings so that it looks like an archery target. Have one more ring than the most number of times a student was chosen. Start outside the last ring and number the spaces from the outside inward starting with zero.

5. Write each student's name in the space corresponding to the number of times he was chosen.

6. Draw arrows from each student to the student chosen by him or her.

7. Survey the diagram to assess popularity and interaction preferences. This information should remain confidential.

Activities and
Discussion Questions

1. Find two containers. Choose any ten names and write each name on two separate pieces of paper. Place one set of names in each container. Container #1 represents the person making the choice. Container #2 represents the person chosen. Pick a name from Container #1, then pick a name from Container #2. Tally the responses and return the second name to Container #2. Do not return the first name to Container #1. Repeat until Container #1 is empty. Make a target sociogram with arrows indicating choices.

2. Complete a mock sociogram using friends, classmates, or other adults. Provide the directions for them, tally the number of times each person was chosen, and make a target sociogram with arrows indicating choices. Discuss the implications of the results.

For More Information

Gronlund, N. E. (1962). *Sociometry in the classroom.* Englewood Cliffs, N.J.: Prentice-Hall.

Moreno, J. (1953). *Who shall survive? Foundations of sociometry, group psychotherapy and sociodrama,* 2nd ed. New York: Beacon House.

Northway, M. L. (1940). A method for depicting social relationships obtained by sociometric testing. *Sociometry, 3,* 144–150.

Review issues of the journal entitled: *Sociometry.*

5

Behavioral Recording

Another method of evaluating a student's behavior that provides you with a very precise estimate of its severity is behavioral recording. The teacher or aide observes the student directly and records how long or how often a certain behavior occurs. Using this method, you can compare the degree of occurrence of the behavior with the degree to which it is exhibited by other students. This can be used as support for enrolling the student into a certain educational placement. This method may also be used to obtain an accurate idea of whether the student's behavior is improving over time. There are three basic types of behavioral recordings: frequency recording, duration recording, and interval recording. The recording procedure you choose will depend on the kind of behavior and type of information that would be most beneficial.

Frequency recording is a simple count of how many times a behavior occurs per designated period during your observation sessions. Those designated periods may be a minute, hour, day, or week. It is most useful with behaviors that are discrete and short lived (e.g., number of correct math problems, number of swear words, number of short talk-outs without raising hand).

Duration recording monitors the percent of time or the total time that a behavior occurs in a specified time period. To calculate the percentage, the sum of the times (duration) that the behavior occurred is divided by the total observation time. This type of recording is used for behaviors that last for more than a few seconds and/or for varying lengths of time (e.g., paying attention, tapping a pencil, in-seat behavior).

Interval recording is a shortcut procedure for estimating the duration of a behavior. In this method, the teacher periodically looks at the student at predetermined intervals and records whether the behavior is occurring. There are three types of interval recording. In *whole interval* time sampling, you observe the student for a few seconds at designated intervals and notice whether the behavior occurs during the *whole* interval (mark "yes" or "no" as to whether this occurred). In *partial interval* recording, you mark whether the behavior occurred at least once during the short observation interval. In *momentary* time sampling, you look up immediately at designated points and notice whether the behavior is occurring at that precise moment. The teacher then figures the percent of observations that the behavior occurred. Interval recording is used for the same behaviors as duration recording, but this procedure takes less time and effort and does not require that the student be observed continually.

How to Use Behavioral Recording

1. Define the behavior that you wish to observe. Be very specific. Be sure that your definition is so narrow in scope that others would observe only what you had in mind.

2. Decide which type of behavioral recording is best suited to monitor the behavior.

3. Decide when you will observe the behavior. Do you want to observe the behavior in a number of situations or just one (e.g., math class, story time)?

4. Decide how long each of your observations will be. Ten to twenty minutes is usually adequate. Repeat your observations *at least* three more times to give a more representative picture.

5. Observe and record the student's behavior.

6. If you used frequency recording, figure the average number of occurrences per minute, hour, or day. If you used duration recording, figure the percentage of the total observation time that the behavior occurred. If you used momentary time sampling, figure the percent of intervals when the behavior was occurring. Plot the occurrence rate on a graph.

7. Repeat steps 5 and 6.

Activities and Discussion Questions

1. For which of the following would frequency recording be appropriate? For which of the following would duration recording or momentary time sampling be appropriate? (Answers are listed in the Appendix.)

   a. Incorrectly pronounced words

   b. Homework assignments handed in

   c. Correct math problems

   d. Items assembled

   e. On task

   f. Humming

2. Define the following in *very* specific terms. (Answers are listed in the Appendix.)

   a. In-seat behavior

    b. Resists help from teacher

    c. Daydreaming

3. While conducting frequency recording, you find that the student has exhibited a certain behavior eighteen times in a ten-minute observation period. What is the average amount of occurrences per minute? (Answers are listed in the Appendix.)

4. Using duration recording during a twenty-minute observation period, you observe the student displaying the defined behavior for one minute, then two minutes and fifteen seconds, and then forty-five seconds. What percentage of time did the behavior occur? (Answers are listed in the Appendix.)

5. Using interval recording, you look up once a minute for fifteen minutes. You see the designated behavior on or during the 3rd, 8th, 9th, 13th, and 14th observations. What percent of intervals was the behavior observed? (Answers are listed in the Appendix.)

6. Locate a student, relative, teacher, or other person for you to observe. Define three behaviors displayed by that person. Choose one for frequency recording, one for duration recording, and one for momentary time sampling. Remember that the behaviors can be negative or positive in nature. Conduct four ten-minute observation sessions for each of the three recording techniques. Graph your results.

7. List several ways that you could use frequency recording to keep track of a behavior while teaching class. (Answers are listed in the Appendix.)

8. You sit in a chair in the lunchroom and watch a student whose behavior is of concern to you. You have a clipboard and pen. You suspect that the student knows that you are watching and has modified his behavior. What can you do to obtain accurate information?

9. You have defined the behavior "hitting others" and you have observed a certain student for the whole day. He hits another person twice during school hours. When you calculate the frequency per minute, you find that it is near zero. Does this mean that the behavior is not of concern?

For More Information

Brulle, A. R., and Repp, A. C. (1984). An investigation of the accuracy of momentary time sampling procedures with time series data. *British Journal of Psychology, 75*, 481–488.

Cartwright, C. A., and Cartwright, G. P. (1974). *Developing observation skills.* New York: McGraw-Hill.

Swanson, H. L., and Reinhart, H. R. (1984). *Teaching strategies for children in conflict,* 2nd ed. St. Louis: Times Mirror/Mosby.

Taylor, R. (1984). *Assessment of exceptional students: Educational and psychological procedures.* Englewood Cliffs, N.J.: Prentice-Hall.

Special Note Concerning Sections Three, Four, and Five

Through the use of the procedures outlined in Section Two of this book or your general observations and impressions, you have determined that one (or more) of your students is in need of intervention to assist him in learning to control his behavior. Based on your assessment, you will need to plan an appropriate intervention. Selecting a certain procedure to implement requires proper consideration of a number of variables. The techniques from Sections Three, Four, and Five of this book should be closely scrutinized, examined, and compared, noting the benefits and drawbacks of each. Review each procedure to determine if it will fit your needs and personal philosophy regarding behavior management while respecting the rights and meeting the best interests of your student.

After reading the description of each technique, decide if the procedure under consideration is feasible, given its ease of implementation and maintenance, the available resources, available support from parents and school staff, and other variables. Use the practice activities and discussion questions at the end of that chapter to familiarize yourself further with the procedure and assist in evaluation of its usefulness. The references will allow you to conduct further reading on the practice. Further reading is also indicated if you are unfamiliar with the underlying philosophy or theory that supports its use.

After implementation, observe closely to determine whether the procedure is safe, effective, and beneficial.

SECTION THREE

Direct Intervention

6

Assertive Discipline

Assertive discipline is a structured, systematic approach designed to assist educators in running an organized, teacher-controlled classroom environment. Lee and Marlene Canter, when consulting for school systems, found that many teachers were unable to control undesirable behavior that occurred in their classrooms. The Cantors attributed this to a lack of training in the area of behavior management. Based on their research and the foundations of assertiveness training and behaviorism, they developed a common-sense, easy-to-learn program to help teachers take control of their classrooms and positively influence their students' behavior. The Cantors believe that you, as a teacher, have the right to determine what is best for the student and to expect compliance. No pupil should prevent you from teaching or keep another student from learning. Discipline is imperative in creating and maintaining an effective and efficient learning environment.

In this program, teachers are taught to react assertively, as opposed to aggressively or nonassertively. Assertive teachers react confidently and quickly in situations that require behavior management. They have a few clearly stated classroom rules and give firm, clear, concise directions to students who are in need of outside control. Students who comply are reinforced, whereas those who disobey rules and directions receive negative consequences. Assertive teachers do not use an abrasive, sarcastic, hostile style, nor do they react in a timid, nondirective manner. Assertive teachers believe that a firm, teacher-controlled classroom is in the best interests of the student. They believe that the students, indeed, wish to have their behavior directed by the teacher. Society demands appropriate behavior if one is to be accepted and successful. Therefore, no one benefits when a student is allowed to misbehave. Teachers show their concern for today's youth when they demand and promote appropriate classroom behavior. Additionally, educators have the right to request and expect assistance from parents and administrators in their efforts.

How to Use
Assertive Discipline

1. Dismiss the thought that there is any acceptable reason for misbehavior. (Organically caused misbehavior may be an exception.)

2. Decide which rules you wish to implement in your classroom. Devise four or five rules that are specific and easily understood by your students.

3. Determine negative consequences for noncompliance. Choose three to six consequences, each of which is more punitive or restrictive than the previous one. These will be administered if the student continues to misbehave.

4. Determine positive consequences for appropriate behavior. For example, along with verbal praise, you might also include raffle tickets that are given to students for proper behavior. Students write their names on the tickets and drop them into a container for a daily prize drawing. Even if a student is having a bad day, there is a reason to improve, as even one ticket can make him or her a winner. Additionally, students who display appropriate behavior

may receive notes of praise to be shown to their parents. Group rewards are also used. A marble might be dropped into a jar for each predetermined interval that the class as a whole has been attentive and respectful. When the jar is full, a special event is held. Some assertive teachers also write a letter on the board for each period of good group behavior. When the letters spell Popcorn Party (or some other activity), that event is held.

5. Conduct a meeting to inform the students of the program. List the rules on the board along with the positive and negative consequences. Have the students orally recite the rules.

6. Have the students write the rules and take them home to be signed by the parents and returned. Attach a message explaining the program and requesting their help.

7. Implement the program immediately.

8. Become skilled in the use of other assertive discipline techniques.

   a. Communicate your displeasure with a student's misbehavior and be sure to tell the student *what to do*. For example: "Bill, stop writing and pass your paper forward." Notice that the teacher told the student what *not* to do, but also told the student what *to do*. Many students continue to display inappropriate behavior when they have been told to discontinue because they do not know what they *should* be doing. Now that you have given a direction, you can reinforce the student for compliance or punish him or her for noncompliance. Be sure to add emphasis to your directions by using eye contact, hand gestures, and the student's name.

   b. Recognize and quickly respond to appropriate behavior. This will encourage the students to display the desired behavior more often. Be aware that some students may need to be reinforced quietly or non-verbally to prevent embarrassment in front of peers.

c. Learn to use the "broken record" technique. Continue to repeat your command (a maximum of three times) until the student follows your directions. Do not be sidetracked by the student's excuses. For example:

T: "Vince, you have work to do. Get away from that window and sit in your seat."

S: "But I want to see the cop give that guy a ticket."

T: "I understand, but I want you to sit down now."

S: "Just one minute, OK?"

T: "No, Vince, I want you to sit down now."

S: "Aw, OK."

If the command is not followed, you may issue a choice to the student. This can be done after the first, second, or third request. Give the student a choice between following the command or facing a consequence for disobedience. For example: "Vince, you have a choice. You can sit down now or you'll sit with me after school (or during recess)." If you find it necessary to implement the consequence, make it clear to the student that he or she made the decision as to which option will occur. The consequence should be administered quickly and in a calm, matter-of-fact manner. In the above situation, you would move through your list of negative consequences until the student complies.

Activities and Discussion Questions

1. Identify the following teacher responses as being assertive, nonassertive, or hostile. (Answers are listed in the Appendix.)

a. "Jim, I like the way you raised your hand before speaking."

b. "Mary, please start putting your project away. It's been five minutes since I asked you to clean up."

c. "I give up. If this group doesn't want to listen, its your problem, not mine."

d. "Get to the end of the line! (The teacher grabs the student's shoulder and pushes him toward the end of line.) If you want to act like a bully, I'll show you what it's like to get pushed around."

e. Students are working quietly on their projects while the teacher sits at his desk and talks with the classroom aide.

f. Students are off task while the teacher quietly sits at her desk and corrects assignments.

g. "Jamie, stop hitting. You will keep your hands to yourself or you will be placed in time-out."

h. "Louise, you did such a nice job on your composition! Let's go down and show Mrs. Gailey (the vice-principal)."

i. "Hank, when are you going to learn that spitting at people is not a good way to handle conflicts?"

j. "Quit acting like a baby. Act your age."

k. "I want you to stop talking and finish those math problems."

l. "I don't believe it. You finally handed in an assignment that doesn't look like chicken scratchings."

m. "Wow, you only made that one small mistake. Great work, Gerry."

n. Peter is working diligently on his seatwork. He feels a hand on his shoulder and looks up to see the teacher give him a smile and a wink.

2. Provide an assertive response to the following situations:

   a. Five students are gathered around a small table for their reading lesson. While three students read or listen, Bob and Vince are poking each other and making faces.

   b. When told to get back on task, Larry tells you that he is feeling ill today. This is not typical behavior for Larry.

   c. When told to get back on task, Juanita tells you that she is feeling ill today. This is commonly reported by her, and you believe that she uses this as a ploy to avoid classwork.

   d. Rodney rips up his dittoed worksheet and throws it on the floor, mumbling, "I'm not doing this crap."

   e. Diana leaves her seat to tug on your arm and ask for assistance. You tell her to sit down and raise her hand. She starts to cry and accuses you of never helping her.

3. Demonstrate the "broken record" technique by writing responses for the teacher. Show your concern for the student by prefacing your unwavering direction with, "I understand, but . . . ," "That's not the point," or some other similar remark.

   a. Mike is not wearing his goggles during an activity that requires chipping pieces off of a rock with a hammer and chisel.

   Teacher: "Mike, put those goggles on."

   Mike: "It's OK. I've done this before."

   Teacher:

   Mike: "But the goggles get hot and fog up."

   Teacher:

   Mike: "They mess up your hair and leave red lines on your face."

Teacher: (Offer a choice with a negative consequence for noncompliance.)

　　b. The softball beats George to homeplate and he violently pushes Tim who is waiting at the plate for the tag. Tim receives a hard knock on the head as a result of the push-initiated fall.

Teacher: "George, sit down for a few minutes."

George: "For what?!"

Teacher:

George: "They do it in the pros!!"

Teacher:

George: "Bullshit! Why do I have to sit out for playing right? If Tim doesn't want to get hurt, he shouldn't stand in front of the plate!"

Teacher: (Offer a choice with a negative consequence for noncompliance.)

　　c. You see Tyler put the stuffed clown doll in his desk rather than returning it to the toy box. You decide to give a friendly hint or two.

Teacher: "Emmett gets lonely without his clown friends."

Tyler: "I won't play with him Mr. Condino."

Teacher: (Issue a direction)

Tyler: "No!"

Teacher: (Offer a choice with a negative consequence for noncompliance.)

4. To understand how messages are made more effective by the use of the student's name, eye contact, and gesture, practice the following steps with another person.

　　a. Sit ten to fifteen feet apart from your partner who is standing.

b. While looking down or away from your partner, say, "Sit down."

c. While looking down or away from your partner, say "(Name), sit down."

d. Say, "(Name), sit down," while looking assertively into the eyes of your partner. Maintain this eye contact for a few seconds.

e. Say, "(Name), sit down," while maintaining eye contact and gesturing toward the chair.

f. Stand up while completing step (e).

g. Switch roles and repeat steps (a) through (f). Use the phrase, "Thank you for your help" in place of "Sit down."

5. Practice giving positive reinforcement and consequences in different ways by finding a partner.

a. Have someone play the role of a student who is quietly writing a composition and sometimes looks up momentarily to think. Give five different nonverbal signals (e.g., wink, smile, nod, "thumbs up," OK sign, etc.).

b. Use positive touching on the student's back or shoulder and give a nonverbal signal.

c. Give a positive comment to the whole class because they are all working so diligently.

d. Have your partner approach your desk and ask if his or her paper is OK. Say something positive to the student in a personal, quiet voice. Remember to use eye contact and the student's name.

6. Turn to Chapter 10 of this book and complete the exercises at the end of the chapter.

7. Conduct a self-analysis by completing the following:

a. List the names of a few students whose behavior has been the most difficult for you to control.

b. Decide with which of these pupils you failed to set firm consistent limits because:

You feared that they might not like you?

You were afraid of them?

You might cause them psychological harm?

You felt inadequate to handle their unusual behavior?

c. Analyze your typical behavior management style.

Do you set firm, consistent limits for *all* students?

Do you respond to misconduct in a nonhostile, assertive manner?

Do you use a firm, calm, confident voice?

Do you use eye contact, gestures, and the student's name?

Do you have a sequential listing of responses (e.g., warning, detention, send to office) so that you are prepared to administer a negative consequence, and do the students know that you will respond in a consistent manner?

Do you "catch the students being good" (e.g., answering questions, doing requested assignments)?

d. Write down the changes that you must make to develop a style that is consistent with the assertive discipline approach.

8. Follow steps 2, 3, and 4 under the section entitled How to Use Assertive Discipline. Also write the message mentioned in step 6.

9. Visualize a classroom experience you have had when you felt inadequate or reacted in a nonassertive or hostile manner. Now relive that experience and act assertively in it. Say your response out loud. Use an assertive, confident voice.

10. With another, discuss the following:

    a. Should students have an influence in the formation of rules and routines? If so, to what extent?

    b. Are there any legitimate excuses for misbehavior (e.g., misinterpretation of a situation, illness, home problems)?

    c. Is this approach useful for all teachers, students, and educational programs?

For More Information

Canter, L. (1979). Discipline: You can do it! *Instructor*, *89*(2), 106–112.

Mandlebaum, L. H., Russell, S. C., Krouse, J., and Ganter, M. (1983). Assertive discipline: An effective classroom behavior management program. *Behavioral Disorders*, *8*(4), 258–264.

The following materials, along with information on training sessions, are available from:

Canter and Associates, Inc.
P.O. Box 64517
Los Angeles, CA 90064

Canter, L. (1982). *Assertive discipline: Competency based resource materials and guidelines workbook*. Los Angeles: Canter and Associates.

Canter, L. (1982). *Assertive discipline: Follow-up guide*. Los Angeles: Canter and Associates.

Canter, L., and Canter, M., (1982). *Assertive discipline: A take-charge approach for today's educator*. Los Angeles: Canter and Associates.

Canter, L., and Canter, M. (1982). *Assertive discipline for parents*. Los Angeles: Canter and Associates.

7

The Ten-Step Approach

William Glasser, renowned psychiatrist and educational theorist, is best known for his "reality therapy" treatment, which, rather than seeking to discover the past happenings that influence one's behavior, focuses on the present. Proper behavior is paramount; excuses for inappropriate behavior are not accepted. This approach has been extended into the educational realm. Students are made aware of which behaviors are appropriate in the classroom and therefore are expected to display them. According to Glasser, students are in control of their behavior and teachers should not accept any explanations as to why the misbehavior occurred. Misbehavior is a result of a bad choice on the part of the student. The teacher provides consequences to help promote good decision making on the student's part. Over time, the pupil will come to accept responsibility for his or her own behavior.

As part of Glasser's educational approach he has developed the problem-solving meeting (Chapter 14) and the ten-step approach to good discipline. The ten-step approach is a sequential system that becomes more directive and restrictive as the student fails to control her or his behavior. Numerous surveys and reports attest to its effectiveness in schools that had previously experienced numerous severe behavior problems.

How to Use the Ten Steps

1. Set aside a quiet thinking time for yourself. Choose a student whose behavior is a problem. Make a list of things you do when he is disruptive.

2. Analyze your list. Have your interventions been effective in improving the student's behavior? If not, make a commitment to stop using them. It's time to find a strategy that will work.

3. Make a plan to help your student start tomorrow on a better note (e.g., pat on the back, personal compliment, personal hello, extra errand, cookie).

4. If a problem arises, ask the student, "What are you doing?" Thinking about a behavior helps the student to recognize it, own it, and prepare to stop it. When you get an answer that states the actual behavior, say, "Please stop it." Do not accept statements such as "I'm not doing anything" and do not let him take you off on a tangent. Keep repeating "What are you doing?" until the student describes the behavior.

5. If, after steps 3 and 4, the behavior repeatedly continues, have a conference with the student when he misbehaves. Say, "What are you doing?" Upon receiving a response, ask, "Is it against the rules?" Upon receiving an affirmative answer, ask, "What should you be doing?" Expect the unacceptable behavior that was identified to be replaced by appropriate behavior. This helps the student realize that he was displaying inappropriate behavior and forces him to review classroom expectations.

6. If step 5 fails, repeat all of step 5 except for the last question. Substitute "We have to work this out. What kind of plan can you make to follow the rules?" The plan must be a positive action plan rather than lack of action. The

student must tell you what he *will* do in that same situation if it should happen again.

7. If the student disrupts again, isolate him or place him in time-out in the immediate classroom. The student may rejoin the class after having devised a plan for following rules, informed you of this plan, and made a commitment to follow it. If the student disrupts the class while in the quiet part of the room, this results in his removal from the room.

8. If step 7 does not work, in-school suspension is implemented. Say, "Things are not working out for you here. You and I have tried to solve this problem, but now it's time to talk with some other people. Please report to the principal's office." In-school suspension continues until an approved plan of action for appropriate behavior is formulated.

9. If the student is completely out of control, the parents are asked to take him home for the rest of the day.

10. If step 9 is continually ineffective, the student must stay home or is sent to an out-of-school placement.

(Note: Steps 9 and 10 may not be workable and feasible for many schools. One option is having the student stay after school or come in on weekends to sit until a plan is devised. Administrative and parental permission is necessary for this approach.)

Activities and Discussion Questions

1. Complete the first three steps in the ten-step approach. Think of a former or present student whose behavior was or is of concern to you. How did you react to that behavior? Was your response effective in influencing long-

term behavioral changes? Make a plan that might be or have been effective in helping the student start a better day.

2. If you had to move to step 7 with a student, where in your classroom would you place the time-out area? How would it be designed?

3. Would steps 9 and 10 be allowed in your school? If not, devise two steps that would be more restrictive than step 8.

4. With a partner, role play for others the use of the ten steps with a student.

5. With a group of others, discuss the following questions:

   a. Why do the first three steps focus only on the teacher?

   b. Glasser considers step 3, "giving the student the time of day," to be the most important of the steps. Why?

   c. Step 8 recommends that the student be removed from the classroom until he devises an appropriate plan of action. How long should you wait for this to happen?

   d. What differences would there be between the use of the ten-step process with elementary school children and its use with high school students?

For More Information

Glasser, W. (1978). Ten steps to good discipline. *Education Digest, 43*(6), 1–5.

For More Information on
Glasser's Reality Therapy

Glasser, W. (1965). *Reality therapy: A new approach to psychiatry.* New York: Harper and Row.

Glasser, W. (1969). *Schools without failure.* New York: Harper and Row.

8

The 10-R Technique

The prosocial response formation technique, often referred to as the 10-R technique, was developed by Patrick Schloss to assist in the control and change of aggressive or noncompliant behavior. It is promoted as an alternative to traditional approaches of punishing disruptive behavior. The approach recommends the implementation of a sequence of ten steps to be followed whenever a student's misbehavior is unreceptive to warnings and mild interventions. The 10-R technique involves the student in the correction of inappropriate behavior by having him analyze why it was wrong or nonproductive, and requiring the practice of proper actions.

How to Use the 10-R Technique

For maximum effectiveness, it is recommended that all ten steps be followed consistently after each behavioral incident.

1. *Response cost.* When a nonacceptable action is displayed, remove a predetermined amount of reinforcer (e.g., free time, points) and have the student state which rules were

broken. The amount to be removed was known to all students beforehand.

2. *Relaxation*. Have the student go to a preassigned place (e.g., a mat, carrel, or corner) and relax himself. He is to summon you when calm. If the voice is excited or sarcastic in tone, or if the muscles appear tense (you may want to lightly shake his arm or leg to monitor muscle tension), tell him to continue to calm himself.

3. *Rectify*. Have the student provide restitution for damage done. This may involve repair of items, an apology to another, or repayment for damage.

4. *Recognize*. Help the student recognize the cause of his misbehavior and identify more appropriate responses for that situation.

5. *Rehearsal*. Have the student practice the alternative behavior(s) identified in step 4. Role play a situation similar to the one that was handled inappropriately.

6. *Reinforce*. Reinforce, praise, or reward the student for having demonstrated appropriate behavior. Also reinforce the behavior when it is displayed later by the student.

7. *Reflect*. Ask the student to identify the consequences of his disruptive behavior and compare them with the possible consequences of the desired action. This helps the student see the benefits of proper behavior.

8. *Reenter*. The student has missed anywhere from a few minutes to a few hours during this session. He should finish all work missed, or be returned to the least pleasant activity missed, so that these sessions do not become a learned way to avoid school work.

9. *Record*. Record data to assist in evaluating the long-term effectiveness of the prosocial technique.

10. *Repeat*. Use this technique as necessary to change behavior.

Activities and Discussion Questions

1. You are leading Kristen through the ten steps. She refuses to apologize to Shirley for hitting her. Kristen becomes angry again. What can be done? (Answers are in the Appendix.)

2. Dan refuses to go to the relaxation mat as directed. What can you do? (Answers are in the Appendix.)

3. How could these ten steps be revised or condensed if the student (or the teacher) can't remember all ten? (Answers are in the Appendix.)

4. How could two simultaneously misbehaving students be handled at one time by a teacher using this technique?

5. What information do you want to record in step 9 of the 10-R technique?

6. Discuss what might be done if your recording indicates that this technique has not been effective in changing a student's behavior.

7. With a partner, role play the use of the 10-R technique. Have your partner imitate a student who is of concern to you.

For More Information

Schloss, P. J. (1983). The prosocial response formation technique. *The Elementary School Journal, 83*, (3), 220–229.

9

Shaping

The shaping technique is not, in and of itself, a method for controlling inappropriate behavior. Instead, it is a method that assists you in setting goals for the behavior of a certain student. Shaping will provide guidance and direction for your behavior change program, and will help you assess its effectiveness. It can assist you in changing an aberrant behavior or creating an appropriate behavior that is not yet in the student's repertoire.

Shaping is used when you want the student to engage in a certain desirable behavior that is, at present, infrequently or never displayed by him. If you were to wait for the student to show this behavior so that you could reward him, you might wait a very long time. Shaping allows you to build this desired behavior in steps and reward those behaviors that come progressively closer to the one you have chosen as the final goal. As the student masters each substep, you require that he move to the next increment in order to receive an award or reinforcement. For example, John never does his math homework. You would like to have him complete his homework on a daily basis. You realize that if you wait for him to complete his homework before you reinforce him in some way, you may never (or infrequently) have the opportunity to administer a positive consequence. Therefore, you decide to break down the desired behavior into substeps that are progressively more demanding. These steps might be:

1. John will write his name at the top of the worksheet.

2. John will complete one problem of his choice.

3. John will complete five problems of his choice.

4. John will complete either all the odd-numbered problems or all the even-numbered problems.

5. John will complete all problems except one.

6. John will complete all problems.

As John masters each step, you will tell him he must now move on to the next objective to receive a reward. If the jump between two steps is too difficult, then you must break down the steps even further.

How to Use Shaping

1. Identify a desired behavior for this student. Determine the final goal.

2. Identify the student's present level of performance in displaying the desired behavior.

3. List the steps to take the student from his present level of performance to the desired behavior. These should be progressively more demanding.

4. Tell the student that he must do step 1 to receive reinforcement.

5. When the student has mastered one step, require that the next step be accomplished to receive reinforcement.

Activities and
Discussion Questions

1. Avion has difficulty kicking the kickball while playing with the class during recess and physical education class. The steps in her shaping program are in the wrong order. Place them in the correct order. (Answer is in the Appendix.)

    a. Avion will run to an approaching ball rolled slowly by the teacher and kick it firmly.

    b. Avion will stand in place and kick a stationary ball.

    c. Avion will run to a quickly approaching ball that has "spin" or "English" on it and kick it firmly.

    d. Avion will stand in place and firmly kick a slowly approaching ball rolled by the teacher.

    e. Avion will run to an approaching ball rolled quickly by another student and kick it firmly.

2. Willy has done well in his shaping program which is helping him lose his fear of dogs. However, he is unable to make the jump from step d to step e. Devise at least two more intermediary steps to gradually help him reach stage e. (Answer is in the Appendix.)

    a. Willy will look at photographs of dogs.

    b. Willy will watch dogs in a movie or television program.

    c. Willy will watch a dog through a window.

    d. Willy will watch a dog from the other side of a fence.

    e. Willy will play with the neighbor's Saint Bernard.

3. List at least five steps to shape behavior in the following situations. (Answers in the Appendix.)

    a. Rose never participates in Show and Tell. You have

asked her to become involved, but she appears frightened to do so.

Desired behavior:
Present behavior:
Substeps: (1)
          (2)
          (3)
          (4)
          (5)

b. Andy has never raised his hand to volunteer an answer to your activity or lecture questions.

Desired behavior:
Present behavior:
Substeps: (1)
          (2)
          (3)
          (4)
          (5)

For More Information

Bootzin, R. (1975). *Behavior modifiers and therapy.* Cambridge, Mass.: Winthrop Publishers.

Suran, B., and Rizzo, J. (1979). *Special children: An integrative approach.* Glenview, Ill.: Scott, Foresman.

Wright, J., and James, R. (1974). *A behavioral approach to preventing delinquency.* Springfield, Ill.: Charles C. Thomas Publisher.

10

Contracting

A contract is a written agreement between a student and a teacher that is directed toward changing behavior. It is a motivational device in which you agree to provide a reward to the student if he completes a designated task or displays a certain behavior. The behavior chosen is usually one that is exhibited less frequently than you would like. Therefore, you offer an incentive to the student to increase the occurrence of that behavior. The contract outlines time or amount constraints, the reinforcer to be administered, and any other necessary conditions. Most contracts are positively oriented. That is, they attempt to build desirable behavior. However, some do include penalty clauses to punish the student if he fails to meet stated expectations. Here are two examples of contracts:

Room 226 Contract

Date _____

During the week of: _____ I will: _____

_____

If I do this, I will receive: _____

_____

We agree to the above terms.   Teacher _____
Student _____   Witness _____

Contract

The following is an agreement between _____
                                                    (student)

and _____ . The terms of the agreement are as follows:
        (teacher)

The student will _____

_____

In return, the teacher will _____

_____

The following conditions apply:

1. _____

2. _____

3. _____

This contract is rendered void if the student fails to achieve

the designated goal. The contract will be reviewed on

_____ .
  (date)

                                    Student signature _____

                                    Teacher signature _____

                                    Witness signature _____

Date _____

How to Use Contracting

1. Arrange a meeting with the selected student.

2. Discuss your concern about his performance and let him know that you are willing to make a deal in order to help him improve.

3. Explain contracting and give a few examples. Tell how movie stars, sports heros, and persons in other professions of interest to the student are involved with contracts.

4. Be sure that the student understands the concept of contracts by asking him to give an example of what a contract is.

5. Inform the student of which behaviors you would be willing to reward. You might also wish to ask the student which behaviors he feels need to be improved.

6. Have the student tell you for which activities or items he is willing to work.

7. Negotiate the ratio of task to reinforcement and agree upon the amounts. Decide what must be done to receive the reinforcement.

8. Decide on the achievement level to be met by the student (e.g., 80 percent correct, less than three talk-outs per day). You may wish to start at a low level initially and renegotiate later for a higher level of performance.

9. Determine the amount of time allotted to complete the task.

10. Determine who will monitor and evaluate the student's performance. (The teacher usually does this.)

11. Determine how and when the reinforcement will be awarded.

12. Set a date for renegotiation of the contract. This allows dissatisfied parties to state grievances and close loopholes.

13. Read the contract with the student and sign your names if both are in agreement.

14. Have a witness read and sign the contract. Obtaining a witness who is perceived positively by the student may be a motivational tool.

15. Have all parties shake hands and congratulate each other.

Activities and Discussion Questions

1. Find a partner and assign her or him the role of the student. You, as the teacher, lead the contract development meeting by following the steps outlined in this chapter. If you do not have a specific task or behavior in mind, use the following situations:

    a. Judy is regularly truant. When she does attend your class she refuses to do any work.

    b. Brian rarely does his homework.

    c. Robin dislikes remedial reading instruction. He will not bring a book to the tutoring sessions as requested and complains if you ask him to go to the library and choose one. When asked to read orally in a small group, he places his head on the table and rests quietly.

2. Write three different contract forms, one for primary grades, one for intermediate grades, and one for high school. Be careful with your wording. Use drawings on the contract for the primary grade level.

3. Make a contract sheet for grading. Outline what needs to be accomplished to earn an A, B, C, or D grade.

For More Information

Swanson, H. L., and Reinhart, H. R. (1984). *Teaching strategies for children in conflict*, 2nd ed. St. Louis: Times Mirror/Mosby.

Walker, J. E., and Shea, T. M. (1984). *Behavior management: A practical approach for educators*. St. Louis: Times Mirror/Mosby.

11

Token Economies

One of the most often used behavior management techniques, especially in settings for students who have learning or behavioral difficulties, is the token economy system. A token economy involves awarding tokens (chips, stickers, checkmarks, points, or other items/markings) to students who demonstrate desired behaviors identified by the teacher. The student may periodically exchange the tokens for rewards, which are items or activities desirable to him. It is often compared to a national economic system in which we work for money, which has no value in and of itself, and later exchange it for items and activities that are valuable to us.

Token economies are often quite effective for students who are resistant to other types of motivational or behavior management techniques. Other benefits of this system are ease of administration, the use of immediate reinforcement (tokens) while teaching delayed gratification (holding tokens until trade in time), lack of boredom or satiation for the student due to the availability of a variety of back-up reinforcers, and lack of competition between students as the student competes against himself.

When a token economy is used for one or a few students only, it is often devised through a contract. Procedures for implementing this variation are presented in Chapter 10 of this book. In this version, along with a token economy for groups, the tokens are periodically devalued so that the student(s) must perform at a higher level to earn the same value in back-up reinforcers. This promotes continual improvement in behavior or performance by the student(s). Token economies have great flexibility and utility; they have been shown in research studies to be effective with many types for students with various kinds and severities of handicapping conditions. Perhaps the reason it is so effective is that a token or checkmark is visible evidence of progress. It also reminds the student to display proper behavior, and assures that the teacher will notice appropriate behavior and interact with the student in a positive manner.

How to Use Token Economies

1. Select the behavior(s) to be rewarded. The behavior(s) reinforced should be in concert with classroom rules and guidelines.

2. State the desired behavior(s) in specific and observable terms. Phrase them in a positive manner. Be sure to tell the student what *to* do, rather than what *not* to do (e.g., "Raise hand before talking" rather than "No speaking out").

3. Decide how you will measure the behavior(s) (e.g., percentage correct, number of minutes engaged in proper behavior, number of times student displays appropriate behavior).

4. Decide where to monitor the behavior(s) (e.g., only in the classroom or also in the lunchroom and on the bus).

5. Select the initial reinforcers. Use a reinforcer that is easy to administer and convenient to store. Devise a token/item/marking that will inhibit theft or counterfeiting.

6. Select your back-up reinforcers. Involve your students in the selection to insure that the reinforcers will be perceived as being valuable. (For instance, have the students list things that they would work to obtain, or complete one of the many published reinforcement inventories or set out possible reinforcers and observe which ones are selected most often.) Be sure that the reinforcers are appropriate. Consider educational value, cost, possible misuse, or danger involved.

7. Place a price (in tokens) on your back-up reinforcers. Record the actual price of any purchased items. Higher priced items will demand more tokens. Place a value on back-up reinforcers that is activity-oriented such as free time, listening to music, or painting. Develop a wall chart that lists the number of tokens needed to purchase each back-up reinforcer.

8. Place a value on the tokens. Give the tokens a value that is worth more now than in the future. As students begin to function more appropriately, tokens will have to be devalued to motivate them to improve continually. Next, develop a wall chart that lists the number of tokens to be given for each desired behavior, and decide whether inappropriate behavior will result only in a withholding of tokens or whether you will place a fine and take away tokens for that misconduct. If this is the case, make a wall chart that indicates the amount to be fined for each misbehavior.

9. Finalize the details by developing your own monitoring sheet to keep track of awards and fines and deciding how often and when tokens can be exchanged for back-up reinforcers (e.g., at the end of each day, at the end of each week). Develop storage containers/procedures for yourself and the students and devise a method for displaying the back-up reinforcers.

10. Start your program. Have the materials ready to show to

students as you explain the program in language that they can understand. Make your presentation very positive and upbeat. Post the wall charts and review them periodically. Implement the program, providing the tokens as soon as they are earned. Add to your back-up reinforcer menu as necessary.

11. Periodically modify your system to wean your students from the token economy. This might involve requiring more positive behavior for a longer period of time in order to obtain a checkmark or token.

Activities and Discussion Questions

1. List twenty-five items that could be used as tokens in a token economy.

2. Make a reinforcement inventory to determine the rewards desired by your students. Use open-ended sentences (e.g., "If I had 15 minutes of free time, I would like to _____ .") and choices (e.g., "Given free time, which would you rather do? (a) talk with a friend; (b) play a game; (c) read; (d) listen to music). List only those choices that you would alow in your classroom.

3. Complete steps 1 through 9 in the section entitled How to Use Token Economies. Make all the materials and indicate what items you would use for tokens and back-up reinforcers. Write your introduction of the system to the students.

4. Read Chapter 10 of this book on contracting. With a partner, role play a situation in which a token economy will be set up for one student through contracting. Put that contract in writing.

5. A parent feels that your token economy is bribery. How do you respond to this parent?

6. Hamilton comes to you to report that someone stole his tokens. How can you prevent this from occurring in the future? (Answers are in the Appendix.)

7. You caught Jeff bringing poker chips from home that look like the ones you use to reinforce students. You had this problem once before when you gave checkmarks and the students made their own. How can you prevent this behavior? (Answers are in the Appendix.)

8. Is it fair to take away tokens that have already been earned by the student? Shouldn't he be able to keep tokens he has earned previously by displaying appropriate behavior?

For More Information

Stainback, W. C., Payne, J. S., Stainback, S. B., and Payne, R. A. (1978). *Establishing a token economy in the classroom.* Columbus, Ohio: Merrill.

Walker, J. E., and Shea, T. M. (1984). *Behavior management: A practical approach for educators.* St. Louis: Times Mirror/Mosby.

12

Differential Reinforcement of Other Behaviors

One behavior modification technique that has proven to be useful in decreasing frequent, severe, or repetitive behaviors, especially in those students who are labeled mentally retarded, is known as differential reinforcement of other behaviors (DRO). DRO is a technique that involves rewarding or reinforcing a student if an undesired behavior is not displayed during a designated time period. It is positive in nature in that the student's behavior is either reinforced or ignored. No punishment is involved. Although the standard form of DRO requires a one-to-one teacher-student ratio with independent observers to record data, modifications can easily be made to allow for its use in the classroom, workshop, or home environment. These modified steps for implementation are presented below.

How to Use DRO

1. Define the behavior of concern in very specific, observable terms. Be sure that your definition is so precise that oth-

ers, after reading your definition, will be observing the exact same behavior.

2. Conduct a frequency count (see Chapter 5). How often does the behavior occur on the average?

3. This interval (see step 2) is how long the student must withhold the undesirable behavior in order to be reinforced. During this time, the student is engaged in normal, everyday tasks. If a reward other than verbal praise is involved, be sure to tell the student why he is being rewarded each time you do so.

4. If the behavior does occur during the designated time period, restrain that behavior (e.g., hold the head still if rocking; hold the hands still if hand flapping; close the mouth if vocalizing) for two to four seconds and say, "No (behavior) ." Or, while restraining, state the behavior you wish to see (e.g., "Sit still"; "Hands on lap"; "Be quiet"). If the behavior occurred during the designated time period, give no reinforcement at the end of that period. Or, after you release your restraint, start the designated time period again.

5. Return to step 2 to monitor progress and determine the length of the next day's time periods.

Notes

1. The behavior of concern may occur *more frequently* for the first day or two. It will then drop drastically. On the average, intervals will double in length each day. The behavior usually disappears by the third week.

2. You may have to decrease instructional time at the beginning of the program in order to deal with the behavior of concern, but you will gain instructional time as the program progresses.

Activities and Discussion Questions

1. Define the following behaviors in specific, observable, and measurable terms. Be *very* precise. (Answers are in the Appendix. See also activity number 2 in Chapter 5.)

   a. Spits

   b. Curses

   c. Rocking

   d. Throws objects

   e. Slams top of desk

   f. Turns out classroom lights

   g. Leaves work area

   h. Screams

   i. Hand flapping

   j. Bites self

   k. Mouthing

2. Pretend that you have been observing your students' behavior. For each of the following examples, figure the designated time period that the undesired behavior must be withheld by the student in order to receive reinforcement. (Answers are in the Appendix.)

   a. Steve screamed twelve times in fifteen minutes.

   b. Amber started to rock sixteen times in ten minutes (before you restrained her).

   c. Cary threw materials on the floor seven times in twenty-five minutes.

   d. Rashad bit himself three times in twenty minutes.

3. You find it difficult to keep track of time periods that last thirty-seven seconds, or three minutes and seven seconds,

and so on. What can you do to monitor the behavior accurately while still attending to your other students and tasks? (Answers are in the Appendix.)

4. Your student exhibits many undesirable behaviors. How can you deal with more than one behavior at a time? (Answer is in the Appendix.)

5. You wish to conduct DRO procedures with many students at once. What can you do to accommodate the different time periods that you calculated for each student? (Answer is in the Appendix.)

6. Some of your students' behaviors last a few seconds to a few minutes. How can you do a frequency count of a behavior that might usually be regarded as best recorded with a duration count (e.g., prolonged humming, rocking, walking)? (Answer is in the Appendix.)

7. With a partner, have the other person imitate a behavior of concern while he or she is completing a typical task presented to your students.

   a. For three minutes, record the number of behavior outbursts. Do not intervene at this time.

   b. Calculate the time period to be used.

   c. For the next three minutes, monitor your partner's behavior while reinforcing and intervening as appropriate. Restart your time period after either reinforcement or intervention. Continue to record the frequency of the behavior during this time.

   d. Calculate the new time period to be used.

For More Information

Barton, L. E., Brulle, A. R., and Repp, A. C. (1984). *Programming DRO to reduce multiple behaviors of multiple subjects.* Kent, Ohio: Kent State University. (ERIC Document Reproduction Service, ED # 4198.)

Barton, L. E., Brulle, A. R., and Repp, A. C. (1986). Maintenance of therapeutic change by momentary DRO. *Journal of Applied Behavior Analysis. 19,* 277–282.

Barton, L. E., Meston, L. A., and Brulle, A. R. (1984). A brief note on the differential reinforcement of other behavior (DRO) and multiple problem behaviors in a group setting. *Special Education in Canada, 58,* 55–58.

Brulle, A. R., and Barton, L. E. (1987). The reduction of maladaptive behavior through DRO procedures: A practitioner's reference. Unpublished manuscript. Available from Dr. Andrew Brulle, Department of Special Education, Eastern Illinois University, Charleston, IL 61920.

Deitz, S. M., Repp, A. C., and Deitz, D. E. D. (1976). Reducing inappropriate classroom behavior of retarded students through three procedures of differential reinforcement. *Journal of Mental Deficiency Research, 20,* 155–170.

Repp, A. C., Barton, L. E., and Brulle, A. R. (1983). A comparison of two procedures for programming the differential reinforcement of other behaviors. *Journal of Applied Behavior Analysis, 16,* 435–445.

Repp, A. C., and Deitz, S. M. (1974). Reducing aggressive and self-injurious behavior of institutionalized retarded children through reinforcement of other behaviors. *Journal of Applied Analysis, 7,* 313–325.

13

Time-Honored
Techniques

Most misbehaviors in the classroom can be controlled by minor changes in teacher style. Becoming a more effective behavior manager involves being familiar with numerous intervention techniques, knowing when to use each one, and implementing the selected technique in an assertive manner. For centuries, effective behavior managers have used the many quick and simple intervention techniques listed in this chapter. These strategies are especially useful in that they are easy to learn and implement and they can be used in any setting in which children and youth are present. In addition, they can be used as a behavior management system in and of themselves for students with mild behavioral problems, or used with a more structured technique offered in the other chapters when dealing with students with more severe behavioral problems.

These teacher-tested, time-honored strategies are divided into three categories. The first grouping includes ideas that help prevent the occurrence of undesired behavior. The second group includes strategies that are effective in stopping unwanted displays of behavior. The third category contains techniques that are useful in dealing with students after their behavioral outburst has ended. As you read each strategy, think of when you might use each and for which students each might be effective. Effective behavior managers learn from their experiences, discontinue ineffective behavioral interventions, and continue to search for answers to behavior problems that are resistant to present interventions.

How to Use Time-Honored Techniques

Prevention

1. Keep your classroom neat and organized.
   A messy, uncared for atmosphere promotes lax, uncaring, disorderly behavior. On the other hand, a neat and organized environment promotes mannerly and organized behavior.

2. Make your classroom attractive and colorful.
   This helps to create a place where it's nice to learn. Consider using soft music and flowers; they have been demonstrated to promote nonviolent, task-oriented behavior.

3. Create work and interest centers.
   The presence of learning centers in the classroom tends to promote productive rather than nonproductive activity during less structured time periods.

4. Arrange the seating to fit the activity.
   Students may display undesired behavior if they cannot view an activity or see or hear the speaker. Use more structured seating plans to promote a quiet, noninteraction-oriented environment. Utilize less structured seating to promote discussion and interaction.

5. Provide special seating for the disruptive student.
   Some possible options include seating the student near the teacher for seatwork, movies, and demonstrations, being sure that the student is not hidden from the teach-

er's view by furnishings or another student, and sur-
rounding the student with classmates who display appropriate behavior. Seat distractible students away from
windows, doors, chalk trays, material displays, and other
stimulating areas.

6. Insure that your classroom has adequate lighting, heating,
and ventilation.
An uncomfortable room can affect the mood of both the
teacher and student. Request repairs immediately.

7. Set up carrels or offices.
These cubicles can be used with students who are easily
distracted in the larger classroom. By facing a blank wall
and being flanked by dividers, the work becomes the most
interesting stimulus and the distracting stimuli are
blocked.

8. Get to know you students quickly.
Anonymity gives a sense of security to a misbehaving student. Get to know the names of your "ringleaders." Additionally, socialize with your students outside of the
classroom if possible. This can improve your image in the
students' eyes. A friendly discussion in the hallway or at
a basketball game can build a bond with the student that
will help prevent future misbehavior.

9. Begin your lesson promptly.
Don't give misbehavior a chance to start. Focus the student's attention onto the task immediately. This also helps
reduce tardiness.

10. Plan ahead.
Review your lesson plan during the evening or breaktime
before that lesson. Think of students who are disruptive.
What behaviors can you expect to see? Devise a plan to
prevent those behaviors by modifying your presentation,
lesson seating, or assignment demands. Think of how you
will intervene effectively if the students do display undesirable behavior during that lesson.

11. Devise rules.

    It is important to set guidelines or limitations for student behavior. Have five or fewer rules stated in positive terms. That is, state what behavior you would like to see rather than behavior you wish to eliminate (e.g., "Walk" rather than "Don't run"; "Follow directions the first time they are given," rather than "No backtalk"). Your students may test the limits initially. Therefore, it is important to enforce the rules strictly and consistently at the beginning of the school year. You may decide to become more lenient in your interpretation as the students prove their ability to control their behavior.

12. Have routines.

    Disorganization causes confusion, which can lead to misbehavior. Have a set, structured method for dismissal of students, leaving the room, choosing teams, taking turns, and cleaning up after activities. Decide how books, papers, and materials can be distributed and collected quietly and quickly with a minimum of confusion or disruption.

13. Develop a positive and assertive teaching style.

    a. Catch the students being good. Too often, teachers give attention only when students are misbehaving. Praise, reward, and recognize desired behavior *constantly*. Never ignore appropriate behavior.

    b. Mark the correct answers on assignments instead of the incorrect answers.

    c. Give recognition for correct oral responses to questions. When an incorrect response is given, provide another question, statement, or hint to allow the student to improve upon his answer. If this next attempt is also incorrect, respond to a part of the answer that is correct or compliment the student for trying.

    d. Develop a warm and friendly classroom atmosphere

by developing rapport with your students and showing an interest when listening, conversing, or interacting with them. Students are more likely to be cooperative and nondefiant when they like their teacher.

e. Start the day on an upbeat note. Greet your students with a warm hello and a nice personal comment. Smile! Believe it or not, after a while this actually becomes a pleasant activity rather than a chore.

f. Stand near the door as students enter or leave. This personalizes greetings and goodbyes and provides more control over student behavior. Do not allow students to enter your room if they are misbehaving. Have them walk back down the hallway and return to your room in an appropriate manner. Set the tone of your room as being a place where disruptive behavior is not allowed. Do not allow students to leave your room until materials are neatly stored, trash is thrown away, and the classroom was left in its original state.

g. Be prepared. It is difficult to present an interesting lesson when you are not sure of where your materials are, what to say to the students, or what is expected of them. Plan your lesson carefully and specifically, and practice it at least once before presenting it to your students.

h. Don't try to talk over noise. Be sure that the class is quiet and attentive before speaking. If interrupted, do not continue teaching until all students are silent.

i. Vary the tone, speed, and intensity of your speaking to maintain the interest of your pupils. Be dramatic in voice and mannerism. Ooze enthusiasm.

j. Vary the mode of presentation. Intersperse activities, movies, discussions, or role playing between periods of lecture to maintain the students' interest. Ask questions of students whose interest has waned to bring them back on task.

k. Give your directions in sequence, pausing between each one or each part of your direction to be sure that everyone has obeyed you to that point (e.g., "Quiet please." (pause) "Take out your books." (pause) "Turn to page 36." (pause) "Write the answers to the odd-numbered questions."). This method assures that all students understand and follow your commands.

l. Avoid saying "OK?" at the end of a command. A direction should be in the form of an imperative sentence. Do not say "OK?" unless you really want the student to make a decision.

m. Get out from behind your desk! Roam to all parts of the room, praising students who are behaving appropriately and moving closer to those who are off task.

n. If you must sit at the desk to complete your work, look up frequently and scan the entire classroom to assure that all is going well.

o. When bending over to assist a student, do so from the side of the desk that allows you to face the largest number of students or potential trouble areas. In this manner, misbehavior can be detected with your peripheral vision.

p. Model the behavior you wish to see in your classroom. Be courteous and polite. Reward the same behavior in your students.

q. Never argue with a student. If you have given a direction, there should be no debate. Go through your sequential list of interventions as needed. If you have not given a command to the student yet, *give one!*

r. Know each student's personal frustrations and how he reacts to that frustration. With this information, you can attempt to prevent the frustrating situations or can react effectively if the undesired behavior does occur.

s. When speaking with students, use a firm, calm, yet friendly voice. Carry yourself in a manner that appears confident and self-assured.

14. Learn from experience.

After school, think about the low points and highlights of your day. Where did you make mistakes? If you could relive those moments, what *could* you have done? In those high points, what did you do correctly that you'll want to do again? Make your experience work for you.

Stopping Misbehavior

1. Ignore the behavior.

This is usually effective only for a well-behaved student who is temporarily off task and can be expected to return to task momentarily. Unless the behavior is intended to gain your attention, attention from peers will often suffice. You will need to obtain the cooperation of all students in ignoring this behavior in order for this plan to be effective. Be aware that misbehavior increases when you first ignore it. To be effective, you must not give in too soon.

2. Refocus the student's attention back to the work.

Walk over to the off-task student and while looking at the student's assignment, inquire as to how he is doing. This draws the student's attention back to the work. Evaluate the student's work while you are present to determine if assistance is needed to complete it.

3. Use nonverbal signals.

   One study (Repp, Barton, and Brulle, 1982) found this to be the *most* effective method of bringing a student back on task. Some well-known signals are: glaring at the student (especially effective when the teacher stops in midsentence to do this); a finger to the lips to indicate that the student should be quiet; a finger to the ear to indicate that the student should listen; or point to a seat to indicate that the student should sit down. Don't forget to catch your student being good with positive, nonverbal signals such as a smile, a wink, an OK sign, or a nod. A signal system can also be set up between you and the student. In a meeting, inform the student that you will use a nonverbal signal when he is not on task. To indicate that the behavior will improve immediately, the student returns an agreed upon nonverbal signal.

4. Tell the student to stop.

   A nonverbal signal cannot be given to a student who isn't looking at you. Often, misbehavior occurs because the student is not aware of expectations or has forgotten what he is supposed to be doing. Therefore, rather than telling the student what *not* to do (e.g., "Stop looking out the window"), tell the student what he should be doing (e.g., "Turn to page 99 and write down the causes of the boycott").

5. Get close to the misbehavior.

   Undesired behavior is most likely to occur in the part of the classroom furthest from where you are standing. When misbehavior starts to occur, continue to teach while slowly moving toward that area, or nonchalantly stroll to that area to straighten some books or water a few plants. Upon seeing your approach, the student will become attentive again. If you have approached from his blind side, a hand on the shoulder is effective in regaining attention. More permanent proximity control can be obtained by seating the disruptive student near your desk.

6. Remove tempting objects.

   Certain items and materials draw students like a magnet. These include balls, toys, cards, and unsupervised overhead projectors. Keep these and other tempting objects out of sight in locked cabinets or in your closet. If the objects must be stored on open shelves or in unlocked drawers or cabinets, be sure that the pupils are aware that they must ask for permission to use those items.

7. Use humor to defuse tense situations.

   Humor can be especially effective when situations arise in which a teacher and a pupil are going to butt heads. When you feel that any other type of intervention might escalate the problem, some good natured, nonsarcastic humor can let the student know that you'll allow him to get away with that behavior this time, but you are aware of the behavior, you want it to stop, and you won't allow it again. If done correctly, the teacher appears very confident and in control. For example, after an earlier argument in the hallway, Arnie is frustrated over some difficult seatwork and tears up the ditto sheet while yelling, "I ain't doing this crap! It stinks!" The teacher, grabbing a clothespin that holds papers together on his desk, places it on his nose and says, "You're right. This work does stink. Do you need one of these?" Humor is often effective in defusing difficult situations and providing an opportunity to conduct some personal counseling.

8. Follow through on your words.

   In order to show your dedication to creating a learning atmosphere that is orderly, it is important that potential consequences for misbehavior only be identified if the teacher will indeed use them under the conditions stated. Idle threats make you appear ineffective.

9. Implement your hierarchy of interventions.

   When a student disobeys rules, directions, or otherwise misbehaves, implement a predetermined series of responses until the misbehavior stops and your direction is followed. These responses should progress from least to most punitive (e.g., warning, loss of part of a privilege or activity, loss of the whole privilege or activity, detention, in-school suspension).

10. Use an assertive intervention style.
    When giving a direction to the student who is being defiant or disruptive:

    a. Stand up. This gives you more of a physical presence.

    b. Get out from behind the desk. This makes you look more assertive and removes the barrier between you and the student.

    c. Use an assertive "command voice." Keep your voice calm and low in tone. Do not raise the tone of your voice at the end of the sentence. This makes you sound unsure of yourself.

    d. Look the student in the eye. Eye contact adds to the appearance of confidence.

    e. Use the student's name. This personalizes the message or direction.

    f. Use hand gestures (e.g., pointing to the chair that you wish the student to sit in, pointing to your ear while telling the student to listen, or making a twisting motion with your fingers near your lips while saying "Put a lock on it" to indicate that the student should stop talking).

11. Reprimand the student in private whenever possible.
    This eliminates the need for the student to retaliate in order to save face in front of his peers. It also keeps other students from witnessing any blunders in your decision making that might occur.

12. Punish only the misbehaving student.

Punishing the whole class for the misbehavior of one or a few students may build resentment toward the teacher. Periodic use of this technique should not be ruled out entirely, however. Threatening to remove a class privilege if a student doesn't behave appropriately can place peer pressure on that student to stop the misbehavior. If you need to implement the consequence occasionally, the blame falls on the misbehaving student, and continuing peer pressure may help in behavioral change.

13. Never get physical.
    Reacting in anger is unprofessional and shows a lack of ability in behavior management. It might also result in a court appearance for you. If you feel that you might strike, push, or otherwise "strong arm" a student, *stop yourself!* Tell the student that you will deal with him later, or allow another professional to intervene.

After the Incident

1. Punish the student.
   Although a positive, reinforcing environment can be highly effective, students will sometimes misbehave, and consequences for this misbehavior must be present. Move down your sequential listing of consequences as necessary. Some severe behaviors may require that steps be passed over to a more severe consequence. Some unusual behaviors may require special consequences. For example, a student pushes a plant out of a second-story window. The teacher might require the student to repot the plant and do extra work in the classroom to pay the price of a new flower pot. For behavior that is nonresponsive to present consequences, the teacher must identify activities whose removal would be punishing to that particular student, or consequences that would be aversive.

2. Require the student to display the correct behavior.

When misbehavior occurs, it may be appropriate to have the student demonstrate or practice the proper behavior for that situation. For example, while walking through the courtyard to the library, a student breaks from your small group and runs to the door near the library. You catch up to him in the library after walking in with your group. You escort him back to the classroom while advising him on proper walking behavior. The two of you then walk back to the library. If this approach did not appear to get the message to the student, making him wait five minutes before going to a popular activity so that you can "practice walking" may be effective. Another application of this technique can be used with the student who either refuses to work, hands in inadequate work, or skips school. The teacher can obtain permission from the parents to keep this student after school until all work is completed correctly. This usually changes the student's behavior after one or two after-school sessions.

3. Help the student cool off.
   There may be times when one or two students become violent, defiant, or overly excited during an activity. The activity might be such a good learning experience, however, that you wish to have all students participate in it. In this case, you might choose to remove the students temporarily from that situation, tell them to calm down, and have them calmly tell you that they are ready to re-enter the activity before you allow them to do so. A description of expected behavior might also be given, along with obtaining the students' pledge that they will conduct themselves in that manner.

4. Have a long talk with the student.
   Oftentimes, a situation requires personal counseling by the teacher. This should be conducted in a private setting where interruptions will not occur.

Activities and Discussion Questions

1. Observe another teacher or student teacher. Use the strategies listed in this chapter as a checklist. Mark those strategies that are used effectively by that instructor. Also mark those that are used ineffectively, at the wrong time, with the wrong student, or not at all. Based on your observation, write a few paragraphs regarding how this instructor could improve his or her style.

2. Conduct a self-analysis. Mark those strategies that you use effectively and those that you wish to develop and include in your repertoire. Each week, select one that you will practice using. Review your progress at the end of that week.

3. By yourself or in a group, view videotaped sequences of students misbehaving. (These can be purchased or can be made by filming friends or classmates who are role playing situations that they have seen.) Decide which of the strategies could have been used effectively by the teacher in that situation. In a larger group, form three smaller groups with each being in charge of one category of strategies.

4. List twenty-five ways to praise a student for good behavior other than by saying "Good."

5. Become more personal and specific in giving praise. Reword the listings from number 4 so that all comments are stated in complete, complex sentences and include *why* you think the behavior was "good."

6. Make a list of the four or five rules for your classroom. State or restate them so that they are written in positive and observable terms.

7. With a partner, role play the part of the teacher. Sit in a

chair and have your partner stand next to a chair that is about three or four body lengths from you. Practice each of the following and assess the degree of impact that each had.

  a. While looking down or away from your partner, say, "Sit down" in a meek voice.

  b. In a firm tone, say, " __(name)__ , sit down."

  c. Say, "Sit down" in a firm tone while looking assertively into the eyes of your partner. Maintain this eye contact for a few seconds.

  d. Repeat step c, but this time stand up to speak.

  e. Repeat step d while pointing to the chair.

  f. Switch roles and repeat steps a through c. This time, say, "I really appreciate your help."

8. During your free time, look around the classroom. What images does it project? Look at suggestions 1–7 for organizing classrooms. Devise a plan for change if it is needed.

9. Imagine the following situation: You gather around a small table with three students for reading instruction. The students start to poke each other and kick each other under the table. How could you rearrange the furniture or seating arrangement to prevent this from occurring in the future?

10. Look at one of your lesson plans. Are there any potential problem areas in your presentation? Which students might misbehave during this lesson? What behavior(s) can you expect to see? How could you prevent this misbehavior? How will you react if this misbehavior does surface?

11. If you do not already have routines set for daily activities, devise organized, structured ways to dismiss the class,

travel as a group through the hallway, distribute and collect assignments, take turns, and the like.

12. Practice catching the students being good. Give praise to various students at least twenty times during the class period. Keep track of this by placing checkmarks on a card, tying knots on a string or using a counter. Each day, try to beat the previous day's total. After four or five days, ask yourself the following questions:

   a. How did the students react to the praise?

   b. Did behavior improve?

   c. Did the students seem to be happier?

   d. Did I enjoy doing this and did it become less of a chore over the course of the experiment?

13. When correcting papers, mark only the correct answers. Observe the students' response (if any) over the course of a week.

14. Locate one of your troublesome students outside of the classroom (e.g., hallway, dance, lunchroom) and start a discussion on a topic of interest to him. Determine if rapport between the two of you seems to improve over time.

15. Make a pledge to yourself to teach one lesson in which you use each of the following *at least once* during that lesson:

   a. A whisper

   b. A loud voice

   c. A strong, fast, physical movement (e.g., running, jumping, clapping)

   d. A walk through the aisles between student's desks

   e. Talking from the back of the room

   f. Touching a student on the shoulder

g. A fifteen-second pause between sentences while looking into the eyes of various students

h. Telling a nonoffensive joke

i. Sitting in a student's desk and talking in a personal manner to the class from that position

Assess the effect (if any) on the attention level of your students. What level of anxiety did each of these cause you? Would this level of anxiety lessen over time?

16. List the names of students who misbehave in your class. Next to the names, write their typical responses to frustration. Also list what seems to frustrate each student. Devise a plan to limit these frustrating points for each student.

17. Think of two situations in which you acted inappropriately or felt inadequate in handling a behavior problem. If you could relive that situation, what would you do this time to handle the situation more effectively? Each time you have another of these experiences, analyze it in this manner in order to learn from your experience.

18. Find a partner. While this partner displays various positive and negative behaviors, give messages to this student by using nonverbal signals. Use at least fifteen different nonverbal signals before switching roles.

19. If you do not already have a listing of a hierarchy of interventions, list a series of four or five reactions to continued misbehavior, progressing from least to most punitive.

For More Information

Biehler, R. F. (1974). *Psychology applied to teaching*, 2nd ed. Boston: Houghton-Mifflin.

Knoblock, P. (1983). *Teaching emotionally disturbed children.* Boston: Houghton-Mifflin.

Reinert, H. R. (1980). *Children in conflict,* 2nd ed. St. Louis: Mosby.

Repp, A. C., Barton, L. E., and Brulle, A. R. (1982). Naturalistic studies of mentally retarded persons: V: The effects of staff instructions on student responding. *Applied Research in Mental Retardation, 3,* 55–65.

SECTION FOUR

Using Peer Influence

14

The Pow-Wow

Developed by Nicholas Hobbs, the pow-wow is but one component of a comprehensive institutional program developed for students with severe emotional/behavioral problems. Project Re-Ed, as its name might indicate, is based upon the assumption that misbehavior is learned. These children, however, are receptive to an intensive program of reeducation both in academics and behavior. Hobbs recognized the importance of the group in creating, changing, and maintaining behavior. The pow-wow meeting uses the group as a positive force for change. Although originally designed for use with institutionalized youths, it can be utilized effectively in other educational environments.

Held on a regular basis in academic settings, the pow-wow is a structured, teacher-directed meeting of students who spend much time together. It provides an opportunity for each student to evaluate personal behavior in terms of goals that he set for himself. Peers also evaluate each other's behavior and provide peer pressure to improve. It is also an effective method for teaching students how to take turns and providing an opportunity for students to give and receive positive commentary.

How to Use the Pow-Wow

1. Seat the students in a circle or around a table.

2. Choose a student or ask for a volunteer. All others give a positive comment to this student. Other students are chosen in turn or you may continue to accept volunteers. This process can be shortened by having each student give one positive comment to one other student. Each student in the group *gives* one positive comment and each *receives* one positive comment. The teacher keeps a checklist of who has given and received compliments.

3. Choose a student or accept a volunteer to state his personal goal that was set in the previous meeting and to describe his progress in meeting that goal. If this is the first meeting, students will set a goal and evaluate progress at the next meeting.

4. After this student has reviewed his progress toward the goal, recognize any other students who have information or perceptions regarding the goal under consideration.

5. Allow the student whose goal is under consideration to decide whether to continue working on the present goal or set a new one. The teacher may overrule this decision if necessary.

6. Repeat steps 3, 4, and 5 until all students have reviewed their goals.

7. Last, hold a short gripe session with a set time limit. The students should be directed to identify possible solutions for stated problems rather than just complaining.

Activities and Discussion Questions

1. With other persons, take one of the following roles listed below. Participants will periodically drop their assigned

role to take their turn in playing the revolving part of the teacher who is directing the pow-wow. If enough people are involved, also include the role of teacher aide. After a few minutes of role playing, the person playing the part of the aide will take the role of the teacher and the teacher will return to the assigned student role. Someone else will then become the teacher aide. (It may be helpful to have the teacher and teacher aide wear nametags to avoid confusion.) This role-playing situation is a shortened version of the pow-wow in which each student gives a positive comment to one other student only. The person playing the part of the teacher should keep a record of which students have given and received a positive comment. The teacher will also be calm, assertive, and directive. Insure that students do not talk out or respond inappropriately. The teacher aide may choose to roam quietly behind the group to troubleshoot. Students should have place cards in front of them that identify their personality traits and stated goals.

Student #1

Positive statement for: Student #2 (Be the first student to volunteer to say something positive.)

Your personality/problem: You're known as a troublemaker. Your hallway gang terrorizes other students. Student #2 is one of your cohorts.

Your last goal: Proper hallway behavior.

Your goal performance: You will claim that you stayed out of trouble and will threaten Student #8 when he or she squeals on you in the meeting.

Student #2

Positive statement for: Student #1 (Be the second student to volunteer to say something positive.)

Your personality/problem: You are a prankster and a member of Student #1's hallway gang. You are a follower and want to stay on good terms with Student #1. You will defend him or her. Display appropriate behavior during the meeting unless you are defending Student #1.

Your last goal: Refrain from playing pranks on others.

Your goal performance: You will state that you met your goal.

Student #3

Positive statement for: Student #4 (Say something nice about his or her clothes.)

Your personality/problem: You are very fashion conscious and frequently prim and prep yourself in class. You're self-centered and never miss a chance to tell how attractive and wonderful you are.

Your last goal: Come prepared for class.

Your goal performance: You did not meet your goal, but you will initially try to avoid the question by saying, "How can anyone as great as me do anything wrong?" When Student #8 gives a positive compliment to you, which also includes some tattling, you will respond by saying, "At least I don't tattle like a little kid."

Student #4

Positive statement for: Student #5

Your personality or problem: You are very distractible. During the meeting, you often look out the window, tie your shoes, doodle, and groom your nails and hair. You are responsive to teacher directions, but will often go off task again quickly and be unaware of what's happening in the meeting.

Your last goal: Proper behavior (i.e., sit in seat, not bother others).

Your goal performance: You met your goal.

Student #5

Positive statement for: Student #6

Your personality/problem: You are an active, talkative student who touches people a lot and grabs objects (e.g., pens, toys) that you would like to touch. You are impulsive (but don't overact). Claim that Student #10 bit his or her nails.

Your last goal: Raise hand before speaking in class.

Your goal performance: You have improved. You raise your hand about one-third of the time.

Student #6

Positive statement for: Student #7

Your personality/problem: You are a slow learner who is unmotivated and does not complete classwork. You don't interact with others well. Display appropriate behavior during the meeting.

Your last goal: To complete all work in class.

Your goal performance: You did not meet your goal. Your performance was at about the same level as before your goal setting.

Student #7

Positive statement for: Student #8 (You will wait to be the last person to give a positive comment. You won't say anything for a minute or so, but after making everyone wait for a while you'll give a sarcastic compliment saying, "You didn't fart much today.")

Your personality/problem: You are a street-wise kid who makes derogatory comments. Some of the names you'll give others when talking to or about them are along the lines of "Loose Lisa," "Jerky John," and "Truant Teresa." Refer to Student #9 as the teacher's pet.

Your last goal: Be on time to classes.

Your goal performance: You met your goal except for gym class because the teacher really doesn't care if students arrive promptly.

Student #8

Positive statement for: Student #3 (You will say, "(name) brought all the needed materials to class, even though he (or she) was late.")

Your personality/problem: You are an unpopular student who is often picked on and scapegoated by others. You will tattle on Student #1 and a few other students during the peer reaction phase of the goal review session (e.g., (name) slammed a locker door on Bill's hand, etc.).

Your last goal: No tattling and criticizing others. You were to criticize others only when you have proof that can be verified by another student or teacher.

Your goal performance: Tell the teacher that it's difficult to find proof and that you don't lie because you're an honest person.

Student #9

Positive statement for: Student #10 (Say that he or she helped you with your homework.)

Your personality/problem: You're basically a nice student although were once known as being a very mean and nasty person. You've changed so drastically that now others often call you the teacher's pet.

Your last goal: Do homework in all classes.

Your goal performance: Did all except for social studies where you are having difficulty understanding the material and don't like the teacher very well.

Note: During goal review for Student #10, you will nicely report that you saw Student #10 biting his or her nails.

Student #10

Positive statement for: Student #9 (Say that he or she walked to class with you and introduced you to a new friend.) Mumble your comments in a very soft voice.

Your personality/problem: You are painfully shy. You use a soft voice, don't talk much, and avoid eye contact. You don't respond if others taunt you.

Your last goal: Not to bite your nails.

Your goal performance: You will meekly state that you met your goal. When confronted by others, you will become quiet unless questioned by the teacher. Then say that you were biting your cuticles, not your nails.

All other persons should ad lib student roles or observe.

2. What can you do to control the situation when many students are speaking at once during the meeting?

3. What can you do to control the presentation of rude comments by some of the students (e.g., "That's stupid")?

4. A student gives a superficial positive comment about the clothing of another student. Will you request that the stu-

dent present a more thoughtful comment or are there some students for whom this is acceptable?

5. What, if anything, will you do for two students who are always the first to volunteer to give a positive comment in order to be able to compliment each other?

For More Information

Hobbs, N. (1964). Project Re-Ed: A demonstration project for the re-education of emotionally disturbed children. Nashville, Tenn: Project Re-Ed.

Hobbs, N. (1966). Helping disturbed children: Psychological and ecological strategies. *American Psychologist, 21,* 1105–1115.

Hobbs, N. (1967). The re-education of emotionally disturbed children. In E. M. Bower and W. G. Hollister (Eds.), *Behavioral science frontiers.* New York: Wiley & Sons, 335–354.

Hobbs, N. (1982). *The troubled and troubling child. Re-education in mental health, education and human services for children and youth.* San Francisco: Jossey-Bass.

Lewis, W. W. (1967). Project Re-Ed: Educational intervention in discordant child-rearing systems. In E. L. Cowen, E. A. Gardener, and M. Zax (Eds.), *Emergent approaches to mental health problems.* New York: Appleton-Century-Crofts, 352–368.

15

The Problem-Solving Meeting

William Glasser, renowned psychiatrist and lecturer on education, believes that students must learn to accept responsibility for their behavior. He recommends that his program, entitled Reality Therapy, be implemented in order to help students with behavior problems learn to function in a more responsible manner. Glasser also believes that if students are going to become involved and develop a stake in their school, they should share responsibility in the management of the classroom. In order to allow for an opportunity for teachers and students to discuss mutual concerns, he recommends the implementation of classroom meetings.

Three different types of meetings are advocated: open ended, in which the students discuss various topics; diagnostic curriculum, in which the teacher evaluates the knowledge possessed by the students; and problem solving, in which students deal with their behavior, emotions, and troubling situations. Possible discussion topics in a problem-solving meeting might include seating plans, rules, home problems, and recent classroom incidents.

In this type of meeting, students, with the guidance of the teacher, attempt to resolve either individual, group, or school problems that are important to class members. These meetings are held on a regular basis, anywhere from once a week to daily. Students are exposed to the values and opinions of others and are provided with the opportunity to practice thinking and brainstorming in a group. Peer support and pressure also evolve to promote the improvement of behavior. The students help to set the conditions regarding meeting conduct (e.g., taking turns, proper language, etc.). The tone of the meeting is always positive in nature. Fault finding and criticism are downplayed. The teacher is never judgmental as this might stifle interaction and communication. However, the teacher may express an opinion on a topic under consideration, or if necessary, inform the students that one of their ideas or solutions is inappropriate.

Students are encouraged to challenge one another constructively in a nondemeaning manner; the teacher insures that the meeting is directed toward solving the problem. Although it may initially be difficult to direct the meeting and prevent the voicing of negative comments, with time and practice, meetings become more productive as students seek socially acceptable solutions to problems. These solutions should not blame or punish anyone, however. One subject should not be the topic of concern at numerous meetings. Repeatedly discussing the same topic is viewed by Glasser as being nonproductive.

How to Use the Problem-Solving Meeting

1. Seat the students in a circle to promote participation and to allow all group members to see and hear each other. (Vary your position in the circle from meeting to meeting.) Students may be seated by you in a manner that is most productive. You will run the meeting.

2. Designate a time period of ten to twenty minutes for younger pupils, and thirty to forty-five minutes for older students. Enforce the designated time limit. This will prevent the students from avoiding other daily responsibilities.

3. Open the meeting by allowing students to discuss a topic that involves behavior, emotions, or situations of concern.

Rules for taking turns may be necessary. If a student monopolizes the conversation, goes off on a tangent, or lapses into fantasy or lying, the teacher may call on another student to speak or ask the other students if they believe that the student is monopolizing the discussion or telling the truth. Rules regarding foul language, degrading comments, or other concerns should be set with the help of the students. Guide the students toward a resolution of the problem.

Activities and Discussion Questions

1. With a group of teachers or other adults, take the role of teacher in a mock problem-solving meeting. You may wish to assign the following personalities and use the following situations.

   Student #1: This student, who is larger than the others, often uses his or her size to intimidate others. She or he is known to resort to force to make other students comply with her or his wishes.

   Student #2: This student is a group leader. He or she is humorous, intelligent, very talkative, and somewhat of a wise guy.

   Student #3: This student is rather quiet, has a poor self-concept, and will present an opinion if asked, but will back down and withdraw if confronted by other students.

   Student #4: This student is extremely bright, but often says and does things that point to his or her immaturity. This student often plays pranks and makes fun of others.

   Student #5: This student is belligerent, foul mouthed, and has difficulty controlling his or her verbal outbursts.

Other Students: The other students are generally cooperative and mild mannered.

Situation #1: Students #1 and #2 have been mean to Student #3, who has attempted daily to sit next to them at lunch. The first two students have destroyed the lunch of Student #3, dropped food on him or her, and threatened him or her with harm. They consider it to be embarrassing to be near Student #3. He or she has a few friends, but they eat lunch at other times. Student #3 continues to sit near Students #1 and #2 despite the abuse received.

Situation #2: The students enjoy having the option of working in their carrels if they desire. You're also rather pleased because the portable bookshelves that you have extended from the side wall have prevented interaction among the students during work periods and helped them concentrate on their assignments. During homeroom period the next day, you are conversing in the hall with another teacher. Upon entering the room, you see that Students #2, #4, and #5 have redesigned their carrels. Two have taken the removable shelves from the bookcases and placed them over the tops of the cases to form roofs. You are concerned about the lighting in the carrels and the possibility of the boards falling and hurting the students. You are also concerned about the music star posters brought in by Students #2 and #4, and the foldouts of nude bodies decorating the carrel of Student #5. You ask that this be the topic at today's daily problem-solving meeting.

2. How can you promote taking turns in conversation and prevent interruptions or many students talking at once?

3. With a group of youths other than your students, lead a problem-solving meeting.

For More Information

Glasser, W. (1969). *Schools without failure.* New York: Harper & Row.

Classroom Counseling

16

Transactual Analysis

The way a teacher interacts with his or her students (and colleagues and supervisors) can either escalate or resolve potentially tense situations. The choice of words and the way in which they are spoken convey an attitude that can cause or alleviate tension. The manner in which we interact with others can be analyzed and improved in order to make our contacts more effective and productive. One method for doing this is an approach known as Transactual Analysis (TA). According to TA, we act or react toward others in one of three ways: as a parent, an adult, or a child.

The Parent

The parent part of us operates on "old information" and beliefs thought to be true and valuable. We internalized these by listening to our parents when they gave us stern commands and all-knowing truisms. We have also incorporated the memories of our parents' actions that made us feel secure and cared for. Therefore, we have certain beliefs and ideas as to how a child should act and be treated. Sometimes we feel the need to be stern; other times we feel the need to be nurturing. Typical comments from our negative parent side include the words: *never, always, do,* and *don't.* The negative part tends to talk *at* or *down to* others, rather than talking *to* them. The nurturing part of the parent role tries to console others and make them feel better.

The Child

The child part of our personality feels powerless and inadequate on one hand, yet can be energetic, fun-loving, exploring, and mischievous on the other. When we act explosively, impulsively, irrationally, or uncontrollably, that is the child in us. When we are playful and exuberant, that, too, is the surfacing of the child facet of ourselves. Additionally, when we feel inadequate in a situation and try to gain the approval of another, that is our child part.

The Adult

The adult part of us thinks and reacts in a rational, logical manner. The adult tests the beliefs of the parent to determine if they really are true. The adult also tries to quell the inadequate feelings and irresponsibility of the child, while deciding when to allow this part of us to surface. The adult in us is the wise mediator that attempts to gain more information in a situation and act in an informed, confident, restrained manner. The adult state is organized, adaptable, intelligent, practical, and predictable. A strong adult part still allows the child and parent to be expressed when appropriate, but if the adult part is underdeveloped, the parent and child will express themselves more frequently and perhaps cause problems in interacting with others. Our students also have an adult part (e.g., when a youngster tells friends that it is time to go home and eat dinner with his or her family), but they need practice to further develop it.

To illustrate the three states further, the following is an example of what might pass in the mind of a teacher who stayed out late last night and wants to go back to sleep when the morning alarm rings.

The Child: "Call in sick and go back to sleep."

The Parent: "I have an obligation to show up unless I'm really ill."

The Adult: "I could get away with this, but I've got a meeting to attend and kids who are depending on me. I'll nap during lunch hour."

When someone speaks to you, he or she speaks from one of their three states to one of your three states. They may speak as a parent to your child, a child to your child, an adult to your adult, or any other of the nine possible combinations. You, in turn, respond to this person through one of the nine interaction patterns. As you speak with others, analyze the type of interaction that is taking place and decide which is the best way for you to respond each time.

How to Use
Transactual Analysis

1. Listen to the other person.

2. Think. Analyze the situation using the adult mind-set. From which state is this person talking, and to which state of yours are they speaking?

3. Respond in a manner designated by your calm, rational adult part.

Activities and
Discussion Questions

1. Identify the following actions as being indicative of the parent, child, or adult state. (Answers are in the Appendix.)

    a. Patting another person on the top of the head

    b. Pointing a finger and shaking it at someone

    c. Pouting

    d. Hands on hips with pursed lips

    e. Temper tantrum

    f. Sitting, leaning forward, eyes focused on speaker

    g. Speaking in a calm, confident tone of voice

    h. Teasing another

    i. Laughing

    j. Raising a hand for permission to speak

    k. Arms folded across the chest while tapping a foot on the floor

    l. Biting nails

    m. Leading another quickly and firmly by the hand as he or she resists

2. Identify the following phrases as being indicative of the parent, child, or adult state. Also decide which part of the other person is being spoken to. (Answers are in the Appendix.)

    a. _____ to _____ "Now listen here, young man."

    b. _____ to _____ "Good point. I hadn't considered that."

    c. _____ to _____ "I wish. . . . "

    d. _____ to _____ "When I get bigger. . . . "

e. _____ to _____ "What do you recommend?"

f. _____ to _____ "What a lazy oof!"

g. _____ to _____ "You naughty boy!"

h. _____ to _____ "Here. Let me help you."

i. _____ to _____ "You did a nice job, Gina."

j. _____ to _____ "Now! Not later. Now!"

k. _____ to _____ "And then what happened?"

l. _____ to _____ "Can I go now?"

m. _____ to _____ "Never start it until you've made all the checks."

n. _____ to _____ "Don't lie to me!"

o. _____ to _____ "If you don't finish the work by the end of the period, then you can complete it at home this evening."

p. _____ to _____ "Drive safely."

q. _____ to _____ "I blew it again. I'm so dumb."

r. _____ to _____ "Who made this mess?!!"

s. _____ to _____ "These kids are driving me crazy."

t. _____ to _____ "If you would like to contribute to the discussion, please raise your hand."

u. _____ to _____ "Boy, this is great work!"

v. _____ to _____ "Of course you did well. I taught you! Ha-Ha!"

w. _____ to _____ "Girls shouldn't play basketball with boys."

3. Write an adult-mediated response to the statements in number 2.

4. List five critical statements, often heard in school settings, that are representative of the parent state.

5. List five nurturing remarks, often heard in school settings, that are representative of the parent state. In which of these was a parental remark or action necessary? In which of these would remarks from the child or adult state have been effective?

6. Identify situations in which you have criticized your students. Are your actions similar to those of your parents or a former supervising teacher? In which of these was a parental remark or action necessary? In which of these would child or adult state remarks have been effective?

7. Identify situations in which you have nurtured your students. In which of these was a parental remark or action necessary? In which of these would remarks from the child or adult state have been effective?

8. List five child state remarks or actions often heard in school settings. They can be either inferiority oriented or exuberant in nature.

9. Identify situations in which your child state surfaced in school. Was it appropriate and acceptable in those school situations?

10. List five adult state remarks or actions witnessed in school settings.

11. Identify situations in which your adult state surfaced in school.

12. The exuberance of your child state should surface periodically during the school day. List three situations in which your child state might appropriately surface.

13. When, if ever, should your parent state surface during the school day? List appropriate times and situations.

14. Are adult-to-adult state interactions always preferable to

those involving child and parent state interactions? Write or voice your opinion.

15. Imagine that one circle represents the sum of your three states in your home situation, a second circle your social life, and a third circle your school situation. Divide each of the circles into three parts representing the percentage of each state shown in those situations. Does the percentage of each state change depending on the environment? Ask a friend to evaluate your portraits. Do they agree? Do changes need to be made?

16. Karen just spilled paint (or milk, or chemicals, or something else). Give a possible response from each of the three states. Which one shows the most respect for the student and models appropriate interaction?

17. Ken shows his frustration with his seatwork by tearing it up, throwing it on the floor, and walking toward the door. Give a possible response from each of the three states. Can more than one of these responses be appropriate?

For More Information

Berne, H. (1964). *Games people play.* New York: Grove Press.

Ernst, K. (1973). *Games students play, and what to do about them.* Mellbrae, Calif.: Celestial Arts.

Freed, A. M. (1971). *T.A. for kids.* Sacramento, Calif.: Jalmar Press.

Harris, T. A. (1969). *I'm O.K.—You're O.K.: A practical guide to transactual analysis.* New York: Harper and Row.

17

Nondirective Counseling

Although most often used by certified counselors, psychologists, and psychiatrists, nondirective counseling provides a number of techniques that can be used effectively by teachers and staff when talking with students about their undesirable behavior. Attributed to Carl Rodgers, this approach was designed to allow the individual in emotional turmoil to talk out problems and resolve difficulties with a minimum of direction being provided by the person serving as counselor. Rodgers believes that everyone has the motivation and ability to change in order to become a better, more self-actualized person. To help your students achieve this state, you, as teacher-counselor, act as a sounding board—observing, listening, and deliberately responding according to certain guidelines while the student explores and analyzes the problem and devises a personal solution. The teacher-counselor's demeanor is always accepting and nonpunitive. This encourages the student to feel comfortable in expressing his or her feelings and thus facilitates positive change.

There are five basic responses to student commentary. The first, *reflection*, is restating the student's comment. This may be done by restating the exact same terminology, repeating part of the comment, or rewording the student's statement. Reflection lets the student know that you are listening and promotes continued commentary.

The second response, *a leading statement or question*, is designed to encourage the student to elaborate on a topic or devise a solution to a specific problem. Examples of a leading remark include, "I'd like to hear your opinion," "Tell me more about yourself," and "What happened then?"

The third response, *clarification*, involves stating the implied feelings behind a student's verbal communication. Examples of clarification include, "You sound sad," and "It appears as if you're very angry at Samantha." Clarification helps the student identify his feelings. It can also be used to focus the student's thoughts on ways to deal with the emotions that are present.

The fourth, *summarization*, is a review of what has been discussed thus far in your counseling session. This summary allows both participants to reflect briefly on what has occurred, view it clearly, and use it as a new starting point from which to build.

The fifth response, *questioning*, is comprised of two main types: closed questions, which are intended to yield brief, specific information; and open-ended questions, which are used to encourage the student to talk at greater length on a topic. Examples of closed questioning include, "How old is Don?" and "Did you complete your homework?" Examples of open questioning include, "How's it going in science class?" and "How do you feel about losing recess?"

Rodgers believes that this approach resolves inner conflicts and feelings that manifest themselves in undesirable behavior. Therefore, the reduction of this inner turmoil can reduce inappropriate actions. This technique is useful with students who can be "reasoned with" and are seeking a solution to their problems or just want to talk. Certainly, the student must be motivated to be involved in a therapeutic discussion. This is not a technique that can be imposed upon someone. Yet, because the student is involved in the program and chooses the most appropriate solution for himself, he is more likely to follow the proposed solution that was decided upon.

The nondirective approach is also useful with students who

have speech and language problems that make their verbalizations difficult to understand. Reflection can be useful in these situations. Repeat the words that are well pronounced, thus continuing the conversation and allowing the student to vent his emotions.

How to Use
Nondirective Counseling

1. Arrange for a time and place that will provide privacy for your conference.

2. If the student does not open the session, use a leading statement or question to focus the student on the topic of concern.

3. Listen to the student in an interested, nonpunitive, accepting manner.

4. Respond as necessary, using one of the recommended techniques.

5. After the concerns have been thoroughly voiced by the student, focus him on finding a solution for the difficulty (e.g., "How will you handle this in the future?" "What do you do now?"). Allow the student to choose the solution that is best for him.

Activities and
Discussion Questions

1. Identify the following responses to student commentary as being a leading statement or question, reflection, clarification, open question, closed question, or summarization. (Answers are in the Appendix.)

    a. "How are you feeling?"

    b. "I wonder how that happened?"

    c. "The other kids won't let you play baseball with them."

    d. "Is he five or six years old?"

    e. "It sounds to me like you're feeling rejected."

    f. "How are you doing on your science project?"

    g. "I'd like to know how you're doing on meeting this week's goal."

    h. "OK. Thus far we've discussed your tardiness to class, your dislike for the instructor, and the poor quality of your classwork and homework. On which one would you like to focus?"

    i. "They say you're the teacher's pet."

    j. "You're feeling very tired."

2. Provide a reflection response for the following remarks.

    a. "I was so embarrassed. I could have died right then and there."

    b. "He just stood there, stunned. He was shocked and couldn't believe what he was seeing."

    c. "It's a strange feeling. I felt lost. It's like being in a giant cornfield and not knowing which way is out."

    d. "It was great. She was all smiles and happier than a pig in mud."

    e. "You're looking at me like it's my fault. Why don't you talk to Doreen?"

    f. "I'm so dumb. I'm useless. I can't do anything right."

3. Provide a clarification response to the remarks in number 2.

4. Provide a response to the following comments:

a. "I'm really tired. My grandfather died over the weekend and we've been running around like crazy."

b. "It's not fair. You treat Julie and Betsy like they're something special. They get to do all the fun activities. Everyone says they're the teacher's pets."

c. "The other guys won't let me play ball with them. They call me a pansy."

d. "I'm so dumb. I can't figure these out. They're too tough. I can't wait until I'm sixteen and can drop out of school."

e. "I should have killed that fool when I had the chance. Next time he squeals on me, I'll kick his rear end all over the playground."

f. "I was so embarrassed. He's always talking about my legs or breasts or bra or something. Can't you tell him to stop?"

g. "Why don't you ever say anything? All you ever do is say the same thing I already said. Are you a jellyfish? Don't you have your own opinions?"

h. "But what do I know? I'm only the teacher's aide."

5. Identify the type of response you gave for each example in number 4. Were you able to avoid being directive and giving opinions? Which other types of responses might have been appropriate for each?

6. With two others, role play nondirective counseling for the situations provided below. One person plays the role of the teacher, another plays the part of the student, and the third person records the types of responses given by the teacher. The recorder should have a sheet with the different types of responses listed. A tally mark should be placed next to the respective response as each is used by the teacher. After the role-play situation has been resolved, the three participants should review the teacher's

technique and make suggestions for improvement (e.g., use less questioning, avoid giving opinions and solutions to the student).

  a. The teacher pulls aside a student who has been involved in a fight. The student opens the conversation with the comment, "I hate Oscar." It will be revealed later that the student's father has been receiving radiation treatments and chemotherapy for cancer. This has caused his father to become bald and Oscar said the father's head looked like a melon. Alternatives to fighting should be discussed.

  b. You have a student report to you after school to complete some classwork. He throws it on the floor and says, "I'm not doing this crap, you jerk." You hear laughter from students in the hallway and suspect that this student is testing your authority.

  c. You call a student aside. You've seen the welts and bruises on his arms, neck, and face. You suspect abuse. The student initially denies this. Remember your legal *obligation* to report suspected abuse.

  d. You catch a student removing your purse (or money collection envelope) from your desk. He defiantly says, "Hey, you gotta have money to impress the ladies (or boys)." You want to have the student analyze morality and personal values.

For More Information

Hilgard, E. R., Atkinson, R. C., and Atkinson, R. L. (1975). *Psychology*, 6th ed. New York: Harcourt, Brace and World.

Rodgers, C. (1961). *Becoming a person*. Boston: Houghton Mifflin.

Rodgers, C., and Stevens, B. (1967). *Person to person: The problems of being human*. Lafayette, Calif.: Real People Press.

18

The Life Space Interview

The Life Space Interview (LSI), accredited to Fritz Redl, is a classroom counseling approach used to manage and change aberrant behavior patterns of students. It is a crisis-intervention technique in which the student's behavior is discussed with him at the time of the problem's occurrence. Practitioners of this approach believe that the student is most receptive to ideas for change when he is in crisis.

There are two types of LSI. Both are immediate reactions to an event or experience in a student's life. Emotional first aid is used when you wish to "cool off" the student, resolve the problem quickly, and return the student to an activity. Clinical exploitation of life events is a more in-depth technique in which you help the student gain insight into his habitual behavior pattern and change inappropriate ways of acting.

Emotional First Aid

There are five different types of emotional first aid. Deciding which one should be used will depend on the situation encountered.

1. Drain off frustration acidity.
   Allow the student to vent his emotions, but assist him in regaining control and calming down. When he is calmed, gently but firmly explain why a rule or direction is necessary and why it must be followed (e.g., "I realize that it's your turn at bat, but we must go in now before the bell rings to go to the next class").

2. Support for the management of emotions.
   Provide support to the student when pent-up feelings and emotions surface. Oftentimes, this technique is used when the student has been victimized or has a personal problem. Help him sort through events and put the problem in perspective.

3. Communication maintenance.
   Often, upon intervention, the student withdraws. This type of interview attempts to prevent the student from breaking off communication with others. Try to keep the student talking and communicating regardless of the topic of conversation.

4. Regulation of behavior and social traffic.
   This involves the consistent application of rules and guidelines by a calm, patient adult. The situation is handled by enforcing the rules of the school or classroom.

5. Umpire services.
   The teacher makes a judgment in cases of interchild and intrachild conflict after having reviewed all available information. A fair, impartial decision is presented and enforced.

Clinical Exploitation of Life Events

This is the more involved of the two LSI techniques. Redl provided no steps for its use, believing that the adult must be flexible in his or her approach to each new situation. There are, however, five different recommended approaches for counseling a student who has been involved in a severe emotional or behavioral flareup. One, a few, or all of these might be used during the discussion.

1. Reality rub.
   The teacher helps the student realize that he has misinterpreted or refused to recognize certain information pertinent to an incident. He is made aware that perceptions are not correct, and he is misinformed as to the truth of the situation under discussion.

2. Value repair and restoration.
   The teacher attempts to awaken dormant values such as respect, empathy, trust, and so on. Many students are unable, at present, to display emotions that represent vulnerability. They tend to act out aggression, nonchalance, and anger most often. The teacher attempts to "massage" the numb value areas and help develop appropriate emotional responses to certain situations.

3. Symptom estrangement.
   A student may not realize that his behavior is inappropriate or bizarre in the eyes of others. The teacher brings the student's attention to the specific behaviors and how they are viewed by others. It is hoped that he will come to realize the problem and talk about other ways to meet his needs.

4. New tool salesmanship.
   In this interview, the student is helped to improve his ability to react appropriately in a problem-solving situation. Socially acceptable tools, or ways of solving problems, are taken from past experience, discussed, and applied to new situations.

5. Manipulation of the boundaries of the self.
   This interview is used with two types of students—those who allow themselves to be used by others, and those

who victimize or take advantage of others. The student is made aware of his behavior pattern in an attempt to make him more receptive to new reaction patterns.

Deciding which technique is appropriate will depend on the incident, the time and personnel available, the teacher's analysis of the situation, and the receptivity of the student.

How to Use Life
Space Interviewing

1. Intervene.

2. Listen to the parties involved in a nonjudgmental manner.

3. Analyze the situation and determine whether this incident is an isolated happening or part of a recurring theme.

4. Choose a specific LSI approach.

5. Implement the chosen approach while being polite.

6. Change or combine approaches as necessary.

Activities and
Discussion Questions

1. Identify which type of emotional first aid was used in each of the following. (Answers are in the Appendix.)

   a. "Bill, you need to sit down in your seat right now. If you don't, you will go to the office."

   b. You restrain a student until he calms down, and then you say, "I know that you want to go with the other kids, but we have a rule that says all classwork must be done before you can have free time and privileges."

c. "I realize that Betty knocked over your project, but I cannot allow you to hit other students. You have lost fifteen minutes of recess and will lose the whole recess period unless you apologize to her."

d. Dierdre enters your room in tears. You call her aside and talk briefly about the relationship with her boyfriend. This seems to help. The tears subside and she is ready to reenter the class activities.

e. Izzie is so angry about an incident in the hallway that he violently slams the door to your room. He appears very tense. You ask him what happened, but he says, "Nothing," through his clenched teeth. You start up a conversation about the Buffalo Bills, his favorite football team, to get him talking, get his mind off the hallway incident, and loosen him up.

f. Herbert comes into the room, slamming the door and throwing playground equipment that was in a box by the door. He is apparently mad because the children on the playground had been calling him names (e.g., Herbie the Lovebug). You say, "I realize you are upset. No one likes to be called names. But you know we don't throw playground equipment in the room. Take a minute to calm down and then I want you to go pick up the playground equipment."

g. Johnny and Dave were fighting. Johnny apparently stole an object from Chris. You listen and then talk to both students separately. Based on the information presented, you state that the object must be returned to Chris before Johnny goes out to recess or he will lose that and future recess periods.

h. Pedro is adopted. The other students tell Pedro that his real parents didn't want him and that they left him on a door step. Pedro returns early from recess and tells you that the other students teased him. You listen and allow Pedro to express his emotions. Then you explain reasons why parents may have to give up children and how his new parents wanted him and went through the adoption procedure.

   i. Ted received an F on a paper and is extremely upset. He doesn't say a word, but makes many gestures that indicate he is tense. When the class period is almost over, you situate yourself and Ted by the door and ask him what is making him upset. The student says, "Nothin." You reply, "Oh, by the way, did you go to the chess tournament last night?" Ted and you exchange quips, but the topic does turn back to the paper grade and ends with Ted saying, "If I get an F in this subject, I'll be ineligible for the chess team." You respond by saying, "What can we do about this situation to insure that you will pass this class?"

   j. Corine is being disruptive by being out of her seat or looking around at other students' projects during reading group. You say, "Corrine, you need to be sitting in your seat and paying attention because it's reading time."

2. Often, a teacher must choose between the use of two types of LSI, deciding whether to resolve a situation quickly or engage in a more in-depth conversation. In the following situation, decide whether you would use emotional first aid or clinical exploitation of life events, and with which students. Assume that an aide, parent, or other teacher is present.

   a. While on a trip to a soda bottling company, the students are watching thick-bottomed bottles go by on a conveyor. Some of the students quietly joke about Sandy's eyeglasses being as thick as the bottom of cola bottles. Marvin, who overhears this discussion, decides that this is funny and yells out, "Hey, Sandy's glasses look like the bottom of cola bottles!" Sandy, shedding tears, runs further into the bottling plant, turning periodically to yell obscenities back toward the other students. He runs through a doorway labeled "Restricted Area. Danger."

3. With a partner, or a group of others, discuss which LSI technique you would use in the following situations.

   a. During lunch, Quincy pours ketchup into Marie's milk. Maria pushes Quincy's tray of food onto his lap. You witnessed only the yelling and shoving after the tray push. What type of interview will you use? Why?

   b. Jason, a student in your classroom, is known for being aggressive and assaultive. He frequently, and with no apparent reason, hits other students. You have had many consultations with Jason about this behavior and know that Jason once lived in a very violent home, where he was frequently exposed to unnecessary physical attacks. Today, while you are teaching, Jason unexpectantly turns around and smacks his best friend, Hank, across the mouth saying, "Quit staring at me!!" You immediately intervene and are prepared to conduct a life space interview. What type of interview will you use? Why?

   c. Lucy is a large, verbally aggressive but very intelligent student in your classroom. She is a new member of your class and is having difficulty forming friendships. She frequently reprimands other students, believing that her view is the correct one and that no one else's opinion matters. For example, Lucy dislikes the Chicago Cubs and berates Mike for wearing a Cubs' cap to school. Yesterday, Lucy told Mike that the St. Louis Cardinals were the best team in baseball and that the Cubs stink. She told him that he had better not wear the Cubs' cap ever again. Today, Mike shows up with his Cubs' cap on and a big smile. As soon as Lucy sees him, she runs over and rips the cap off his head and throws it across the room saying, "You mother f_____, I told you the Cubs stink!" What type of interview will you use? Why?

d. You are having difficulty managing the behavior of three students in your classroom. Ted, Keith, and Susan are continually fighting. They often call each other names and play cruel tricks on each other. You have decided to have a discussion with them. At the onset of the discussion, you realize that Ted and Keith are heaping all the blame on Susan who serves as a scapegoat. What type of interview will you use? Why?

e. At the onset of the class day, Slim and Sid begin arguing. Yesterday, Slim let Sid borrow a record album on the condition that he return it the next day. Sid, however, forgot to bring the album to school as promised. Slim claims that Sid has stolen his record album and calls him a thief. Sid desperately yells back at Slim, trying to defend himself and explain the situation. The two boys begin cursing at each other when you intervene. What type of inteview will you use? Why?

f. Bud presents the image of a teen-age hoodlum. He is known for being a bully and a tough guy. He frequently scares other students with threats of physical abuse. However, Bud is really not the tough guy that he pretends to be. Deep down, he feels rather threatened by others. He likes to make other students afraid of him because it makes him feel more powerful and eliminates the chance of them ever scaring him. During recess today, Bud becomes very angry because Tom hasn't passed him the basketball during the entire game. Bud walks over to Tom, grabs him by the shirt collar, and shakes him violently, while accusing him of being a "ball hog." Your aide breaks up the dispute and tends to Tom while you take Bud aside for a talk. What type of interview will you use? Why?

g. Steve passes a note to Carl, a bully, as requested by a group of girls. The notes says, "You're ugly. Signed, Steve." Steve is often the brunt of other's humor. You witness only Carl threatening to "kill" Steve after school. Assume that recess or your free period is about two or three minutes away.

h. Conrad uses extortion and strong-arm tactics to gain money for a second lunch.

i. While on a camping trip with your Boy Scout troop, Ernie has been sent for left-handed smoke shifters, bacon stretchers, and egg peelers. He was also left in the woods by others after dark during a "snipe hunt." He is often victimized by others as he attempts to please them to become part of the "in group."

For More Information

Brenner, M. (1969). Life space interviewing in the school setting. In H. Dupont (Ed.), *Educating emotionally disturbed children*. New York: Holt, Rinehart and Winston.

Morse, W. (1971). Worksheet on life space interviewing for teachers. In N. Long and R. Newman (Eds.), *Conflict in the classroom: The education of emotionally disturbed children*, 2nd ed. Belmont, Calif.: Wadsworth.

Morse, W., and Wineman, D. (1957). Group interviewing in a camp for disturbed boys. *Journal of Social Issues, 13* (1), 23–31.

Newman, R. G. (1963). The school-centered life space interview as illustrated by extreme threat of school issues. *American Journal of Orthopsychiatry, 33,* 730–733.

Redl, F. (1959). Strategy and techniques of the life space interview. *American Journal of Orthopsychiatry, 29,* 1–18.

Redl, F. (1966). *When we deal with children.* New York: The Free Press.

Redl, F. (1971). The concept of the life space interview. In N. Long, W. Morse, and R. Newman (Eds.), *Conflict in the classroom.* Belmont, Calif.: Wadsworth.

Reinert, H. (1980). *Children in conflict.* St. Louis: Mosby Company.

Walker, J., and Shea, T. (1984). *Behavior management: A practical approach for eduators.* St. Louis: Times Mirror/Mosby.

19

Classroom Conferencing

When we see misbehavior in the classroom, it is oftentimes necessary to call the student aside to discuss his inappropriate actions. Whereas other counseling techniques provide specific types of responses or a general focus, classroom conferencing is different in that it offers an outline or format for conducting a long talk with the student. These procedural guidelines provide structure to the counseling situation and allow you to use the interaction or counseling style with which you are most comfortable. This is important due to our differing personalities and philosophies that make some of us more directive, reflective, reserved, understanding, nondirective, collegial, or authoritarian than others. Classroom conferencing provides a series of steps to assist you in directing behavioral changes in misbehaving students. This approach actively involves the pupil in the change of personal interaction behavior, thereby giving the student a stake in the behavior change program. Over a period of time, by reasoning with the student, one can promote inner control of behavior and produce more permanent changes.

How to Use Classroom Conferencing

1. Meet with the student as soon as possible after the incident. Arrange for a minimum of distractions by meeting in private or informing other students that they are not to interrupt. Assure that your conference cannot be overheard by others.

2. Ask the student to review what happened. Immediately correct any misconceptions, differences of opinion, or lies so that both of you are dealing with the same perceptions of the situation.

3. Discuss morality and common courtesy, and question the student as to what was right and wrong in that given situation. Discuss whose rights or privileges were violated and by whom.

4. Discuss the student's pattern of behavior. (Each student with behavioral or emotional problems tends to have his own stereotypic reaction frustration.) Let the student know that his ideosyncratic behavior is unacceptable in the classroom (or school, playground, etc.) and cannot be tolerated.

5. Agree on a new reaction pattern. Have the student suggest other possible ways of handling the situation should it occur again. Ask the student to list as many alternative reactions as possible, even if he disagrees with their use. Write these possible solutions on paper. Ask the student to identify one that he will use in the future. Discuss the pros and cons of that decision. Choose another if that one is not acceptable.

6. Reconvene your conference as necessary to review the student's progress. Expect the change to take time and perhaps many conferences.

Activities and
Discussion Questions

1. With others, discuss the importance of steps 1, 2, and 3 of the classroom conferencing.

2. How many classroom conferences do you conduct and how long do you wait for behavior to change before you give up and decide on another intervention?

3. What do you do if the student fails to cooperate during the conference?

4. Fran reacts to teasing by others by hitting them. The following is a list of alternative solutions given by Fran for handling the teasing:

   a. Kick them.

   b. Spit at them.

   c. Give them "the finger" while cursing at them.

   d. Call the teacher.

   e. Call others names in return.

   f. Ignore the teasing.

   When asked which she will use in the future, Fran sees them as being in order of her preference. What are the concerns you have with each? At which point will you say, "OK. This one sound good."? (Possible concerns are listed in the Appendix.)

5. What other solutions might you recommend for Fran's consideration? (See number 4.)

6. With a partner who plays the part of the student, practice classroom conferencing with the following situations:

   a. During a softball game, a ground ball gets by Nick and rolls toward the far end of the playground. Nick chases after it and runs through an area where other students are playing with marbles. After throwing the ball too late to tag the runner at home plate, Nick, in anger, blames the marble players for slowing him down, kicks a pile of marbles, and throws a few over a distant fence. You call Nick over to you. He approaches you but is still contaged by his angry feelings.

b. Nancy leaves her seat to throw away a wad of paper. Because you are teaching a lesson, you tell her to sit down. After a short argument and a repeating of your direction, she reluctantly returns to her desk, mumbling. A few minutes later, Nancy arises again and, despite your command for her to return to her seat, she throws away the paper before doing so. In your conference you find that she asked the aide if she could throw away the paper after you told her no. The aide said yes. (Will you also talk to the aide?)

c. Two boys make faces, groan, and say rude remarks when a rather plump girl enters the room or is called upon during a lesson. She often becomes belligerent because of this teasing. During one incident she chases these boys around the classroom. You convince her to walk with you into the hallway to talk.

For More Information

McIntyre, T. (1987). Classroom conferencing: Providing support and guidance for misbehaving youth. *Teaching Behaviorally Disordered Youth*, *3*, 33–35.

20

Play Therapy

Play therapy is a technique whereby a child's natural means of expression (play) is used as a therapeutic method to assist him in coping with emotional stress or trauma. It has been used effectively with children who have an understanding level of a normal three- to eight-year-old, who are distraught due to family problems (e.g., divorce or sibling rivalry), nail biters, bed wetters, aggressive or cruel, socially underdeveloped, or victims of child abuse. It has also been used with special education students whose handicap is a source of anxiety or emotional turmoil.

Practitioners of play therapy believe that this method allows the child to manipulate the world on a smaller scale—something that cannot be done in the child's everyday environment. By playing with specially selected materials and with the guidance of a person who reacts in a designated manner, the child plays out his feelings, bringing these hidden emotions to the surface where he can face them and cope with them.

The teacher is unconditionally accepting of anything the child might say or do. The teacher never expresses shock, argues, teases, moralizes, or tells the child that his perceptions are incorrect. An atmosphere should be developed that lets the child know that he can express himself in a nonpunitive environment. Yet, even though the atmosphere is permissive, certain limits may have to be imposed, such as restrictions on destroying materials, attacking the teacher, or going beyond a set time limit.

Many psychologists, counselors, and other professionals may view this technique as being within their jurisdiction only. They may be correct when referring to long-term, in-depth counseling. However, although this technique is usually practiced by school counselors, social workers, and psychologists, it can easily be modified for use by the teacher in the classroom for less intensive problems. If you plan to conduct preplanned sessions, it is best to obtain the permission of administrators and parents.

How to Use Play Therapy

1. Select a student who might benefit from play therapy.

2. Decide if you will have a separate session with this child or whether you will sit near the student during your class play period or recess.

3. Obtain materials for the session. Recommended items include:

   > Manipulatives (e.g., clay, crayons, painting supplies)
   >
   > Water and sand boxes
   >
   > Toy kitchen appliances, utensils, and pans
   >
   > Baby items (e.g., bottles, bibs, rattles, etc.)
   >
   > Dolls and figures of various sizes and ages
   >
   > Toy guns, rubber knives
   >
   > Toy cars, boats, soldiers, and animals
   >
   > Blocks, erector sets
   >
   > Stuffed animals

4. Position the materials in specific places where they can be located for each session.

5. Meet the student and introduce him to the play area.

6. Inform the student of limitations and how long the session will last (usually thirty to sixty minutes).

7. Allow the student to choose materials. Do not suggest materials or activities. If the student wishes to leave before the session ends, that is allowed. However, the student is not allowed to return that day. He is informed of the time of the next scheduled session.

8. Use the reflection technique (see Chapter 17, Nondirective Counseling) to respond to the student's comments. If the student is nonverbal, your role will change. You will be describing what the student is doing.

9. As the end of the session nears, inform the student of that fact, stating the number of minutes left.

10. Upon reaching the time limit, inform the student in a manner similar to the following: "Our time is up for today. We'll have to stop now and put the toys back where we found them." The student is not allowed to continue playing.

11. Inform the student as to when the next session will be held.

Activities and Discussion Questions

1. Read Chapter 17, entitled Nondirective Counseling, for pertinent additional information.

2. Write or verbalize a reflection for each of the following comments spoken by a student during the play therapy session. You can restate the comment exactly, restate part

of the comment, or reflect the content of the comment. (Answers are in the Appendix.)

  a. While holding the head of one figure of a dog to the back of another, the student says, "The big dog is biting the little dog."

  b. While spanking a baby doll, the student says, "The baby is bad. She went to the bathroom in her diapers. She's a bad baby."

  c. While pretending that she is cooking, the student says, "I'm cooking a roast. I'm really good at cooking. I can cook anything."

  d. While manipulating soldier figures and knocking some down, the student says, "Bang. Another soldier is dead." The child then picks up the fallen soldier, looks at it, and says, "Nope, they missed. He's still OK."

3. Have a partner play the part of a student in a play therapy session. Practice your reflection technique.

4. If a student is nonverbal or is not talking much during part of a session, your role is to describe the action. Write or verbalize descriptions for each of the actions given in the following sequences. (Answers are in the Appendix.)

  a. The student is holding a car in each hand and is pushing them around on the floor. He starts to make loud engine noises and crashes the cars together.

  b. The student is sucking on a baby bottle and rocking back and forth. The child then looks at the bottle, shakes it as if it is empty, and pretends to cry. The child then says, "It's full again" and contentedly sucks on the bottle.

  c. The student has nearly unintelligible speech. You can only understand a few words that he is saying. He is holding two adult doll figures, one of each sex.

He mumbles some words very loudly in a low voice. The only word you can understand is *bad*. The student then makes the male doll lunge at the female doll and hit it. He is still mumbling in a low tone of voice, but you do not recognize any words. The child then imitates crying and mumbles words in a higher frequency voice. You recognize two words: *stop* and *hurt*.

5. Describe the proper reaction (according to the play therapy approach) to the following situations. (Answers are in the Appendix.)

   a. The student takes a black crayon and scribbles on a sheet of paper for ten minutes.

   b. The student quietly looks out the window for twenty minutes.

   c. The student paints a very lovely picture, using many colors and excellent proportions.

   d. The student takes paint and smears it on his face and shirt.

6. Locate play therapy materials. Price those that are not available for use on a free basis.

7. On paper, design your play therapy room or a section of your room that can be used for play therapy.

For More Information

Axline, C. (1947). Play therapy: A way of understanding and helping reading problems. *Childhood Education, 26,* 156–161.

Axline, V. (1969). *Play therapy.* New York: Ballantine Books.

Bills, R. E. (1950). Non-directed play therapy with retarded readers. *Journal of Consulting Psychology, 14,* 140–149.

Bills, R. E. (1950). Play therapy with well adjusted readers. *Journal of Consulting Psychology, 14,* 246–249.

Bishop, J. K. *Change as a function of play: Toot! Toot!* Canada. (ERIC Document Reproduction Service No. ED 234 889.)

Brody, V., Fenderson, C., and Stephenson, S. (1976). *Sourcebook for finding your way to helping young children through developmental play.* Tallahassee: State of Florida, Department of State.

Burt, M. A., and Myrick, R. D. (1980). Developmental play: What's it all about? *Elementary School Guidance and Counseling, 15,* 14–21.

Carlson, B., and Ginglend, D. (1961). *Play activities for the retarded child.* New York: Abington Press.

Clement, P. W., and Milne, D. C. (1967). Group play therapy and tangible reinforcers used to modify the behavior of eight-year-old boys. *Behavior Research and Therapy,* 301–312.

Fisher, B. (1953). Group therapy with retarded readers. *Journal of Educational Psychology, 44,* 356–360.

Ginott, H. (1961). *Group psychotherapy with children.* New York: McGraw-Hill.

Grahamm, B. (1975). Non-directive play therapy with troubled children. *Corrective and Social Psychiatry and Journal of Behavior Techniques, Methods and Therapy, 21,* 22–23.

Moustakas, C. (1973). *Children in play therapy.* Michigan: Jason Aronson, Inc.

Nystul, M. S. (1980). Nystulian play therapy: Applications of Adlerian psychology. *Elementary School Guidance and Counseling, 15,* 22–30.

Schaefer, C. E., and O'Connor, K. J. (1983). *Handbook of play therapy.* Boston: John Wiley & Sons.

21

Bibliotherapy

Most of us realize how therapeutic reading can be. We find ourselves entering the world described in the pages of a good book and becoming involved with the characters within. We often close the cover having gained new insight and ideas. That is the purpose behind the use of bibliotherapy—to assist a student in overcoming the emotional turmoil related to a real-life problem by having him read a story on that topic. This story can then serve as a springboard for discussion and possible resolution of that dilemma. Thus, the teacher provides guidance in the resolution of personal crisis through the use of directed readings and follow-up activities.

The student is believed to receive the benefits of bibliotherapy by passing through three stages:

1. *Identification* The student reader identifies with a book character, either real or fictional.
2. *Catharsis* The student is able to release pent-up emotions under safe conditions.
3. *Insight* Possible solutions to personal problems are identified.

Bibliotherapy can be conducted with individuals or groups.

In individual bibliotherapy, literature is assigned to a student for a specific need. The student may read the material, or the literature may be read to him. The activities that follow the reading are also conducted individually with the student. The student discusses the literature with a teacher, writes a report, talks into the tape recorder, or expresses his reaction artistically. Through this process he is able to unblock emotions and relieve emotional pressures. Additionally, by examining and analyzing moral values and the stimulation of critical thinking, he develops self-awareness, an improved self-concept, and improved personal and social judgment. This results in improved behavior and increased empathy, tolerance, respect, and acceptance of others through identification with an appropriate literary model.

In its use with groups, the students read literature orally or listen while the teacher reads to them. Group discussion and activities follow. Group discussion encourages the students to be aware that they are not alone in their feelings and that perceived problems are shared by others and can be resolved. By observing the limitations and strengths of others, students may begin to deal with their negative feelings and actions that were produced by the personal problems.

Although bibliotherapy encourages change within an individual, its use is not restricted to times when a crisis is present. However, it is not a cure-all for deep-rooted psychological problems, either. These are best served through more intensive therapeutic interventions. Other students may not yet be able to view themselves in a literary mirror and may use literature for escape purposes only. Others may tend to rationalize their problems away rather than facing them. Still others may not be able to transfer insights into real life. However, these vicarious experiences with literary characters prove to be helpful for many students.

How to Use Bibliotherapy

1. Identify student needs. This is done through observation, parent conferences, student writing assignments, and the review of school records.

2. Match the student(s) with appropriate materials. Find books that deal with divorce, a death in the family, or whatever student needs have been identified. Keep the following in mind:

   a. The book must be at the student's reading ability level.

   b. The text must be at an interest level appropriate to the maturity of the student.

   c. The theme of the readings should match the identified needs of the student.

   d. The characters should be believable so that the student can empathize with their predicaments.

   e. The plot of the story should be realistic and involve creativity in problem solving.

3. Decide on the setting and time for sessions, and how sessions will be introduced to the student.

4. Design follow-up activities for the reading (e.g., discussion, paper writing, drawing, drama).

5. Motivate the student with introductory activities.

6. Engage in the reading, viewing, or listening phase.

7. Take a break or allow a few minutes for the student to reflect on the material.

8. Introduce the follow-up activities.

9. Assist the student in achieving closure through discussion, a listing of possible solutions, or other activity.

Activities and Discussion Questions

1. Locate various books, stories, and filmstrips that deal with personal problems. Decide if the materials are appropriate

for bibliotherapy. List why or why not. If they are appropriate, decide which age group, sex, and so on would be the target of these materials.

2. With the materials you have located, devise introductory and follow-up activities.

3. Give a report to others, complete with a demonstration on the use of bibliotherapy.

For More Information

Adult bibliotherapy: Books help to heal (1979). *Journal of Reading, 23* (1), 33–35.

Axelrod, H., and Teti, T. R. (1976). An alternative to bibliotherapy: Audiovisiotherapy. *Educational Technology, 16* (12), 36–38.

Brown, E. F. (1975). *Bibliotherapy and its widening applications.* Metuchen, N.J.: Scarecrow Press.

Cornett, C. E., and Cornett, C. F. (1980). *Bibliotherapy: The right book at the right time.* Phi Delta Kappa Educational Foundation, Library of Congress 80-82584.

Dreyer, S. S. (1977). *The bookfinder.* Circle Pines, Minn.: American Guidance Services.

Edwards, B. S. (1972). The therapeutic value of reading. *Elementary English, 49* (2), 213–218.

Olson, H. D. (1975). Bibliotherapy to help children solve problems. *Elementary Street Journal, 75* (7), 422–429.

Schrank, F. A. (1982). Bibliotherapy as an elementary school counseling tool. *Elementary School Guidance and Counseling, 16* (3), 218–227.

Examples of Books
for Bibliotherapy

Acceptance by others:

Estes, E. (1944). *The hundred dresses.* New York: Harcourt Brace Jovanovich.

Accidents:

Wolff, A. (1969). *Mom! I broke my arm!* New York: Lion Press.

Adoption:

Caines, J. (1973). *Abby.* New York: Harper and Row.
Daringer, H. (1973). *Adopted Jane.* New York: Harcourt Brace Jovanovich.

Alcoholism:

Trivers, J. (1974). *I can stop any time I want.* Englewood Cliffs, N.J.: Prentice-Hall.

Anger:

Hitte, K. (1969). *Boy was I mad.* New York: Parents' Magazine Press.
Preston, E. (1969). *Temper tantrum book.* New York: Viking.
Simon, N. (1974). *I was so mad!* Chicago: Whitman.
Watson, J. (1971). *Sometimes I get angry.* Racine, Wis.: Western, Golden Press.
Zolotow, C. (1969). *The hating book.* New York: Harper and Row.

Appearance:

Blume, J. (1971). *Freckle juice.* New York: Four Winds Press, Scholastic Book Service.
Haywood, C. (1949). *Eddie and the fire engine.* New York: Wm. Morrow.
Kerr, M. E. (1972). *Dinky Hocker shoots smack.* New York: Harper and Row.
McGinley, P. (1945). *The plain princess.* Philadelphia: Lippincott.

Behavior:

Cleary, B. (1968). *Ramona the pest.* New York: William Morrow and Co.
Hanson, J. (1972). *Alfred Snood.* New York: Putnam.

Bullies:

Hinton, S. (1967). *The outsiders.* New York: Viking Press.

Courage:

Speare, E. (1958). *The witch of Blackbird Pond.* New York: Dell.

Crying:

Zolotow, C. (1972). *William's doll.* New York: Harper and Row.

Deafness:

Levine, E. (1974). *Lisa and her soundless world.* New York: Human Sciences Press.

Death:

de Paola, T. (1973). *Nana upstairs and Nana downstairs.* New York: G. P. Putnam's Sons.
Viorst, J. (1971). *Ten good things about Barney.* New York: Altheneum.

Disabilities:

Butler, E. (1962). *Light a single candle.* New York: Dodd, Mead.
Lasker, J. (1974). *He's my brother.* Chicago: Whitman.

Divorce:

Blume, J. (1972). *It's not the end of the world.* New York: Bradbury Press.
Berger, T. (1977). *How does it feel when your parents get divorced?* New York: Julian Messner.

Dropouts:

Eyerly, J. (1963). *Drop out.* Philadelphia: Lippincott.

Drugs:

Anonymous (1971). *Go ask Alice.* Englewood Cliffs, N.J.: Prentice-Hall.

Embarrassment:

Alexander, M. (1971). *Sabrina.* New York: Dial.

Emotions:

Berger, T. (1971). *I have feelings.* New York: Human Sciences Press.
Burlingham, J. (1971). *Mr. Grumpy's outing.* New York: Holt, Rinehart and Winston.
Kingman, L. (1953). *Peter's long walk.* New York: Doubleday.
Viorst, J. (1976). *Alexander and the terrible horrible no good very bad day.* New York: Atheneum.

Fears:

Heide, F. (1971). *Some things are scary.* New York: Scholastic Book Services.
Mayer, M. (1968). *There's a nightmare in my closet.* New York: Dial Press.
Watson, J. (1971). *Sometimes I'm afraid.* Racine, Wis.: Western, Golden Press.
Zolotow, C. (1952). *The storm book.* New York: Harper and Row.

Feelings about a mid-year change in teachers:

Cohen, M. (1974). *The new teacher.* New York: Macmillan, Collier Books.

Fighting:

Zolotow, C. (1963). *The quarreling book.* New York: Harper and Row.

Friendship:

Anglund, J. (1958). *A friend is someone who likes you.* New York: Harcourt Brace Jovanovich.
Cohen, M. (1971). *Will I have a friend?* New York: Macmillan, Collier Books.

Cohen, M. (1973). *Best friends*. New York: Macmillan, Collier Books.

De Regniers, B. S. (1974). *May I bring a friend?* New York: Altheneum.

Sharmat, M. (1970). *Gladys told me to meet her here*. New York: Harper and Row.

Glasses:

Raskin, E. (1974). *Spectacles*. New York: Altheneum.

Wolff, A. (1970). *Mom! I need glasses!* New York: Lion Press.

Growing Up:

Blume, J. (1970). *Are you there God, it's me Margaret*. Scarsdale, N.Y.: Holt, Rinehart and Winston.

Breinburg, P. (1974). *Shawn goes to school*. New York: Thomas Y. Crowell.

Watson, J. (1971). *Look at me now*. Racine, Wis.: Western, Golden Press.

Height:

Beim, J. (1949). *Smallest boy in the class*. New York: William Morrow.

Krasilovsky, P. (1959). *Very tall little girl*. New York: Doubleday.

Illness:

Bemelmans, L. (1977). *Madeline*. New York: Penguin.

Charlip, R., and Supree, B. (1966). *Mother Mother I feel sick, send for the doctor quick quick quick*. New York: Parents' Magazine Press.

Shay, A. (1969). *What happens when you go to the hospital*. Chicago: Contemporary Books.

Insecurity:

Justus, M. (1963). *New boy in school*. New York: Hastings House.

Waber, B. (1972). *Ira sleeps over*. New York: Houghton Mifflin.

Life in a ghetto:

Clifton, L. (1973). *The boy who didn't believe in spring.* New York: E. P. Dutton.

Love:

Anglund, J. W. (1966). *What color is love.* New York: Harcourt Brace Jovanovich.

Anglund, J. W. (1960). *Love is a special way of feeling.* New York: Harcourt Brace Jovanovich.

Lying:

Ness, E. (1966). *Sam, Bangs and Moonshine.* New York: Bradbury Press.

Mental retardation:

Fassler, J. (1969). *One little girl.* New York: Haman Science Press.

Mexican child:

Ets, M. (1963). *Gilberto and the wind.* New York: Viking.

Overweight:

Breene, C. (1969). *A girl called Al.* New York: Viking Press.

Pinkwater, M. (1974). *Fat Elliot and the gorilla.* New York: Scholastic Book Services.

Physical handicap:

Wolf, B. (1974). *Don't feel sorry for Paul.* Philadelphia: Lippincott.

Poverty:

Estes, E. (1974). *The hundred dresses.* New York: Harcourt Brace Jovanovich.

Pregnancy:

Sherburne, Z. (1967). *Too bad about the Haines girl.* New York: William Morrow.

Prejudice:

De Angeli, M. (1946). *Bright April.* New York: Doubleday.
Fox, P. (1973). *The slave dancers.* Scarsdale, N.Y.: Bradbury Press.

Puerto Rican:

Keats, J., and Cherr, P., (1960). *My dog is lost.* New York: Thomas Y. Crowell.

Race relations:

Beim, L., and Beim, J. (1974). *Two is a team.* New York: Harcourt Brace Jovanovich.
Randall, B. E. (1956). *Fun for Chris.* Chicago: Whitman.

Rejection:

Wells, R. (1976). *Noisy Nora.* New York: Scholastic Book Services.

Responsibility:

Cleaver, V. (1969). *Where the lillies bloom.* Philadelphia: Lippincott.

Running away:

Alexander, M. (1972). *And my mean old mother will be sorry, Blackboard Bear.* New York: Dial.
Samuels, G. (1974). *Run, Shelley, run.* New York: Thomas Crowell.

School:

Barkin, C., and James, E. (1975). *Sometimes I hate school.* Milwaukee, Wis.: Raintree.
Mannheim, G. (1968). *Two friends.* New York: Alfred A. Knopf.

Self-concept:

Bel Geddes, B. (1963). *I like to be me.* New York: Simon and Schuster.
Gibbons, J. (1974). *There is only one me.* Los Angeles: Science of Mind.
Klein, N. (1974). *Confessions of an only child.* New York: Pantheon Books.
Kottler, D., and Willis, E. (1974). *I really like myself.* Nashville, Tenn.: Aurora.

Sharing:

Bonsall, C. N. (1964). *It's mine!* New York: Harper and Row.

Shyness:

Krasilovsky, P. (1970). *Shy little girl.* New York: Houghton Mifflin.

Siblings:

O'Dell, S. (1960). *Island of the blue dolphins.* Boston: Houghton Mifflin.
Schick, E. (1970). *Peggy's new brother.* New York: Macmillan.
Simon, N. (1970). *How do I feel.* Chicago: Whitman.

Violence:

Dillon, L. (1976). *Why mosquitoes buzz in people's ears.* New York: Dial Press.

22

DUSO Kits

The DUSO program is a packaged curriculum with accompanying activities designed to help students better understand the social consequences of their behavior and to become more aware of the relationships between themselves, their goals and needs, and other people. Through the use of DUSO, Developing and Understanding of Self and Others, the students are assisted in perceiving the purposes and goals of their behavior and identifying the reasons for their faulty relationships with others. Two different versions allow its use with students from kindergarten through fourth grade.

The materials included in the DUSO kits are: a manual, story books, records or cassettes, posters, puppet activity cards, puppets, puppet props, role-playing cards, and group discussion cards. The DUSO kit is divided into eight units. Each unit has enough activities to last four to five weeks. The eight major units of the DUSO kit (D-1) for younger students are:

1. Understanding and Accepting Self

2. Understanding Feelings

3. Understanding Others

4. Understanding Independence

5. Understanding Goals and Purposeful Behavior

6. Understanding Mastery, Competence and Resourcefulness

7. Understanding Emotional Maturity

8. Understanding Choices and Consequences

Each of the units is subdivided into different cycles. In each of these cycles, the following activities are included: a story to be followed by discussion, a problem situation to be followed by discussion, a role-playing activity, a puppet activity, several supplementary activities to be used as desired, and recommended supplementary readings that can be read to the class by the teacher or read independently by individual pupils.

The DUSO kit (D-2) for students seven to ten years of age also contains eight major themes:

1. Self Identity: Developing Self-Awareness and a Positive Self Concept

2. Friendship: Understanding Peers

3. Responsible Interdependence: Understanding Growth from Self-Centeredness to Social Interest

4. Self-Reliance: Understanding Personal Responsibility

5. Resourcefulness and Purposefulness: Understanding Personal Motivation

6. Competence: Understanding Accomplishment

7. Emotional Stability: Understanding Stress

8. Responsible Choice Making: Understanding Values

Each of the eight major themes is subdivided into four or five cycles that contain activities involving: a story and poster, a problem situation to be followed by discussion, a role-playing activity, a puppet activity and discussion picture, a career awareness activity, several supplementary activities, and recommended supplementary readings.

The goal of the DUSO kits is to help students see themselves in a positive light. There are three main objectives: to teach more words for feelings; to teach that feelings, goals, and behavior are related; and to teach students to talk freely about feelings, goals, and behavior. The kits arrange learning activities to strengthen the students' self-esteem and, by doing this, meet their social, emotional, and academic needs. The activities make extensive use of listening, inquiry, discussion, and an experiential approach to learning. There are enough lessons in each kit to last for a full school year.

Activities and
Discussion Questions

1. Obtain the DUSO kits and become familiar with them. Give a presentation on the kits to classmates or a group of peers.

2. Analyze the materials in the kits. Would they be appropriate for your students? If you were going to give only a few lessons/activities, which ones would you choose for your students?

3. Lead a group in a lesson outlined in the kits.

4. Obtain a curriculum on coping skills from your school system. Review it.

5. Devise a curriculum on coping skills for your school system if one does not exist.

For More Information

To obtain information regarding the kits or to purchase them, contact:

American Guidance Service, Inc.
Publisher's Building
Circle Pines, MN 55014
Phone: (800) 328-2560.

SECTION SIX

Related Areas

23

Legal Considerations in Behavior Management

by Larry Janes

Education does not occur in a vacuum, void of legal and political realities. As an educator, you are bound by the increasing volume of statutes, rules, regulations, and case law decisions impacting school personnel in general as well as you in your role as a teacher. No longer are a teacher's supervisory and instructional skills a matter for consideration only in the schoolhouse. Educators are increasingly faced with defending actions and decisions in the arena of the courthouse. In the courthouse, good intentions and a sincere desire to help a student in need of special services are not the best defenses against actions that are viewed as having damaged the body, mind, or good name of a pupil. Nor is your ignorance of the law held in high esteem by hearing officers, judges, or juries if you have inadvertently treaded upon the civil or constitutional rights of a student.

This chapter addresses several issues regarding your liability as an educator. No attempt is made to be all-inclusive; to do so is a near impossibility in view of the expanding body of education law. Neither is the chapter an attempt to make you an expert on the liability of educators. Hopefully, though, you will become more aware of the legal ramifications of your relationships with students and the safeguards that will protect your liability status. One brief caution should be observed: Even the most responsible individuals may find themselves facing litigation. Should you face this possibility, you must be prepared to document your actions and present a factual account grounded in sound teaching theory and practice. Consequently, the records you maintain and your conduct as a teacher should be accurate, current, and reflective of competent professional practice.

Avenues into the Courts

Educators must be concerned with the two divisions of law: criminal and civil. Criminal law governs an individual's relationship to society, is grounded in criminal statutes, and relies on a political subdivision and a prosecuting attorney for initiating actions that could lead to imprisonment and/or fines. An educator accused of assault or battery would be facing a criminal charge.

Civil law governs duties owed to individuals. It involves taking or not taking an action that causes harm to an individual. Civil action is grounded in precedent from past cases and general principles of law. Action is typically initiated by a private practice attorney. A teacher accused of failing to properly supervise a student who is injured while in the teacher's classroom would face a civil suit.

In a criminal action, proof beyond a "reasonable doubt" is necessary for an educator to be found guilty. However, the lesser standard of a preponderance of proof is required to be met for an educator to be held liable for a civil wrong. The preponderance standard requires only that the scales of justice be tipped in favor of the plaintiff's case when all the evidence has been presented.

The educator in the classroom is most frequently concerned with civil actions related to negligence or actions resulting in injury to a person. Negligence comprises a major segment of the law of torts, which includes those acts or omissions that infringe on the rights of individuals, or cause damage by the failure to perform an implied, noncontractual obligation.

When negligence is considered, a single question will be used to evaluate the educator's conduct that gave rise to alleged loss or damage: What would a reasonably prudent person have done in the same or a similar situation? In addressing the actions of the prudent person, a court will determine if four elements exist that are necessary for recovery under tort:

A duty to adhere to a particular standard of conduct or to exercise reasonable care

Breach of a duty, or violation of a standard of care

Causal connection between the breach and injury

Resultant injury

A special area of tort law serves to protect a person's federally granted civil and constitutional rights. Civil action related to these torts originates in federal courts; whereas injury torts are state issues grounded in state law and are decided in state courts. Consequently, each state has its own body of law by which your actions will be judged. In most states though, instructors are expected to conduct themselves as reasonably prudent teachers. You are not a common and ordinary citizen. You are an expert in a variety of areas reflective of your profession: curriculum, classroom management, discipline, and supervision of children, to name but a few. A few states still hold teachers to a lesser standard of expertise in juding a teacher's actions as negligent, but no state permits its citizens, be they teachers or otherwise, to act or fail to act such that they are malicious or willful or wanton in their conduct that leads to injury. If placed in the role of defendant, the classroom teacher will typically try to establish that the injury could have occurred even if common and ordinary care was being provided, or that the teacher's actions were not the cause of injury. In any case, the defendant will still suffer the personal stress that comes from the legal action. Additionally, in our society many actions end with an out-of-court settlement without regard to findings of fault, leaving defendants to face their publics who too often perceive those settlements as de facto admissions of negligence.

A Test for the Teacher

To help you better understand your responsibilities under the law, a brief quiz is provided. Each question is answered and analyzed in the Appendix, based on current legal standards. However, observe this caution: Law is a living entity, growing and changing everyday. What might be true today could be swept aside tomorrow by a decision or statutory change, leaving a need to modify your classes or your supervisory actions.

T F   1. A teacher who leaves his or her areas of supervision will always be found liable if a student is injured during the absence.

T F   2. An educator who uses corporal punishment may be charged with child abuse if his or her actions are viewed as excessive and unreasonable, or if the student is injured.

T F   3. If a parent signs a permission slip for his or her child to go on a field trip, the teacher bears no legal responsibility for injuries or accidents to the student during that trip.

T F   4. The use of a time-out room or area is acceptable as long as parental consent has been obtained.

T F   5. A teacher may search a student's locker or desk. However, a warrant is necessary unless immediate danger to the school, staff, or student exists.

T F   6. Teachers may be liable for gossip they spread about students in the teachers' lounge, even if they believe that they are representing the truth.

T F   7. A teacher may reduce a student's grade as a disciplinary action for that student's behavior.

T F   8. Temporary suspension of a handicapped student

is a change in placement that triggers the procedural protections of P.L. 94–142.

T F   9. Very little can be done on a short-term basis beyond a temporary change in placement to discipline a handicapped student.

T F 10. If a student under your direct supervision attacks
or causes injury to another student, you will be
held liable.

T F 11. You may deny a parent the right to access your
personal notes about his or her special education
child in matters related to the disciplining of the
student or of an injury to the student.

Some Final Thoughts

"Before the enactment of compulsory education laws, those children who did not fit into the system suitable for the majority failed
to attend school, or were excluded by act of the school itself. Subnormal children have always existed, doubtless in about the same
proportion as they now exist, but the school did not become acutely
aware of them until the law decreed that every child must receive
an education, if physically and mentally able to attend school. The
state then hired truant officers to bring in those who of their own
volition failed to attend, and the school was prohibited from ex-
pelling children. Thus the subnormal child and the school were
forced into a reluctant mutual recognition of each other" (Hollingworth, 1920).

Written in 1920, the above statement failed to consider the
slow and treacherous path that the special education student would
have to take to achieve their "reluctant mutual recognition," but
the statement is certainly now at hand and you, as the one charged
with teaching and supervising the child, face substantially more
diverse legal considerations than those who do not teach the special
needs student. As such, you would be wise to follow the advice

of Rothstein (1985), who lists four areas to address in order to avoid liability:

Knowledge of handicapping conditions and implications of those conditions. All teachers and related service personnel should have a basic understanding of the common types of handicapping conditions and the effect those conditions may have on achievement, abilities, and behaviors. Depending on the educator's role, there may also be a need to know what accommodations are necessary to meet the needs of students with certain handicaps.

Knowledge of behavior management techniques. With the inclusion of children with handicaps such as mental retardation, behavior disorders, and emotional disturbance, it has become more essential that teachers and other educational personnel understand and use appropriate behavior management techniques.

Knowledge of law. All professional educational personnel should have an understanding of P.L. 94–142, including an understanding of its underlying principles, the fundamental requirements for due process, and the deadlines and mandates for evaluation and placement.

Communication capabilities. Educational personnel should be able to communicate and consult with other professionals, such as physicians, psychologists, and social service providers, along with the student and family members, and other educational professionals within the system.

You do have a professional obligation toward the behaviorally disordered student, but do not ignore the personal obligation to yourself. To act on instinct and good intentions may well be humane, but such an act may also be negligent. Ultimately you stand alone with your competencies and knowledges as your guide.

For More Information

Appenseller, H. (1983). *The right to participate.* Charlottesville, Va.: The Michie Company.

Fischer, L., Schimmel, D., and Kelly, C. (1981). *Teachers and the law.* New York: Longman Publishers.

Hindman, S. (1986). The law, the courts, and the education of behaviorally disordered students. *Behavioral Disorders, 11* (4), 280–289.

Contact your state department of education for rules and regulations regarding the rights of handicapped students.

24

Mainstreaming Students with an Emotional/ Behavior Problem

The ultimate goal that we hold in mind for a student with an emotional/behavioral disorder is to return him someday to the regular education classroom on a full-time basis. Infusion into regular education can be good for a student's self-concept as it shows that he has "made it." We also know that the behavior of this student is likely to improve as he is exposed to, and models, the actions of regular education peers (Yaffe, 1979).

In the special education setting, we watch the slow progress of this student as behavior improves and structure is progressively removed from the program. The day finally arrives when it's time for the student to test the waters of regular education, entering slowly at first and wading in progressively deeper as he proves himself worthy. However, to insure success, both the student and the system must be prepared. The student must be emotionally, behaviorally, intellectually, and academically ready so that failure—which would be disastrous to his self-concept—is avoided. The regular educator must be prepared and receptive because an unreceptive teacher can consciously or unconsciously sabotage the mainstreaming attempt (Vacc and Kirst, 1977). The regular education pupils need to be prepared for the entry of this student in order to promote his acceptance. In general, students with behavior disorders are less accepted than others in the regular education classroom (Keogh and Levitt, 1976). The administration must be supportive in the provision of assistance, be it monetary, material, service, or emotional. Also, the parents, who may have negative memories of their child's past experiences in regular education, must be informed of the benefits of this approach. Difficulty is to be expected as the effort moves forward, but with proper support and preparation, it can be a positive experience for all involved. To assist in the development of a successful program, guidelines and considerations are offered below.

Checklist for Successful Mainstreaming

_____   1. The regular classroom is the next step in the cascade of services. (The student should be placed in the regular classroom only after he has performed well in a public school special classroom.)

_____   2. All involved parties agree with the placement and want to see the program succeed.

       _____ regular education teacher(s)

       _____ special education teacher or consultant

       _____ parent

       _____ student

       _____ administration

       _____ other service providers (e.g., counselors, aides)

_____   3. The student is academically/intellectually ready.

       _____ ability level

       _____ reading level (or modifications agreed upon)

_____ at the present point in the regular classroom curriculum

_____ proper study skills

_____ punctual

_____ homework always completed

_____ works independently

_____ 4. The student is behaviorally ready and has good inner control of his behavior.

_____ 5. The regular education teacher has the skills to be effective with this student.

_____ open minded and willing to allow modifications

_____ able to individualize instruction

_____ tolerant

_____ organized

_____ structured

_____ good behavior management skills

_____ confident

_____ friendly, yet firm with students

_____ 6. The regular education teacher has met and talked with the student.

_____ introduced self

_____ friendly conversation

_____ talked about class in general

_____ talked about rules

_____ talked about curriculum

_____ talked about expectations

_____ 7. The student and the regular education teacher have

signed a contract to assure that both are aware of required behavior (optional).

——— 8. The students in the regular education classroom have been prepared for the entry of a new student.

——— 9. The student is slowly entered into the class if necessary.

       ——— brings note to regular classroom teacher and leaves

       ——— stands with new teacher on playground

       ——— meets regular education students on the playground

       ——— sits with aide in classroom for increasing amounts of time

       ——— student stays for full time in classroom

——— 10. The special education teacher or consultant continues to advise and work with the regular education teacher and student to ensure success.

Activities and Discussion Questions

1. Identify a regular classroom teacher with whom you are familiar and complete the listing of characteristics under step 5 of the checklist for successful mainstreaming. Would this teacher be a good candidate for accepting a student with a behavior problem into his or her classroom?

2. Rate yourself as you rated another teacher in number 1. Would you be a good receiving teacher?

3. Find a partner who will role play the part of a student with a behavior problem who is about to be mainstreamed into your class. Have a conversation with this student

along the guidelines outlined in step 6 of the checklist for successful mainstreaming.

4. Decide how you would prepare the students in your class for the entrance of a student with a behavior disorder. Would you mention that this student was in a special education classroom? Would you mention his past behavior? What would you ask of your students?

5. With a partner, role play the development of a contract for entrance into the regular education classroom as mentioned in step 7. (Refer to Chapter 10 of this book.)

6. How can you prove to other unconvinced parties that the student is behaviorally ready to enter into the regular classroom as mentioned in step 4? (Answer is in the Appendix.)

7. Why is it important for the special education teacher to continue working with the student and the regular education teacher?

For More Information

Kavanaugh, E. (1977). A classroom teacher looks at mainstreaming. *Elementary School Journal, 77*, 318–322.

Keogh, B., and Levitt, M. (1976). Special education in the mainstream: A confrontation of limits? *Focus on Emotional Children, 8*, 1–12.

Lasher, M., Mattick, I., Perkins, F., and Hailey, J. (1979). Mainstreaming children with emotional disturbances. *Teacher Education.*

Meissler, S. J. (1977). First steps in mainstreaming: Some questions and answers. *Young Children, 33*, 4–13.

Owen, L. (1978). The placement and preparation of the handicapped child in the regular classroom. *Kappa Delta Pi Record, 15*, 58–59.

Pappanikou, A. J., and Paul, J. L. (Eds.) (1977). *Mainstreaming emotionally disturbed children.* Syracuse, N.Y.: Syracuse University Press.

Vacc, N., and Kirst, N. (1977). Emotionally disturbed children and regular classroom teachers. *Elementary School Journal, 77*, 308–317.

Yaffe, E. (1979). Experienced mainstreamers speak out. *Teacher Magazine, 84*, 19–21.

25

Burnout: Prevention and Remediation

Teaching is undoubtedly one of the most stressful occupations that one can enter. In addition to the difficulties associated with the important task of educating our nation's youth, teachers must deal with societal, parental, collegial, and administrative demands on a daily basis. Add to these one of the most often reported stressors—problems with discipline. This, according to surveys of teachers, is a major source of stress and burnout.

Stress is not necessarily bad for us; a certain amount of stress helps us to get "psyched up." This is known as *eustress*, as opposed to *distress*, which results when too much stress affects our ability to think and act rationally. It is when the stress of teaching exceeds a teacher's ability to cope and adjust that burnout occurs. The teacher begins to feel emotionally exhausted, tired, and irritable. If the problem persists, the teacher may start to develop negative feelings toward students or attempt to cope with the problem by becoming emotionally detached and thus less caring and concerned. Instruction and interactions become less personalized and more removed and calculated. Physical problems and illnesses may also develop. If the stress continues unimpeded, the teacher feels a lowered sense of professional accomplishment. Although many teachers will make a career change, many others will remain in the school systems, feeling bitter and professionally unfulfilled.

The stress that we feel is individualized. That is, because of our different personalities, abilities, skills, and situations, what is stressful to one may not be stressful to others and vice versa. In general, though, the amount of stress that you feel is equal to the stress of the job minus your ability to cope. If your coping capacity (i.e., personality, nonprofessional activities, and hobbies) is adequate, you will experience few manifestations and reactions to stress. However, if your coping techniques are inadequate, given the level of your job-related stress, you may experience some degree of burnout. It is when stress is handled poorly that it becomes an enemy. The purpose of this chapter is twofold. First, it will assist you in determining if stress is affecting your teaching performance. Second, if your performance is suffering, the following activities will help you cope with personal and professional stressors and relieve the effects of stress.

There are three ways to deal with stress: acceptance (letting stress affect you negatively); withdrawal (e.g., switching careers, using sick-leave days); or developing a plan to relieve the stress. This chapter will focus on the third option—developing a new plan of action. Responses to stressful situations are primarily learned; therefore, adequate coping methods can also be learned. You *can* make your classroom a less stressful environment and you *can* reduce and relieve the effects of stress. You're a good teacher. We don't want to lose you!

Symptoms and Manifestations of Burnout

As you review the traits listed below, reflect on the frequency and severity of each. Use these to determine if your stress level needs to be addressed.

Emotional Domain

Excessive worry, anxiety, or frustration

Feeling emotionally or mentally exhausted

Feelings of not wanting to go to work on school mornings

Feelings of dislike toward one or more students in your class

Feeling insecure

Feeling unable to cope

Feeling depressed

Feeling that teaching is the wrong career for you

Behavioral Domain

Sleeping more or less than usual

Conversations with colleagues and students become less personal

Avoidance of school-related tasks and preparation

Excessive absences

Excessive use of drugs or alcohol

Physical Domain

Stomach acid

Stomach cramps

Headaches

Loss of voice

Physical exhaustion

Nausea

Dizziness

Back pains

Change in appetite

Increased heart rate

Techniques for Coping with Stress

1. Focus on the positive things you have accomplished in the last six months or one year. Make a list of your accomplishments. Think of both professional and personal areas. Take pride in these.

2. Identify professional stressors. List those things that are stressful to you at school. Consider the students, other teachers, the administration, parents, curriculum, pay scale, degree of professional fulfillment, your role, job description, paperwork, and so on. Be as specific as possible.

3. Become aware of how stress affects you. List your behavioral, emotional, and physical reactions to stressful, job-related situations.

4. Now that you have identified your job-related stressors (see number 2), decide how much control you have over each stressor. Which ones could you change? Devise a plan to change those over which you have control.

5. Goals can give our professional lives more purpose. Set a long-term goal for yourself. What would you like to accomplish within a year? Five years? Break down these goals into subgoals. List these in sequential order and decide how you can work toward accomplishing the first subgoal. Upon achieving the first subgoal, work toward the second step. Be sure that your goals are measurable and achievable so that you will know when you have achieved them.

6. Each night, list situations that were stressful that day. How could you have handled that situation more effectively? Learn from your experience.

7. Find or form a support group. Discuss stressful aspects in your school. Don't just complain, however; discuss possible solutions for problems.

8. Make your day more organized and structured through the use of time management. Divide a piece of paper into three columns. List those activities that *must* be done tomorrow in column A. List those activities you would *like* to complete tomorrow in column B. List other activities in column C. Never complete a B task before an A task or a C task before an A or B task.

9. Talk to the person(s) in charge of arranging inservice sessions for your school. Ask for workshops on stress and burnout to be scheduled.

10. To what degree are classroom behavior problems adding to your stress level? Determine if the behavior problems are primarily evident in a few students or a larger segment of your class. Review the various chapters on behavior management to find ideas for gaining more control over the class as a whole. For one or a few students, do the same, but also look at the ideas in the strategy sheet section.

For More Information

Alschuler, A. S. (1980). *Teacher burnout.* Washington, D.C.: National Education Association.

Lakein, A. (1973). *How to take control of your time and life.* New York: Signet.

McIntyre, T. C. (1983). *Teacher stress and burnout: A review of research literature.* Charleston: Eastern Illinois University. (ERIC Documentation Service Reproduction No. ED 236 868.)

Schafer, W. (1978). *Stress, distress, and growth*. Davis, Calif.: Responsible Action.

Schwab, R. L. (1983). Teacher burnout: Moving beyond "psychobabble." *Theory into Practice*, 22 (1), 21–26.

Selye, H. (1974). *Stress without distress*. Philadelphia: J. B. Lippincott.

Walker, C. (1975). *Learn to relax: 13 ways to reduce tension*. Englewood Cliffs, N.J.: Prentice-Hall.

Woolfolk, R., and Richardson, F. (1978). *Stress, sanity, and survival*. New York: Monarch.

26

The IRS Plan for Parents

Co-authored by Karol Cowell

When confronted in the classroom by disrespectful, defiant, or irresponsible behavior, we react by implementing a behavior management program that provides consequences for this misbehavior while insuring that appropriate actions are reinforced. Parents, for the most part, have not had the professional training afforded us and do not have a systematic support system available as we do in the schools. When they are faced with noncompliant behavior on the part of their child, some respond in a manner that is harsh and punitive in nature, and others feel helpless and complain that they have "lost control" of their children. Their behavior results in the youth's continued rebellious behavior and intensified feelings of disappointment, frustration, or embarrassment. Guilt, shame, anger, and resentment tear at the fabric of the family structure, deteriorating family interaction into a pathological state.

What can a teacher do to assist the parents in developing an effective, comprehensive parenting system that is responsible for caring? How can we help parents change the course of their child-rearing practices when our contacts with them usually are only periodic phone calls and infrequent face-to-face meetings? A frequently used strategy is to set up a home-based contingency management program. (See references at the end of this chapter.) In this approach, the student's classroom behavior determines the amount of reinforcement received at home. Although these programs may improve in-school performance and behavior, and increase positive interactions at home, they are not capable of rearranging aberrant interaction patterns and promoting effective, directive, positive parenting.

The Investment and Reward System (IRS) includes the home-school component of other programs while going beyond them to extend help to the parents in developing appropriate behavior management skills and promoting healthy family interaction patterns. This program has been used successfully with youths described by their parents as being incorrigible, disrespectful, troublemakers, delinquents, and "black sheep." Their behaviors ranged from disrespect and sibling rivalry to violence, drug usage, and running away from home. Feedback from the families indicated that parents, siblings, and the student of concern all found the program to be fair and effective. The parents felt "in control," and the youths involved felt that they were fairly and impartially treated and were recognized for their assistance and accomplishments at home and school. Both parties enjoyed a renewed sense of family. Additionally, teachers discovered a newly motivated student sitting in class, seeking better grades and demonstrating more desirable behavior.

The IRS plan utilizes the principles of banking to achieve these changes. It is organized in a manner similar to a personal financial system. For example, one works, earns a paycheck, deposits it in a bank account, writes checks on it, and/or saves part of it for future use. In the IRS program, the student earns points for completed daily/weekly responsibilities and enters them into his "bankbook." The deposits are verified during a family meeting, which also involves other planned interactions. The points are totaled on Thursdays (payday) and deposited into his account. The child may then choose to save the earned points or spend them on privileges that have assigned costs. A lack of earned points results in being "grounded." To motivate the student to participate, his allowance is also determined by the number of points earned.

How to Use the IRS Plan

The following instructional steps are for use by the parents and can be given or explained to them.

1. Obtain checkbooks, complete with checks, deposit slips, and transaction record sheets. These are usually available free of charge from local banks.

2. Develop your own record sheet to be sure that your child's recording of earned/spent points is accurate.

3. Call a family meeting. You should lead the meeting unless a third party facilitator (e.g., teacher, neighbor) would be beneficial.

4. Explain the program in a calm, assertive voice. Tell your child that you love him and cannot allow him to continue to act in this way. Explain that in order to earn privileges such as television, telephone, dances, and time with friends, he must complete school and household responsibilities that are worth a certain number of points.

5. List on paper the daily and weekly duties that must be completed by your child (e.g., vacuum, clean room, make bed, wash dishes, go to church, pass weekly test in math, etc.).

6. Have your child list the activities in which he wants to participate (e.g., friends over, use of car, going to the shopping mall, staying overnight at friend's house, etc.).

7. Negotiate point values for the desired duties and privileges. List these on paper (see Figures 1 and 2). Your child's allowance can be included in this program, making him responsible for paying for earned privileges (e.g., going for a meal after school with friends, going to a football game). Assign a certain money value to each point earned (e.g., 5 cents for each point).

Weekly Responsibilities

Making bed (daily)	2 pts.	Take laundry to basement	5 pts.
Vacuum room (weekly)	5 pts.	Respectful of family	
Dust room (w)	5 pts.	members	5 pts.
Change sheets (w)	5 pts.	Clean bathroom (w)	5 pts.
Remove dishes		Closing windows (d)	1 pt.
from room (d)	2 pts.	Turning out unused	
		lights (d)	1 pt.

Extra Credit Responsibilities

(All positive points)

A on a paper or test	20 pts.	Participation in a family	
B on a paper or test	15 pts.	activity (camping,	
C on a paper or test	10 pts.	movie, picnic,	
A on report card	100 pts.	etc.) (per event)	10 pts.
B on report card	50 pts.	Daily Family Conference	1 pt.
C on report card	25 pts.	Do dishes (d)	1 pt.
One week perfect		Laundry (per load)	5 pts.
school attendance	10 pts.	Dust living room	3 pts.
Being involved in an		Vacuum	5 pts.
extracurricular activity		Read a "parent-	
(school, church,		approved" book	10 pts.
community)			
(per week)	5 pts.		

(Negatives only)

D on report card	−50 pts.
F on report card	−100 pts.
On phone after	
10:00 P.M.	−5 pts.

Figure 1 Point Values for Weekly Responsibilities

Have boyfriend over for a visit	10 pts.
Go to visit boyfriend (per visit)	20 pts.
Date with boyfriend	30 pts.
Stay overnight at a friend's	25 pts.
Have an overnight guest	15 pts.
Go to a ball game	20 pts.
Go to McDonald's after school	5 pts.
Go to a movie with friends	15 pts.
Go out with friends (for soda or similar brief activity)	15 pts.
Go shopping	15 pts.
Go to a rock concert	300 pts.

Figure 2 Privilege Prices

8. Set a daily family meeting time and distribute the materials to your child. At future meetings, a topic of discussion will open or close each meeting (see Figure 3). Each family member must, in turn, speak to the topic.

9. Start the program. Your child should enter points for completed tasks in his bankbook. He should inform you of duties performed by telling you or leaving notes in a certain place. You should inspect and verify that your child has performed the duty to your satisfaction. Compare totals at the nightly meetings. On Thursday ("payday") your child is presented with his earned allowance. He may write checks at any time to spend earned points for privileges, but he must never overdraw his account. *Never* make loans. Your child must *earn* his privileges and allowance.

Activities and Discussion Questions

1. What can parents do if their child refuses to engage in this program? (Answers are in the Appendix.)

I know something good about you and it is _____
If I could change something about you it would be _____
The nice thing about you is _____
What can I do to help your self-esteem?
What I like most about you is _____
What I see you going through now is _____
What means the most to me in our relationship is _____
"Trigger words" you use that irritate me are _____
What are your emotional needs concerning me?
I thought I knew everything about you until _____
What would you like to see changed in our family?
What can I do to help meet your ego needs?
This is the way I feel about sharing the responsibilities of being a family
    member _____
I perceive our relationship to each other as _____
The kind of family life I want is _____
My view of myself physically is _____
Some inner resources I would like to develop are _____
What are some areas we can rediscover as points of sharing?
How am I doing at recognizing, supporting, and sharing in your feel-
    ings and ideas?
How am I doing at listening to what you have to say?
A recent thing you did that pleased me was _____

Figure 3 Family Conference Topics

2. Before the first payday, the child asks for money which
   he says he's already earned by completing various responsibilities. What can be done in this situation? (Answers are in the Appendix.)

3. Practice the explanation of the program to your child (step
   4).

4. Design your own record sheet (see step 2).

5. Devise a list of daily and weekly responsibilities (see steps
   5 and 7) similar to that in Figure 1.

6. In some cases, daily meetings do not seem to be feasible

due to varying schedules. What can be done? (Answer is in the Appendix.)

For More Information

McIntyre, T., and Cowell, K. C. (Unpublished manuscript submitted for publication). The I.R.S. (investment and reward system) plan for helping families cope with non-compliant, defiant children. (Available from Thomas McIntyre, 151 77th Street, Niagara Falls, New York 14304)

Home Support of Schools

Coleman, R. G. (1973). A procedure for fading from experimenter-school-based to parent-home-based control of classroom behavior. *Journal of School Psychology, 11,* 71–79.

Schumaker, J. B., Jovell, M. F., and Sherman, J. A. (1977). An analysis of daily report cards and parent-managed privileges in the improvement of adolescent's classroom performance. *Journal of Applied Behavior Analysis, 10,* 449–464.

Taylor, V. L., Cornwell, D. D., and Riley, M. T. (1984). Home-based contingency management programs that teachers can use. *Psychology in the Schools, 21* (3), 368–374.

Trice, A. D., Parker, F. C., Furrow, F., and Iwata, M. M. (1983). An analysis of home-contingencies to improve school behavior with disruptive adolescents. *Education and Treatment of Children, 6* (4), 389–399.

27

Working with Black Streetcorner and Minority Youth

By Herbert L. Foster

Most teachers begin their careers with very little, if any, coursework or practical experience regarding how to work with minority youths. However, most schools, especially in urban areas, have students from culturally different minority groups. These students may be poor, black, Hispanic, recent immigrants, or members of some other minority group. Some of these students behave in a "streetcorner" way. Usually, in an inner-city classroom, only two or three students in a class of thirty are streetcorner youngsters. These students enter the schools with a value system that is oppositional to the middle-class values held by the school's faculty and most of its students. They are more aggressive and manipulative. They bring a behavior and mindset, necessary for survival on the street corner, to the classroom where it confuses and frightens others.

In many urban areas, because educators do not understand a streetcorner youngster's behavior, teachers feel he represents the majority of students. Furthermore, because of a teacher's misunderstanding and misinterpretation of a streetcorner youngster's behavior, these youngsters are often subjected to the Emmett Till Syndrome[1] or are allowed to misbehave.

---

[1] Emmett Louis Till was a fourteen-year-old black youngster from Chi-

Because of this misunderstanding, there exists an overrepresentation of minority youths, particularly males, suspended from school and assigned to special education classes. This phenomenon starts in the community outside of the school where whites, nonwhite minorities, and poor youngsters, for the most part, grow up not really knowing one another. Consequently, unknowing, overt, or covert ethnocentrism and racism is reinforced.

To overcome school problems related to the streetcorner student, today's educator needs to understand the rules, regulations, and conditions of the ritual coping and survival techniques that urban lower-class males in general developed and black lower-class males in particular have refined in response to the majority culture that they believe has rejected them. Indeed, the streetcorner youngster has been conditioned by his environment to act in an aggressive and physical way, whether on the street or in the school. His language and behavior is often played out in our schools through concerns, games, or events, some of which include:

1. *Playing the Dozens*   This is talking in a negative way about someone in the student's family, usually his or her mother. Such behavior very often ends in a fight.

2. *Ribbin'*   Usually this is making fun of someone's clothing, body makeup, size, stature, or just about anything. The white middle-class term of *mocking out* is similar but causes fewer, if any, problems with middle-class students.

3. *Signifyin'*   A common form usually takes place when a student tells two different students that one said something negative about the other. Students will sometimes play the game on teachers.

---

cago, who, in 1955, went to Mississippi to visit with relatives. While visiting, he was lynched for not "knowing his place" in relation to a white woman. Hence, the Emmett Till Syndrome indicates a youngster being punished or disciplined out of proportion to his or her supposed inappropriate behavior.

4. *Woofin'*   This form of intimidation was used by Eddie Murphy in the movie *Beverly Hills Cop* when he yelled loudly at the desk clerk to get a room for which he did not have a reservation. In essence, the clerk bought his *woof ticket*. In school, a streetcorner youngster may attempt to sell a woof ticket to a teacher by blocking his way in the hall.

5. *Playing the "Cat" or "Gorilla"*   A youngster may want a pass from a teacher. To get the pass, he may first try to sweet talk the teacher, referring to her pretty dress. If that approach does not work, he may start yelling and throwing his body around.[2]

Because of racist psychosexual beliefs and expectations that so many whites have about culturally different youth in general, and black males in particular, the streetcorner behavior and language of some of these students creates a fear and threat to many teachers. Very often, this misunderstanding and misinterpretation of the streetcorner behavior, as noted earlier, results in suspension or placement in special education.

Additionally, there are urban, suburban, and rural youngsters who are equivalent to the streetcorner youngster in relation to the inability of educators to understand and work with them. For example, in Buffalo, New York, special education students are negatively referred to as *rumps* and *woodies* by their fellow students and some teachers. In some suburban, rural, and urban schools these youngsters are referred to as *bo bos, brews, burnouts, drakes, freaks, greasers, grubies, hard kids, heads, hoods, project kids, rats, rocks, sweathogs, titeres,* or *vokies*. The ostracization by the "school system" of these students reinforces their behavior as they strive to preserve their self-concept, sometimes rebelling against authority.

---

[2] For additional examples, see H. L. Foster, *Ribbin', jivin', and playin' the dozens: The persistent dilemma in our schools*, 2nd ed. Cambridge, MA: Ballinger, 1986.

Furthermore, as this behavior is layed out in the classroom, a mismatch often results between the urban lower-class youngster's concept and expectation of the teacher's behavior and role as compared with the teacher's concept and expectation of his or her teaching behavior and role.

Techniques for Working with Culturally Different Youth

1. Avoid a rigid-punitive or ignoring-passive approach to teaching this youngster. If teacher's could (a) come to grips with their conscious or unconscious racist and or ethnocentric feelings about these youngsters, and (b) assiduously become more familiar with their language and behavior, they could then work with these students on a more even and fair approach and make desirable and appropriate discipline and academic demands. Indeed, what has gone on currently just has not worked for anyone.

2. Do not use the youth's upbringing or racial background as an excuse for accepting inappropriate behavior. No one benefits by allowing the student to continue his inappropriate behavior. For example, many white administrators and teachers will make excuses, from "I don't want him to catch a cold," to "It is part of his cultural background," for allowing black male students to keep their hats on in school.

3. Insure that classroom rules and consequences apply equally to all students in your classroom. Do not play favorites or fail to enforce rules for some students.

4. Explain why you enforced your rules and why a different behavior is more appropriate.

5. Change your interaction style. Become familiar with the language and behavior of your students. (However, the

suggestion is not being made that teachers begin to speak and behave as their students speak and behave.) Such understanding and behavior on the part of the educators will hopefully assist them in better understanding these students. It will also help students to master another repertoire of language and behavior that is more appropriate for the school and work setting. Helping these students to become flexible in this manner provides them with the skills required to function better within society as a whole.

Activities and Discussion Questions

1. With a number of your fellow students, discuss the group names (i.e., *greasers*), behavior, and dress of the students from your high school days who were placed in special education or were often in trouble with school authorities.

2. Make up a dictionary of at least twenty-five words considered to be "black English."

3. Watch a few episodes of *Hill Street Blues*, *Moonlighting*, or other television programs and record any words or phrases that may be black English. Label them as being examples of "Shuckin," "Jivin'," "Woofin'," and so on. Translate these words into Standard American English.

4. Listen to your minority students in class. Write down some of their cultural phrases and words. Identify them as being examples of "Shuckin," "Jivin'," and so on. Translate these words or phrases into Standard American English.

5. If you heard a black student talking about "droppin' a dime" on another student, what would this student be suggesting? (Answer is in the Appendix.)

6. Participate in a class discussion around the feelings and prejudices that you have heard about the various ethnic, religious, racial, or social-class groups in your community. Include in your discussion whether any of the comments you have heard about any of these groups are accurate or inaccurate.

7. Complete a research paper covering the problems faced by your ancestors when they were immigrants.

8. Research and then participate in a class discussion about at least two of the events or games related to streetcorner behavior that were mentioned in this chapter.

9. Discuss the differences between how a teacher, as a professional, and a blue-collar worker are expected to carry out his or her work responsibilities.

10. With a group, describe and discuss at least one positive and one negative incident that happened between you and a teacher in high school. Include in the discussion how you will make sure your teaching style and behavior will reflect only the positive experiences you had in high school.

11. Discuss various modes of teacher dress. What assumptions do we make about those who dress in any of the various styles? Also interview a number of streetcorner students about their feelings about how their teachers dress.

12. When teaching a lesson, include several of your students' phrases. Does your use of these phrases appear to help the students grasp the concept, motivate them, or distract them?

13. Have one of your student's parents escort you and a friend through his or her neighborhood, exposing you and your friend to gathering places, stores, restaurants, and the like. With your friend, compare differences between your

observations in your student's neighborhood and your neighborhood.

14. To better understand your students' experiences before coming to school, record the buses and/or trains they take to get to and from school. On a few mornings and afternoons, ride the same public transportation your students ride. Discuss with your fellow teachers your experiences and feelings about your trips.

15. In a group discussion, discuss to what extent culturally different students should be allowed to use their language in oral discussions and written assignments.

For More Information

Foster, H. L. (1975). Don't be put on! Learn about the games kids play. *Today's Education, 64* (3), 50–52, 54.

Foster, H. L. (1986). *Ribbin', jivin' and playin' the dozens: The persistent dilemma in our schools,* 2nd ed. Cambridge, Mass.: Ballinger.

Kochman, T. (1981). *Black and white: Styles in conflict.* Chicago: University of Chicago Press.

Kochman, T. (1972). *Rappin' and stylin' out.* Chicago: University of Chicago Press.

Marotto, R. A. (1978). "Posin' to be chosen'": An ethnographic study of ten lower class black male adolescents in an urban high school. *Dissertation Abstracts International, 39,* 1234-A. (University Microfilms No. 7814236.)

Appendix:
Answers to Chapter
Activities and Discussion
Questions

Chapter 5:
Behavioral Recording

1. a. Frequency recording
   b. Frequency recording
   c. Frequency recording
   d. Frequency recording
   e. Duration recording
   f. Duration recording

2. a. The student will have buttocks in contact with the seat of the chair and will be facing toward the speaker. All four legs of the chair will be in contact with the floor. (Or something similar.)

   b. When verbally offered assistance by the teacher, the student shakes or lowers his head or verbally tells the teacher that he is not in need of assistance. (Or something similar.)

c. The student is not working on the presently assigned task and is not interacting with other students. (Or something similar.)

3. 1.8 occurrences per minute: $\dfrac{18 \text{ occurrences}}{10 \text{ minutes}} = 1.8$

4. 20 percent of the total time: $\dfrac{4 \text{ minutes}}{20 \text{ minutes}} = .20 = 20\%$

5. 33 percent of intervals: $\dfrac{5 \text{ occurrences}}{15 \text{ observations}} = .33 = 33\%$

7. Carry a string and tie knots in it, switch buttons or pennies from one pocket to another, tape an index card to your trouser leg and make marks with a pencil, carry an automatic counter, rip off pieces of paper and place them in your pocket, or any other useful idea.

Chapter 6: Assertive Discipline

1. a. Assertive. The teacher actively reinforced the desired behavior.

   b. Nonassertive (with a hint of hostility). The teacher allowed Mary to continue working after she was told to clean up. The teacher is now becoming a bit perturbed.

   c. Nonassertive (with a hint of hostility). Teacher feels helpless and makes no attempt to control inappropriate behavior. His or her retaliation is to insult the students.

   d. Hostile. The teacher bullied the bully, thus modeling inappropriate behavior and indicating that the use of force is acceptable in handling disagreements.

   e. Nonassertive. The teacher and the aide could be roaming around the room or observing the class while frequently reinforcing desired behavior.

f. Nonassertive. The teacher is not reacting to undesired behavior, perhaps due to a feeling of helplessness or not knowing what to do in that situation.

g. Assertive. The teacher told Jamie what *not* to do, then told her what *to* do through the use of the choice technique.

h. Assertive. Louise was reinforced through verbal praise and by having her composition shown to someone she views positively.

i. Nonassertive. Hank was not given a consequence or even a warning for his behavior. He also was not told what he *should* be doing. As with most of these examples, the tone of voice has much to do with whether the statement is hostile, nonassertive, or assertive.

j. Hostile. The student was berated by the teacher.

k. Assertive. The student was told what *not* to do and then provided with the desired actions.

l. Hostile. Instead of verbally reinforcing the student, the teacher responded in a mean manner. However, if this same statement was given in a friendly, humorous manner, it could become an assertive response.

m. Assertive. The student was actively rewarded for his near-perfect product.

n. Assertive. Knowing that Peter would be embarrassed by public praise, the teacher privately delivered a positive consequence.

2. a. Your response should tell the students to desist in their misconduct and direct them to attend. Other assertive interventions are also acceptable.

b. To prevent possible legal repercussions of negative parental feedback, Larry should be sent to the school nurse. If a nurse is not available, the pupil should be sent to the main office to insure that an administrator is aware of the possible illness.

c. The same precautions as above still apply. However, you may wish to indicate that the work must be completed later that day, over night, or upon return to class. This will help to prevent bogus excuses of this manner.

d. Many assertive responses are appropriate here. A gentle tone of voice and a suggestion that the two of you talk about this matter might avoid an extreme confrontation. Other teachers might directly confront this behavior. It is important that you know your students and how each responds to various interventions.

e. Diana should be informed that she must return to her seat and raise her hand before receiving any assistance. You should then "catch her being good" by giving her the requested assistance immediately, or by telling her that you are glad to see her hand raised and that you will get to her in turn after helping others who had raised their hands before her.

Chapter 8: The 10-R Technique

1. Return to the relaxation step and restart from there. (Or any other workable idea.)

2. a. Physically lead Dan toward the mat.

   b. Physically restrain Dan until he is relaxed and agrees to walk to the mat.

   c. Have an alternative plan ready (e.g., loss of privileges, send to office, etc.).
   (Or any other practical, workable plan.)

3. Make a wall chart with steps 1, 2, 3, 4, 5, 7, and 8 listed vertically. A paper clip, marker, or student's picture can

be moved along the side of the chart to indicate which step is presently being implemented. Steps 6, 9, and 10 can be remembered by the teacher. Pictures or drawings might be used in place of words on the chart to assist nonreaders. (Or any other workable idea.)

Chapter 9: Shaping

1. b, d, a, e, c

2. More substeps:

   Willy will be in the same yard as a puppy on a leash.

   Willy will pet a puppy on a leash.

   Willy will play with a puppy.

   Willy willl play with a gentle, medium-sized dog.

   (Or any other series of logical steps.)

3. a. Desired behavior: Rose will participate in Show and Tell.

   Present behavior: Rose does not participate at all.

   Substeps: (1) Rose will bring an item to school and show it to the teacher.

   (2) When asked by the teacher to show the item, Rose will hold up the item at her desk without speaking.

   (3) Rose will answer questions about an item held up at her desk.

   (4) Rose will tell about an item from her desk.

   (5) Rose will tell about an item while standing near her desk.

   (6) Rose will tell about an item from the

front of the room while a friend or the teacher stands near her.

(7) Rose will tell about an item from the front of the room without another person present as support.

(Or any other workable sequence of steps.)

b. Desired behavior: Andy will spontaneously raise his hand and volunteer an answer.

Present behavior: Andy does not raise his hand or volunteer answers.

Substeps: (1) Andy will answer a question asked of him as the teacher asks questions in order around a group.

(2) Andy will answer a question asked of him by the teacher who is not asking questions in any specific order.

(3) When asked by the teacher if he knows the answer, Andy will provide the answer if he knows it.

(4) Same as above, but if Andy indicates that he knows the answer, the teacher will tell him to raise his hand to show that he knows.

(5) Andy will raise his hand if he knows the answer when the teacher gives him a nonverbal prompt (e.g., raised eyebrow, wink).

(Or any other workable sequence of steps.)

Chapter 11: Token Economies

6. Give each student his own distinctive type of token or color code your tokens. You could also keep a personal record of tokens given to each student.

7. Choose very novel tokens or keep a personal record of tokens given to each student.

Chapter 12: DRO

1. a. *Spits*   The student propels saliva from his mouth by pursing his lips (or something similar).

   b. *Curses*   At a volume audible to a staff member, the student uses a word that he was previously told not to use (or something similar).

   c. *Rocking*   While sitting, the student moves his body from the waist to a position 30° from upright position and returns to the upright position. Each cycle counts as "one" (or something similar).

   d. *Throws objects*   Using arm movement, the student propels an object from his hand(s) that travels at least one foot from his body (or something similar).

   e. *Slams top of desk*   The student opens the top of his desk at least three inches and forceably closes it to produce a noise which is determined by a staff member to be too loud (or something similar).

   f. *Turns out classroom lights*   Without staff permission, the student turns off the classroom lights by manipulating the light switch (or something similar).

   g. *Leaves work area*   Without staff permission, the student ventures outside of a defined work area (or something similar).

   h. *Screams*   The student vocalizes at a level deemed by a staff member to be too loud (or something similar).

   i. *Hand flapping*   The student wobbles his hand(s) back and forth at the wrist at least twice per second (or something similar).

   j. *Bites self*   The student closes his teeth on any part of his hands or arms (or something similar).

   k. *Mouthing*   The student places any object into contact with his lips or mouth (or something similar).

2. a. (15 × 60 seconds) ÷ 12 times = 900 seconds − 12 times = 75 seconds = 1 minute and 15 seconds

   b. (10 × 60 seconds) ÷ 16 times = 600 seconds − 16 times = 37.5 seconds

   c. (25 × 60 seconds) ÷ 7 times = 1500 seconds − 7 times = 214 seconds (approx.) = 3 minutes and 34 seconds

   d. (20 × 60 seconds) ÷ 3 times = 1200 seconds − 3 times = 400 seconds = 6 minutes and 40 seconds

3. You can round the number to the nearest convenient time (e.g., 6 minutes and 57 seconds rounds off to 7 minutes). Times should be reduced unless the calculated interval is *very* close to a longer convenient time period.

   OR   Set a timer to go off at the end of the interval.

   OR   Make an audiotape that has a tone or the word *Now* inserted at the correct time intervals.

4. Count *all* the outbursts of *all* undesired behaviors and then calculate the appropriate time period in which any and all these behaviors must be withheld.

5. Collect data on behavior outbursts for all students. Use only the shortest time period for *all* of the students. Although some students will get reinforced by withholding their behavior more often than is necessary, it does make group monitoring more manageable.

6. Count each five-second duration of the behavior as one occurrence of the behavior. If the behavior endured for seventeen seconds, count it as three occurrences.

Chapter 16:
Transactual Analysis

1. a. Parent

   b. Parent

c. Child

d. Parent

e. Child

f. Adult

g. Adult

h. Child

i. Child

j. Child

k. Parent

l. Child

m. Parent

2. a. Parent to child

b. Adult to adult

c. Child to any state

d. Child to any state

e. Adult to adult

f. Parent to child (or possibly another parent)

g. Parent to child

h. Parent to child (possibly chosen by adult state)

i. Parent to child (chosen by adult state)

j. Parent to child (possibly chosen by adult state)

k. Adult to adult

l. Child to parent (possibly chosen by adult state)

m. Parent to child (chosen by adult state)

n. Parent to child

o. Adult to adult

p. Parent to child (chosen by adult state)

q. Child to any state

r. Parent to child

s. Child to any state

t. Parent to child (chosen by adult state)

u. Child to child (chosen by adult state)

v. Child to child (possibly chosen by adult state)

w. Parent to any state

Be aware that the answers to the above items may vary depending on the voice tone and actions of the speaker. Also many of the above, even though they represent the child or parent, were chosen by the adult state.

Chapter 17:
Nondirective Counseling

1. a. Open question

b. Leading statement

c. Reflection

d. Closed question

e. Clarification

f. Open question

g. Leading statement

h. Summarization (followed by an open question)

i. Reflection

j. Clarification or reflection depending on what was said previously by the student

Chapter 18:
Life Space Interview

1. a. Regulation of behavior and social traffic. The teacher set firm guidelines in a calm manner.

b. Drain off frustration acidity. The teacher restrained the student until emotions were subdued and then explained the rule.

c. Umpire services. The teacher made a decision based on information available to him or her.

d. Support for the management of emotions. The teacher helped the student to cope temporarily with the problem and return to the classroom routine.

e. Communication maintenance. The teacher kept communication flowing by talking about a subject that took the student's mind off the crisis situation.

f. Drain off frustration acidity. The teacher directed the student to start to calm himself and remedy a class rule that was violated.

g. Umpire services. Based on information available, the teacher made a rational decision.

h. Support for the management of emotions. The teacher provided support in a moment of need.

i. Communication maintenance. The student used a favorite topic of interest to open lines of communication and then redirected the conversation toward the paper grade.

j. Regulation of behavior and social traffic. The teacher demanded appropriate classroom behavior.

Chapter 19:
Classroom Conferencing

4. Although your decision will depend on your personal comfortability and school policy, the following guidelines may apply:

a. *Kicking* This is physical contact, as is hitting. It is probably unacceptable.

b. *Spitting* Although less injurious than physical contact, it is probably unacceptable in educational environments.

c. *Give them the "finger" while cursing at them* Although it involves no physical contact, it is probably not acceptable in school.

d. *Calling the teacher* Much better than the previous ideas, but the teacher may not always be available, it could create an image of a "tattler" for the student, and may keep the student from personally dealing with the problem.

e. *Calling others names in return* Provides retaliation, but sinks the student to the level of his tormentors. It may also escalate the situation.

f. *Ignoring* Certainly this is the best idea thus far, but is it feasible for this particular student? Can she really "change her stripes" that drastically?

Chapter 20: Play Therapy

2. a. "The big dog is biting the little dog."
"He's biting the smaller dog."
"Biting."
"One dog is biting the other."
(Or something similar.)

b. "Bad."
"The baby is bad. She messed her diapers."
"The baby went to the bathroom in her diapers."
(Or something similar.)

c. "You're a good cook."
"__(name)__ is a good cook."
"You can cook anything."
(Or something similar.)

d. "He's still OK."
"They thought he was dead, but they missed."
"The soldier wasn't hurt."
(Or something similar.)

4. a. "The cars are driving around." (Or something similar.)
"The cars have loud engines." (Or something similar.)
"The cars crashed." (Or something similar.)

b. "_(name)_ is a baby." or "_(name)_ is sucking on his bottle." (Or something similar.)
"The bottle is empty. That makes that baby sad." (Or something similar.)
"The baby is happy that the bottle is full again." (Or something similar.)

c. "The man thinks the lady is bad." or "Bad." (Or something similar.)
"The man hit the lady." or "The man jumped at the woman." (Or something similar.)
"The lady wants the man to stop. He hurt her." or "It hurts." (Or something similar.)

5. a. Allow the child to continue. Do not suggest the use of other colors or changing to another activity. You might comment on the child's actions. Two possible responses are: "_(name)_ is using the black crayon." or "_(name)_ is scribbing very fast and hard."

b. Allow the child to gaze out the window. Do not suggest another activity. Possible teacher responses are: "_(name)_ is looking out the window." Or perhaps use a leading statement (see Chapter 17, entitled Nondirective Counseling) such as: "I wonder what _(name)_ is watching." Do not pry any further, however.

c. Do not comment on the beauty of the picture. (Remember: We do not provide judgments in play therapy.) Possible teacher responses might be: "_(name)_ has painted a picture. It has many colors." Or use a leading statement such as "I wonder what the picture is about." Do not continue to pry, however.

d. If this is beyond acceptable limits, calmly tell the student that he must stop and wash. If this is not beyond limits set by you, then you may describe the child's actions. Possible teacher responses are: "__(name)__ is wiping paint on himself." or "__(name)__ is painting himself."

Chapter 23: Legal Considerations

1. False. A teacher is not expected to be clairvoyant or possess abnormal powers in the supervision of students. However, the key question is whether or not the teacher's absence from an area was based on the actions of a reasonably prudent person. In deciding this, the court would consider such factors as the age of the student, the handicapping condition of the student, the activity prior to leaving, safety measures taken prior to leaving the area, the propensity for the unsupervised students to have difficulties related to conduct or environment, and the reason and length of the teacher's absence. Simply stated, stay in your supervisory areas unless you leave for an educationally sound reason.

2. False. Child abuse, under federal and state statutes, relates to a parent or guardian relationship. A teacher who applies corporal punishment in an inappropriate or excessive fashion may face battery charges or a civil suit.

   If you use corporal punishment when it is not permissible under state legislation or local rules, your local district, based upon the particular state's court standards, may find your actions irremediable or insubordinate, and pursue dismissal. If your conduct is found to be remediable, the district may issue a remediation plan, or a disciplinary warning, or both. If the IEP limits or precludes corporal punishment, parents may act in the interest of their child and attempt civil action. If it specifically provides for corporal punishment, all procedural steps must be observed. However, the parents may still pursue action, claiming the signature on the IEP does not waive the rights of the student to entertain legal action.

If you resort to corporal punishment, certain questions must be answered. First, do your state, district, *and* building guidelines permit its use? Second, do limitations exist in the IEP that preclude or restrict the use of corporal punishment? Third, have you followed the procedureal steps from court decisions and your district and building rules?

Common sense and specific court cases dictate that local policies address the instrument(s) that may be used, who may apply the punishment and to what part of the body, the number of times a paddle or other instrument may be applied, and prohibitions against administering punishment when angry, to a member of the opposite sex, or with more than moderate force. Further, you are well advised to maintain a record of the incident and punishment, and to provide the administrator with a copy.

If corporal punishment is permissible, after considering the above, then the following procedural guidelines must be observed:

a. A knowledgeable witness must be present.

b. Unless the student's actions are so gross as to ignore progressive discipline steps, other forms of discipline should have first been attempted.

c. The student must be aware that his actions could lead to corporal punishment.

d. A narrative describing the events leading to the corporal punishment and the punishment process must be provided to the parents or guardians upon their request.[1]

However, be aware that a number of states permit parents to provide a written statement prohibiting the inflicting or corporal punishment on their child. Investigate whether a statement to this effect has been written for this pupil. You should also be careful not to confuse corporal punishment with restraint. Restraint is allowed to prevent a student from harming you, himself, or property. A good local policy defines restraint so that it is not confused with physical discipline. In applying restraint, you are limited to using only the force necessary to neutralize the danger. Excessive force moves one into the arena of the criminal act of battery. In reviewing corporal punishment, you must realize that evidence suggests questions regarding liability. Consequently, its place in the classroom is suspect.

3. False. Simply stated, parents cannot waive the rights of their children to sue for damages and therefore relieve teachers from their liability for negligence. The same may not necessarily be true, however, for the parents who sign the waivers. No correct answer on this question exists, even if you were concerned with a specific state; however, public policy normally prohibits preexempting an institution from it liability for negligence.[2] In states where consideration is given to waivers, the waivers are strictly construed and require that a precise definition of the limits of liability be provided.[3] Your best bet is to select field trip sites carefully and to provide additional adult supervision as needed. Numerous legal decisions exist that tie teachers

---

[1] *Baker* v. *Owen*, 423 U.S. 907.
[2] 66 Am. Jur. 2nd Release 514, 33 (1971).
[3] *Gross* v. *Sweet*, 424 N.Y.S. 3d 365 (1979).

to activities off school grounds or nonschool-related activities. For example, courts have ruled that a field trip or a school-sanctioned activity off school grounds can result in liability based upon the potential for injury and the need for a given level of supervision.[4] However, you are not blessed with foresight or omnipotence, and consequently cannot anticipate all possible happenings and supervise each occurrence.

A second illustration involves the pupil who makes an item in a class, takes it home, and through its use, a person or property is damaged. If the item were made without parental approval and had a high potential for risk (e.g., crossbow), the instructor's liability would be greatly enhanced. Reasonably prudent teachers are expected to know the potential dangers of items made in school.

4. True. Although various states have established different criteria to use in establishing and maintaining a time-out room or space, the discipline technique is well accepted as long as the rules are followed. Confusion sometimes arises when a state's mental health agency has rules conflicting with or in excess of school practices. You must turn to your own state guidelines, if they exist, to determine this relationship. Without guidelines, you would be wise to build the time-out practice along the lines of local policy as well as the IEP. Additionally, follow acceptable practices related to provision for such concerns as access and exit, proper supervision, and appropriate time allocations in a time-out area.

5. False. With the disclaimer that unless a local policy or state legislation exists to the contrary, the United States Supreme Court has ruled that school personnel, acting with reasonable suspicion, may search a student's locker or

---

[4] *Mancho* v. *Field Museum of Natural History*, 283 N.W. 2d 899 (Ill. 1972).

desk or request the student to empty a purse or clothing.[5] *Reasonable suspicion* is a nebulous and poorly defined term. Consequently, unless immediate danger or the potential for the student to remove the object of the search exists, you would be advised to allow the principal or supervisor to conduct the search. In any case, consider the age of the student; the preponderance of the problem to which the search relates; the propensity of the pupil to be involved with either drugs, weapons, contraband, or the like; and the strength of the factors that have made you believe a search is necessary. Procure an adult witness, and if the object is found, secure it for school or police personnel.

Never strip-search a student unless eminent danger exists.[6] In that case, solicit the student's cooperation first and strictly follow all school policies. However, it is best to leave this procedure to the police.

6. True. What you say or write, even if you believe it to be true, may be grounds for a civil suit. Defamatory statements, whether they are written (libel) or spoken (slander), that expose a student to disgrace, ridicule, or shame require that a third party be involved. You cannot defame by what you say or write to the student if he is the only one who receives the comments. Damages for slander or libel will vary based on how the damage to one's reputation has damaged him in the community of interest and the personal anguish involved. When statements are provided within a legal investigation or as a necessary component in the performance of one's job, you will be given qualified privilege, conditional on your acting without malice in communicating what you believe to be true to a party who has a right to the information. Gossip in the teachers' lounge, unfounded statements on records, and

---

[5] *New Jersey* v. *T.L.O.*, 105 S. Ct. 733 (1985).
[6] *Doe* v. *Renfrow*, 631 F2d 9 (7th circuit 1980).

the use of the information with malicious intent do not receive immunity, qualified or otherwise.

Incidentally, a low grade can subject a student to some adversity; however, courts have historically sided with the teacher. Courts typically refuse to review the manner in which grades are formulated and the standards involved.

7. False. However, you must be able to draw a fine line in interpreting this issue. Most standards for grades do not include discipline as a criteria. If you can tie discipline to a legitimate objective of the course as related to its content, though, you may find your decision to reduce a grade upheld. But if you have failed to establish this rationale, you are in danger of denying a student access to his or her property interest or grade.

The most common occurrence relates to a grade sanction for an unexcused absence. The key in cases that see such sanctions upheld is that teachers emphasized their purpose for attendance policies as educational and not disciplinary. In one case, a student's unexcused absences were the basis of grade reduction according to a policy. The court stated, "The policy decision that academic credentials should reflect more than the product of quizzes . . . constitutes an academic judgment about academic requirements."[7] Key to this case were written grade policies that established the relationship between academic learning and attendance. Before using individual policies related to grade reductions, you would be well advised to obtain building (if not district) approval.

8. False. Watch this one carefully, though. By statute, a teacher is usually not authorized to suspend a student unless an emergency necessitates that due process (legal

---

[7] *Campbell* v. *Board of Education and New Milford*, 475 A. 2d 289 (Conn. 1984).

steps) be put aside until the emergency is addressed. Should you elect to remove a student from your class or recommend suspension or expulsion from school, then due process must be considered. Short-time suspensions under P.L. 94–142 have been sustained by federal courts, which hold that when brief in duration, a suspension is not a change in placement and a staffing is not necessary to determine the relationship of the action leading to short-term suspension and the handicapping condition. A federal district court noted: "Such a brief period of enforced absence (five days), possibly equivalent to that often caused by a common cold, simply cannot be reasonably described as a change in a handicapped child's placement or termination of educational services to him."[8] However, long-term suspensions or expulsions require a staffing to determine the relationship of the handicapping condition to the actions leading to the exclusion of the pupil from access to his education—a fundamental property right.

9. False. You should avoid the misconception that a double standard exists regarding the disciplining of handicapped students in contrast with nonhandicapped pupils. As noted above, severe discipline (e.g., corporal punishment and exclusion from school) problems merit special concern. However, nothing in P.L. 94–142 exists that precludes application of routine disciplinary or classroom management measures.

Should specific disciplinary measures exist within an IEP, you are bound to honor those measures except when an emergency necessitates modification. You should document any such situation, as well as maintain an anecdotal file when discipline exceeds verbal warnings and if you

---

[8] See *Board of Education* v. *State Board of Education*, 531 F. Supp. 148 (C.D. Ill. 1982) as one example.

give reprimands that could be questioned as inappropriate as related to a student's handicapping condition.

Regarding the more inappropriate forms of behavior, you may wish to consider some alternatives proposed by Lichtenstein:

a. Use a building or district time-out program for temporary placement.

b. Set up an alternative program that stresses behavior modifications.

c. Use a halfway program to facilitate the transfer of handicapped students from special classes to the mainstreamed class.

d. Initiate an after-hours program for disruptive students.

e. Isolate students in a self-contained room to which the teacher comes to instruct the students.

f. Organize a work-study or cooperative education program for disruptive students.

g. Identify and employ resource help from specialists such as counselors and psychologists.[9]

Lichtenstein cautions that some of the above involve a change in placement and would necessitate appropriate staffings and revisions of the IEP. Unless gross abuse of the practice were to occur, these practices would be recognized as acceptable.

10. False. All cases regarding tort liability necessitate a look at the specific events for each case. However, unless you failed to take necessary precautions based on prior knowledge, or unless you acted in such an imprudent manner that you helped provide the action, you are on safe grounds.

---

[9] E. Lichtenstein, "Suspension, Expulsion, and the Special Education Student," *Phi Delta Kappan* 61 (1980): 459–461.

Teachers have protections that vary from state to state, but most states accord teachers *in loco parentis* status that minimizes liability in the supervision of students. Thus, a court must look to see if a teacher has grossly, willfully, or wantonly violated sound educational practices when a student injures another. Courts will thus consider if the four basic elements of a tort claim have been met:

a. A duty or obligation to conform to a certain standard of conduct, as to protect others against unreasonable risk

b. A failure on one's part to act in a manner that conforms to the standards of conduct required

c. Injury to another caused by failure to act in a manner required

d. Actual loss or damage to the person as a result of the injury.

The second item is the most important. It holds you to a standard of care based not only on appropriate supervisory techniques, but also standards that conform to local district policy, building rules and regulations, and specifics that may be built into an IEP. Should you ignore accepted practices or rules, you will be perceived to have been willful or wanton, having acted in careless disregard for the safety of others by ignoring basic measures of ordinary care. Should you deal with students who have a propensity to fight, your knowledge of this raises the standard of care you are to provide.

11. True. Your personal notes that you have elected not to share with a third party are private. This does not limit their being called forward under court order, but the Buckley Admendment does not allow parents the right to inspect your personal file.

Parents have the right to inspect their child's educational records and to address official complaints regarding the content of a student's permanent and temporary file material. Parents also have the right to allow third parties personal access to their child's educational records. For your part, consent is not required when you elect to share the child's records with other school personnel who have a legitimate educational need. Further, should another person need information to help protect the special education student, or to assure others are afforded protection in regard to the student, you may provide this information. Failure to provide such information could be construed as ignoring those actions characteristic of a prudent teacher.

Chapter 24: Mainstreaming

6. Conduct behavioral recording (see Chapter 5, entitled Behavioral Recording) on various behaviors. Compare these results with a so-called average student in the proposed regular education class. Are the findings similar? If so, this is evidence for the entry viewpoint.

Chapter 26: The IRS Plan

1. Make the child stay at home with no phone or television privileges until he or she agrees to engage in the program and earn points and privileges. If he or she leaves home, call the police or file a "person in need of supervision" form with the state.

2. Refuse to make a loan. Or, you may translate the points earned thus far into money and give it to the child. This money will be subtracted from the amount earned by payday. Do not make loans after the first week.

3. Meet as often as possible during the week. Between meetings, have one adult be responsible for inspection and assigning of points.

Chapter 27: Working with Black Streetcorner and Minority Youth

5. The student would be talking about telephoning someone and snitching or reporting on the other student. The expression originated when a phone call, in some places, still cost a dime.

Bibliography

AAMD (1981). *AAMD adaptive behavior scale (school edition)*. Monterey, CA: CTB/McGraw-Hill.

Aaron, T., and Beck, A. (1967). *Depression*. Philadelphia: University of Pennsylvania Press.

Abel, E. (1983). Marijuana and memory: Acquisition or retreival? In *Behavior and social effects of marijuana*. New York: MSS Information Corp.

Abrahamsen, D. (1980). *The psychology of crime*. New York: Columbia University Press.

Alabiso, F. P. (1977). *The hyperactive child in the classroom*. Springfield, IL: Charles C. Thomas.

Alcoholics Anonymous (1983). *Alcoholics anonymous*. United States of America: Alcoholics Anonymous World Service, Inc.

Aptic, J., and Conoley, J. (1973). *Childhood behavior disorders and emotional disturbance*. Englewood Cliffs, NJ: Prentice-Hall.

Avery, A. Teaching shy students: The role of the family life educator. *Family Relations, 981* (1), 39–43.

Awake (1983). Warning on video games. 30.

Baker, H., and Bayner, A. (1984). *Not just a skinny kid*. Highland Park, IL: National Association of Anorexia Nervosa.

Bakwin, M., and Bakwin, R. (1972). *Clinical management of behavior disorders in children*. Philadelphia: Saunders.

Barkley, R. A. (1982). *Hyperactive children: A handbook for diagnosis and treatment*. New York: Guilford Press.

Baron, Jason D. (1983). *Kids and drugs: A parent's handbook of drug abuse prevention and treatment*. New York: Putnam Publishing.

Bartol, C. R. (1980). *Criminal behavior: A psychological approach*. Englewood Cliffs, NJ: Prentice-Hall.

Bauer, B. (1983). *Bulimia: A model for group therapy*. Columbia: University of Missouri. (ERIC Document Reproduction Service No. ED 236 467).

Beck, A. (1967). *Depression: Causes and treatment*. Philadelphia: University of Pennsylvania Press.

Beck, T. (1981). Classroom attitudes: What are the warnings? *Elementary School Journal, 36,* 42–53.

Berndt, D. J., and Kaiser, C. F. (1983). *The lonely and gifted adolescent: Stress, depression, and anger*. Chicago: Annual Meeting of the Midwestern Psychological Association. (ERIC Document Reproduction Service No. ED 236 495).

Biehler, R. F. (1974). *Psychology applied to teaching*. Boston: Houghton Mifflin.

Bornstein, M. (1977). Social skills training for unassertive children: A multiple baseline analysis. *Journal of Applied Behavior Analysis, 1977, 10,* 185–195.

Bower, E., and Lambert, N. (1982). *Bower-Lambert scales*. Princeton, NJ: Educational Testing Service.

Boyd, L. (1980). Emotive imagery in the behavioral management of adolescent school phobia: A case approach. *School Psychology Review, 9,* 186–189.

Brinkley, G.; Goldberg, L.; and Kukar, J. (1982). *Your child's first journey*. Garden City Park, NY: Avery Publishing Group.

Broadhurst, D.; Edmunds, M.; and MacDicken, R. (1979). Recognizing child abuse and neglect in the early childhood program setting. *Early Childhood Programs, 13,* 19.

Bromberg, W. (1972). *Crime and the mind*. Westport, CT: Greenwood Press.

Brooks, J.; Lukoff, I.; and Whiteman, M. (1980). Initiation into adolescent marijuana use. *Journal of Genetic Psychology, 137,* 133–142.

Brown, L., and Hammill, D. (1978). *Behavior rating profile*. Austin, TX: Pro-Ed.

Bruch, H. (1978). *The golden cage*. Cambridge, MA: Harvard University Press.

Bruch, M. A. (1979). Client fear of negative evaluation and type of counselor response style. *Journal of Counseling Psychology, 26*, 37–44.

Bryan, T., and Bryan, J. (1975). *Understanding learning disabilities.* New York: Alfred Publishing Co.

Bucky, S. F. (1978). *The impact of alcoholism.* Center City, MN: Hazelden.

Bumpass, E. R.; Fagelman, F. D.; and Brix, R. J. (1983). Intervention with children who set fires. *American Journal of Psychotherapy, 37*, 328–345.

Burks, H. (1977). *Burks behavior rating scales.* Los Angeles: Western Psychological Services.

Burton, R. L., and Daly, M. J. (1983). Self-esteem and irrational beliefs: An exploratory investigation with implications for counseling. *Journal of Counseling Psychology, 30* (3), 361–366.

Buser, R. L.; Long, R.; and Tweedy, H. (1975). The who, what, why, and why not of student activity participation. *Phi Delta Kappan, 57*, 124–125.

Bush, R. (1980). *When a child needs help.* New York: Dell.

Bush, W., and Giles, M. (1977). *Aids to psycholinguistic teaching* (2nd ed.). Columbus, OH: Bell and Howell.

Bush, W., and Waugh, K. (1976). *Diagnosing learning disabilities.* Columbus, OH: Merrill.

Butler, R. A., and Whipple J. (1983). *The relationship of self-esteem to depressive cognition.* Anaheim: Annual Convention of the American Psychological Association. (ERIC Document Reproduction Service No. ED 240 469).

Cahalcon, D. (1970). *Problem drinkers.* San Francisco: Jossey Bass.

Callahan, L. (1979). *Screening withdrawn and depressed students in public schools.* Sacramento, CA: Sacramento Public Schools. (ERIC Document Reproduction Service No. ED 233 523).

Campbell, A.; Scaturro, J.; and Lickson, J. (1983). Peer tutors help autistic students enter the mainstream. *Teaching Exceptional Children, 15*, 64–69.

Canfield, J., and Wells, H. (1976). *100 ways to enhance self-concept in the classroom.* Englewood Cliffs, NJ: Prentice-Hall.

Carroll, C. (1970). *Alcohol: Use, nonuse and abuse.* Dubuque, IA: Wm. C. Brown.

Chen, A. (1982). Ask the experts. *Gifted Children Newsletter, 3*, 17–18.

Chernin, K. (1981). *The obsession: Reflections on the tyranny of slenderness.* New York: Harper Colophon Books.

Chess, S., and Massibi, M. (1978). *Principles and practices of child psychiatry.* New York: Plenum Press.

Clark, L.; Hughes, R.; and Nakashima, E. N. (1973). Behavior effects of marijuana: Experimental studies. In *Behavior and Social Effects of Marijuana.* New York: MSS Information Corp.

Clinebell, H. (1968). *Understanding and counseling the alcoholic.* New York: Abingdon Press.

Coffey, C. (1971). *Up the down road.* Omaha, NB: Pacific Press.

Cohen, J.; Millman, H.; and Schaefer, C. (1981). *Therapies for school behavior problems.* San Francisco Jossey-Bass.

Coleman, J. (1964). *Abnormal psychology and modern life* (3rd ed.). Glenview, IL: Scott, Foresman.

Conrad, P. (1976). *Identifying hyperactive children.* Lexington, MA: Heath.

Cox, C. M. (1976). Early mental traits of geniuses. In W. Dennis and M. Dennis (eds.), *The intellectually gifted.* New York: Grune and Stratton.

Darley, C., and Tinklenberg, J. (1974). Marijuana and memory. In L. Miller (ed.), *Marijuana: Effects on human behavior.* New York: Academic Press.

Davids, A. (1974). *Children in conflict: A casebook.* New York: Wiley.

Deffenbacher, J. L., and Kemper, C. C. (1974). Counseling test-anxious sixth graders. *Elementary School Guidance and Counseling, 9,* 22–29.

Derdeyn, A. (1983). Depression in childhood. *Child Psychiatry and Human Development, 14,* 16–29.

Deykin, E. (1984). Assessing suicidal intent and lethality. *Educational Horizons, 62,* 134–137.

Doane, M. (1983). *Famine at the feast: A therapist's guide to working with the eating disordered.* Washington, D.C.: National Institute of Education. (ERIC Document Reproduction Service No. ED 239 191).

Doll, R. C., and Fleming, R. S. (1966). *Children under pressure.* Columbus, OH: Merrill.

Dornbush, R.; Fink, M.; and Freedman, A. (1973). Marijuana, memory and perception. *Behavior and social effects of marijuana.* New York: MSS Information Corp.

Dowdall, C., and Colangelo, N. (1982). Underachieving gifted students: Review and implications. *Gifted Child Quarterly, 26,* 179–183.

Drummie, M. A. (1970). *A research report on New Brunswick school dropout in the academic year 1963–64.* New Brunswick: Department of Youth & Welfare. (ERIC Document Reproduction Service No. ED 029 939).

Dugan, S. P. (1976). *The behaviorally disordered child.* Handout. Special Education Institute.

Duhl, L. (1983). *Technology and learning disabilities.* Washington, D.C.: Office of Technology Assessment.

Ehrlich, V. Z. (1982). *Gifted children.* Englewood Cliffs, NJ: Prentice-Hall.

Eidelberg, W. (1968). *Encyclopedia of psychoanalysis.* New York: Free Press.

Empey, L., and Hubeck, S. (1971). *Explaining delinquency.* Lexington, MA: D. C. Heath Company.

Epstein, N. (1982). What is self-esteem and how can it be measured? Washington, D.C.: The Symposium on *Functioning and Measurement of Self-esteem.* August 27.

Faller, K. (1981). *Social work with abused and neglected children.* New York: The Free Press.

Fidel, R. (1981). Toxic substances and you. *Alcohol, tobacco, marijuana, and hard drugs.*

Fine, S., and Louie, D. (1979). Juvenile firesetters: Do the agencies help? *American Journal of Psychotherapy, 136,* 433–435.

Fischer, A. (1982). Do you stuff yourself one moment and starve yourself the next? *Seventeen, 41,* 106–107.

Frease, R. (1973). Delinquency, social class, and the schools. *Sociology and Social Research, 56,* 445–446.

Frumkes, L. (1982). The neurotic personality: Are you screwed up? *Bazaar, 115,* 148–152.

Gadow, K. (1979). *Children on medication: A primer.* Reston, VA: Council for Exceptional Children.

Gallant and Simpson (1976). *Depression.* New York: Spectrum Publications.

Garfinkel, P., and Moldofsky, H. (1980). The heterogeneity of anorexia nervosa. *Archives of General Psychiatry, 37,* 1036–1040.

Gaudry, E., and Spielberger, C. D. (1971). *Anxiety and educational achievement.* New York: John Wiley & Sons.

Gavain, R. (1954). *Understanding juvenile delinquency.* New York: Oxford Book Company.

Gaylin, W. (1968). *The meaning of despair: Psychoanalytic contributions to the understanding of depression.* New York: Holt, Rinehart & Winston.

Gearheart, B. R. (1976). *Teaching the learning disabled: A combined task-process approach.* St. Louis: C. V. Mosby.

Gholson, R., and Buser, R. (1981). Student activities: A guide for who is participating in what. *NASSP Bulletin, 65,* 43–47.

Giffin, P. (1980). *Social problems*. Boston: Allyn and Bacon.

Gillespie, C. (1977). *Your pregnancy month by month*. New York: Harper & Row.

Glueck, S., and Glueck, E. (1970). *Towards a typology of juvenile offenders*. New York: Grune & Stratton.

Goldenson, R. M. (1970). *The encyclopedia of human behavior: Psychology, psychiatry, and mental health* (Vol. 1). Garden City, NY: Doubleday.

Good Housekeeping (1982). Bulimia: The secret dieter's disease, *194*, 239.

Goode, E. (1970). *The marijuana smokers*. New York: Basic Books.

Goode, E. (1980). Marijuana. *Journal of Sociology, 3*, 124–133.

Gordon, S. R. (1979). *Science news of controversy: The case of marijuana*. (ERIC Document Reproduction Service No. ED 176 282).

Gresham, F. M., and Nagle, R. (1981). Treating school phobia using behavioral consultation: A case study. *School Psychology Review, 10*, 104–107.

Gruber, A. R.; Heck, E. T.; and Mintzer, E. (1981). Children who set fires: Some background and behavioral characteristics. *American Journal of Orthopsychiatry, 51*, 484–487.

Hagtvet, K. A. (1982). *A construct validation study of test anxiety: A discriminant validation of fear of failure, worry, and emotionality*. (ERIC Document Reproduction Series No. ED 222 535).

Halikas, J. A.; Goodwin, D. W.; and Guze, S. B. (1973). Marijuana effects: A survey of regular users. *Behavior and Social Effects of Marijuana*. New York: MSS Information Corp.

Hammill, D., and Meyers, P. (1969). *Methods for learning disorders*. New York: Wiley and Sons.

Hansteen, R.; Miller, R.; Loneero, L.; Reid, L.; and Jones, B. (1976). Effect of cannabis and alcohol on automobile driving and psychomotor tracing. *Annals of the New York Academy of Science, 282*, 240–255.

Hardy, R. E., and Cull, J. G. (1974). *Problems of adolescents*. Springfield, IL: Thomas.

Harris, S. (1980). School phobic children and adolescents: A challenge to counselors. *School Counselor, 27*, 263–268.

Hayward, H. (1982). The irrational beliefs which cause test anxiety.

Hegeman, K. T. (1981). *Gifted children in the regular classroom*. New York: Trillium Press.

Hewett, F. M., and Forness, S. R. (1977). *Education of exceptional learners*. Boston: Allyn and Bacon.

Hill, K. T. (1982). Interfering effects of test anxiety on test performance: A growing educational problem and solution to it. *Illinois School Research and Development, 20,* 8–19.

Hill, K. T., and Wigfield, A. (1984). Test anxiety: A major educational problem and what can be done about it. *The Elementary School Journal, 85,* 105–126.

Hindeland, M. (1973). Causes of delinquency: A partial replication and extension. *Social Problems, 20,* 471–487.

Hinsie, L. E., and Campbell, R. J. (1970). *Psychiatric dictionary* (4th ed.). New York: Oxford University Press.

Hirschi, T. (1969). *Causes of delinquency.* Berkeley: University of California Press.

Hollingworth, L. S. (1920). *The psychology of subnormal children.* New York: Macmillan.

Hollister, L. E. (1973). Hunger and appetite after single doses of marijuana, alcohol, and dextroamphetamine. *Behavior and Social Effects of Marijuana.* New York: MSS Information Corp.

Holt, J. (1969). *The underachieving school.* New York: Dell Publishing.

Ingalls, Z. (1983). Alcohol on college campuses: Patterns and problems. *Chronicle of Higher Education, 25,* 9.

Jablonsky, A. (1970). *School dropout: A review of the literature.* New York: Horace Mann-Lincoln Institute Teachers College. (ERIC Document Reproduction Service No. ED 035 778).

Jensen, G. (1976). Race, achievement, and delinquence: A further look at delinquency in a birth cohort. *American Journal of Sociology, 82,* 379–387.

Jensen, G.; Erickson, M.; and Gibbs, J. (1978). Perceived risk of punishment and self-reporting delinquency. *Social Forces, 57,* 57–78.

Jensen, G., and Rojeck, D. (1980). *Delinquency: A sociological view.* Lexington, MA: D. C. Heath Company.

Johnson, S. B. (1978). Children's fears in the classroom setting. *School Psychology Digest, 8,* 382–396.

Jones, K. L.; Shainber, L. W.; and Byer, C. O. (1969). *Drugs and alcohol.* New York: Harper and Row.

Kashani, J. H., and Ray, J. S. (1983). Depressive related symptoms among preschool age children. *Child Psychiatry and Human Development, 13,* 233–238.

Katzman, M., and Wolchik, S. (1983). *Bulimics with and without prior anorexia nervosa: A comparison of personality characteristics.* Tempe: Arizona State University. (ERIC Document Reproduction Service No. ED 236 463).

Kaufman, I.; Heims, L. W.; and Reiser, D. E. (1961). A reevaluation of the psychodynamics of firesetting. *American Journal of Orthopsychiatry, 31,* 123–126.

Kelly, E. W. (1973). School phobia: A review of theory and treatment. *Psychology in the Schools, 10,* 33–42.

Kelly, L. M., and Lahey, B. (1983). *Irrational beliefs as moderators of the life stress-depression relationship.* Atlanta: Annual Meeting of the Southeastern Psychological Association. (ERIC Document Reproduction Service No. ED 234 335).

Keogh, B., and Levitt, M. (1976). Special education in the mainstream: A confrontation of limits? *Focus on Emotional Children, 8,* 1–12.

Kerr, M., and Nelson, C. (1983). *Strategies for managing behavior problems in the classroom.* Columbus, OH: Merrill.

Kessel, N., and Walton, H. (1967). *Alcoholism.* Great Britain: Penguin Books.

Keutzer, C. S. (1972). Kleptomania: A direct approach to treatment. *British Journal of Medical Psychology, 45,* 159–163.

Kiechel, W. (1982). Looking out for the executive alcoholic. *Fortune, 105,* 117–118.

Kiernan, C. (1983). The use of nonvocal communication techniques with autistic individuals. *Journal of Child Psychology and Psychiatry and Allied Disciplines, 24,* 17–23.

Kisker, G. W. (1972). *The disorganized personality.* New York: McGraw-Hill.

Knickerbocker, L. (1983). *Anorexia nervosa: More than just a teen-age disease.* Teaneck, NJ: The American Anorexia Nervosa Association.

Koegel, R.; Lovaas, O.; and Schreibman, L. (1977). The autistic child language development through behavior modification. *Journal of Autism and Developmental Disorders, 14,* 16–21.

Kolansky, H., and Moore, W. (1978). Sufficient for alarm. In J. Brady and H. Brody (Eds.), *Controversy in psychiatry.* Philadelphia: Saunders.

Kopecky, G. (1980). Why women steal. *Mademoiselle,* 156–157.

Kretschmer, E. (1970). *Physique and character* (2nd ed.). New York: Cooper Square Publishers.

Lake, S. (1984). Study habits of the underachiever. *Thrust, 14,* 1–4.

Lall, G., and Lall, B. (1979). School phobia: It's real. . . . and growing. *Instructor, 89,* 96–98.

Lamanna, M. (1981). Marijuana: Implications of use by young people. *Journal of Drug Education, 11*, 281–310.

Landau, E. (1983). *Why are they starving themselves? Understanding anorexia nervosa bulimia.* New York: Julian Messner.

Lindsay, D. (1977). Project real. *Pointer, 22* (1), 52–56.

Liu, A. (1979). *Solitaire: A young woman's triumph over anorexia nervosa.* New York: Harper and Row.

Lukeman, J., and Sorensen, K. (1984). *Medical-surgical nursing psychophysiological approach.* Philadelphia: Saunders.

MacDonald, J. (1920). *Bombers and firesetters.* Springfield, IL: Thomas.

Mack, J. E. (1970). *Nightmares and human conflict.* London: J & A Churchhill.

MacLeod, S. (1981). *The art of starvation.* New York: Schocken Books.

Macnab, F. A. (1968). *Estrangement and relationship: Experience with schizophrenics.* New York: Dell.

Mallick, J. (1984). Anorexia nervosa and bulimia: Questions and answers for school personnel. *Journal of School Health,* 299–301.

Mann, M. (1950). *Primer on alcoholism.* New York: Rinehart.

Margolis, R., and Popkin, N. (1980). A review of medical research with implications for adolescents. *Personnel and Guidance Journal, 59,* 7–14.

Marks, J. (1983). My husband was an alcoholic. *Ladies Home Journal, 100,* May, 10–12.

Martin, D. L., Jr. (1981). *Identifying potential dropouts: A research report.* Frankfort: Kentucky State Department of Education. (ERIC Document Reproduction Service No. ED 216 304).

Mayer, A. (1982). The gorge-purge syndrome. *Health, 14,* 50–52.

McIntyre, T. (1982). The teacher's role in the detection of child abuse. *Eastern Education Journal, 15* (2), 15–17.

McLeod, P. H. (1973). *Readiness for learning.* New York: J. B. Lippincott.

Merrill, N. A. (1947). *Problem of child delinquency.* Cambridge, MA: Riverside Press.

Miller, J. (1973). *Helping your learning disabled child at home.* California: Academic Therapy.

Miller, L. (1981). *Louisville behavior checklist.* Los Angeles: Western Psychological Services.

Miller, L. L. (1974) *Marijuana: Effects on human behavior.* New York: Academic Press.

Miller, M. (1984). *Training workshop manual.* San Diego, CA: Suicide Information Center.

Millon, (1969). *Modern psychopathology.* Philadelphia: Saunders.

Mitchell, R. M., and Klein, T. (1969). *Nine months to go.* U.S.A.: Ace Printing Co.

Mittenthal, S. (1983). I won't let alcohol destroy another innocent child. *Family Circle,* June, 22–23.

Morse, W. C. (1975). Disturbed youngsters in the classroom. In J. M. Palardy (Ed.), *Teaching today.* New York: Macmillan.

Mussen, P. (1973). *The psychological development of the child.* Englewood Cliffs, NJ: Prentice-Hall.

Myers, G., and Hammill, D. D. (1976). *Methods for learning disorders.* New York: John Wiley & Sons.

Newcomer, P. (1980). *Understanding and teaching emotionally disturbed children.* Boston: Allyn and Bacon.

Nicholi, A. M. (Ed.) (1978). *The Harvard guide to modern psychiatry.* Cambridge, MA: The Belknap Press of Harvard University Press.

Nicholls, J. G. (1976). When a scale measures more than its name denotes: The case of the test anxiety scale for children. *Journal of Consulting and Clinical Psychology, 44,* 976–985.

Niles, T. R., and Mustachio, J. A. (1978). Self-concept, learning styles, and grade achievement. *Community College Frontiers, 7,* 44–47.

Norris, R. V., and Sullivan, C. (1983). *PMS/Premenstrual syndrome.* New York: Berkley Books/Rawson Associates.

O'Neil, C. (1982). *Starving for attention.* New York: Continuum Publishing Co.

O'Neill, C. B. (1982). Starving for attention. *McCall's, 110,* 118–119.

Orbach, S. (1982). *Fat is a feminist issue II.* New York: Berkley Book.

Ornstein, A. C. (1975). Who are the disadvantaged? In J. M. Palardy (Ed.), *Teaching today.* New York: Macmillan.

Oursler, W. (1968). *Marijuana: The facts—The truth.* New York: Paul Erikson.

Padus, E. (1981). *The women's encyclopedia of health and natural healing.* New York: Rodale Press.

Petersen, C. (1982). Test without trauma fearlessly uncovers the quiz whiz in all of us. *Chicago Tribune,* 10.

Peterson, D., and Quay, H. (1979). *Behavior problem checklist.* Unpublished.

Available from D. Peterson, 39 North Fifth Ave., Highland Park, N.J. 08904.

Pfeffer, C. (1981). Suicidal behavior of children. *Exceptional Children, 48,* 170–172.

Pfeffer, C. R.; Conte, H. R.; Plutchik, R.; and Jerrett, I. (1979). Suicidal behavior in latency age children: An empirical study. *Journal of The American Academy of Child Psychiatry, 18,* 679–692.

Pimm, J., and McClure, G. (1978). *Ottawa school behavior checklist.* Ottawa, Canada: Pimm Consultants Limited.

Podolsky, E. (Ed.) (1953). *Encyclopedia of aberrations.* New York: Philosophical Library.

Polk, K., and Schaefer, W. (1972). *Schools and delinquency.* Englewood Cliffs, NJ: Prentice-Hall.

Ramelli, E., and Mapelli, G. (1979). Melancholia and kleptomania. *Acta Psychiatrica Belgica, 79,* 56–74.

Ramsey, A. (1974). Marijuana and health. *Third Annual Report to the U.S. Congress.*

Redd, W. H.; Porterfield, A. L.; and Andersen, B. L. (1979). *Behavior modification: Behavioral approaches to human problems.* New York: Random House.

Reinhart, H. R. (1980). *Children in conflict.* St. Louis: C. V. Mosby.

Resnik, H. L., and Hawthorne, B. C. (1974). *Teaching outlines in suicide studies and crisis intervention.* Bowie, MD: Charles Press Publishing.

Riess, P. (1968). Concepts of autism: A review of research. *Journal of Child Psychiatry and Psychology, 9,* 1–25.

Rimland, B. (1974). *Infant autism: Status and research.* New York: John Wiley & Sons.

Rimm, S. (1984). Underachievement. *G/C/T, 31,* 26–29.

Robbins, P. R. (1976). *Marijuana: A short course.* Boston: Brandon Press.

Rogers, G. W. (1977). *Rationally dealing with test anxiety.* KY: Northern Kentucky University. (ERIC Document Reproduction Service No. ED 177 200).

Rosenbaum, C. P. (1970). *The meaning of madness: Symptomatology, sociology, biology, and therapy of the schizophrenias.* New York: Science House.

Rosenblatt, J. (1981). *Shoplifting.* Editorial Research Report, Vol. 2, No. 20. Washington, D.C.: Congressional Quarterly.

Rosenthal, M. S., and Mothner, I. (1972). *Drugs, parents and children.* Boston: Houghton Mifflin.

Ross, A. O.; Lacey, H. M.; and Parlor, D. A. (1965). The development of a behavior checklist for boys and girls. *Child Development, 36*, 1013–1027.

Rothstein, L. (1985). Accountability for professional misconduct in providing education to handicapped children. *Journal of Law & Education, 14* (3), 349.

Royce, D. (1981). Health in the classroom. *Child Welfare, 141*, 361–364.

Rublowsky, J. (1983). The stoned age. *Family Circle, 159*, 35–42.

Russell, K. P. (1977). *Eastman's expectant motherhood.* Boston: Little Brown, and Co.

Rutter, M. (1978). Diagnosis and definition of childhood autism. *Journal of Autism and Childhood Schizophrenia, 8*, 139–161.

Safer, D. J., and Allen, R. P. (1976). *Hyperactive children: Diagnosis and management.* Baltimore: University Park Press.

Sampson, C., and Velten, E. (1978). *Rx for learning disabilities.* Chicago: Nelson-Hall.

Seligman, J., and Zabarsky, M. (1983). A deadly feast and famine. *Newsweek,* March, 59–60.

Sepie, A. C., and Keeling, B. (1978). The relationship between types of anxiety and underachievement in mathematics. *The Journal of Education Research, 72*, 15–19.

Sewell, T. E. (1981). High school dropout: Psychological, academic and vocational factors. *Urban Education, 16*, 65–76.

Shainess, N. (1984). *Sweet suffering.* Indianapolis, IN: Bobbs-Merrill.

Shea, T. (1978). *Teaching children and youth with behavior disorders.* St. Louis: C. V. Mosby.

Simon, J. B. (1980). *Teaching strategies.* Boston: D. C. Heath.

Slater, E., and Roth (1969). *Clinical psychiatry* (3rd ed.). Baltimore: The Williams & Wilkins Company.

Smith, D. W. (1979). *Mothering your unborn baby.* London: Saunders.

Smith, J. (1981). Adolescent suicide: A growing problem for the school and family. *Urban Education, 16*, 279–296.

Spivak, G., and Spotts, J. (1966). *Devereux child behavior rating scale.* Devon, PA: Devereux Fountion.

Spivak, G.; Spotts, J.; and Haimes, P. (1967). *Devereux adolescent behavior rating scale.* Devon, PA: Devereux Foundation.

Spivak, G., and Swift, M. (1967). *Devereux elementary school behavior rating scale.* Devon, PA: Devereux Foundation.

Spivak, G., and Swift, M. (1971). *Hahnemann High School behavior rating scale.* Philadelphia: Hahnemann Medical College and Hospital.

Spivak, G., and Swift, M. (1975). *Hahneman Elementary School behavior rating scale.* Philadelphia: Hahneman Medical College and Hospital.

Spock, B. (1976). *Baby and child care.* New York: Pocket Books.

Sprick, R. (1981). *The solution book: A guide to classroom discipline.* Chicago: Science Research Associates.

Stein, M., and Davis, J. (1982). *Therapies for adolescents.* San Francisco: Jossey-Bass.

Strachen, J. G. (1981). Conspicuous firesetting in children. *British Journal of Psychiatry, 138*, 26–29.

Stumphauzer, J. S. (1977). *Behavior modification principles.* Springfield, IL: Thomas.

Sugarman, M. D., and Stone, M. N. (1974). *Your hyperactive child.* Chicago: Henry Regnery Co.

Swift, M. S., and Spivack, G. (1975). *Alternative teaching strategies.* Champaign, IL: Research Press.

Tahka, V. (1966). *The alcoholic personality.* Finland: Finish Foundation for Alcohol Studies.

Taylor, J. F. (1980). *The hyperactive child and the family.* New York: Everst House.

Taylor, L. B. (1979). *Shoplifting.* New York: Franklin Watts.

Terman, L. M., and Oden, M. H. (1976). The Terman study of intellectually gifted children. In W. Dennis and M. Dennis (Eds.), *The intellectually gifted.* New York: Grune & Stratton.

Time (1980). Pilfering urges: Is shoplifting an illness? *116* (20), 94.

Tindel, C. (1983). 26 tips for building self-concept. *Academic Therapy, 19* (1), 103–105.

Tippelt, G. G. (1983). A process model of the pregnancy course. *Human Development, 26*, 134–147.

Tobias, S. (1980). Math anxiety: What you can do about it. *Today's Education, 69* (3), 26–29.

Today's Education (1982–83). Annual, 60.

Todt, E. (1983). *Evidence for an anorexic bulmic: MMPI profile.* Salt Lake City: University of Utah School of Medicine. (ERIC Document Reproduction Service No. ED 235 450).

Turner, P. M. (1982). Cueing and anxiety in a visual concept learning task. (ERIC Document Reproduction Series No. ED 223 234).

Vacc, N., and Kirst, N. (1977). Emotionally disturbed children and regular classroom teachers. *Elementary School Journal, 77*, 308–317.

Vandersall, T. A., and Wiener, J. M. (1970). Children who set fires. *Archives of General Psychiatry, 22*, 63–71.

Verville, E. (1967). *Behavior problems of children.* Philadelphia: Saunders.

Walker, H. (1983). *Walker problem behavior identification checklist.* Los Angeles: Western Psychological Services.

Wallace, G., and Kauffman, J. M. (1973). *Teaching children with learning problems.* Columbus, OH: Bell and Howell.

Wallace, G., and McLoughlin, J. (1975). *Learning disabilities: Concepts and characteristics.* Columbus, OH: Merrill.

Webb, N. M. (1982). Group composition, group interaction, and achievement in cooperative small groups. *Journal of Educational Psychology, 74*, 475–484.

Wender, P. H. (1973). *The hyperactive child.* New York: Crown Publishers.

Wesley, G. R. (1972). *A primer of misbehavior.* Chicago: Nelson Hall.

Wheeler, K., and Wheeler, M. (1974). School phobia. *Instructor, 83*, 16.

Wiley, W. (1974). *The series in clinical psychology.* Washington, D.C.: Hemisphere Publishing Corp.

Wirtanen, I. D. (1969). *Why and how young men drop out of high school: Some preliminary findings.* Ann Arbor, MI: Institute of Social Research. (ERIC Document Reproduction Service No. ED 028 491).

Wolf, S., and Berle, B. (1976). *The biology of the schizophrenic process.* New York: Plenum Press.

Wolfgang, C. (1980). Many faces of praise. *Early Child Development and Care, 9*, 237–243.

Wolman, B. (Ed.) (1965). *Handbook of clinical psychology.* New York: McGraw-Hill.

Wooden, W. S. (1985). Little swamis. *Psychology Today, 19*, 16.

World book encyclopedia, 11. Chicago.

Wriely, M. (1982). Student drop outs: When did the problem begin? *Elementary School Journal, 8*, 12–16.

Yaffe, E. (1979). Experienced mainstreamers speak out. *Teacher Magazine, 84*, 19–21.

Young, V., and Reich, C. (1974). *Patterns of dropping out.* Ontario: Toronto Board of Education, Research Dept. (ERIC Document Reproduction Service No. ED 106 720).

Yudkovitz, E. (1983). Bulimia: Growing awareness of an eating disorder. *Social Work, 11*, 472–479.